LISTEN TO PSYCHEDELIC ROCK!

Recent Titles in
Exploring Musical Genres

Listen to New Wave Rock! Exploring a Musical Genre
James E. Perone

Listen to Pop! Exploring a Musical Genre
James E. Perone

Listen to the Blues! Exploring a Musical Genre
James E. Perone

Listen to Rap! Exploring a Musical Genre
Anthony J. Fonseca

Listen to Classic Rock! Exploring a Musical Genre
Melissa Ursula Dawn Goldsmith

Listen to Movie Musicals! Exploring a Musical Genre
James E. Perone

LISTEN TO PSYCHEDELIC ROCK!

Exploring a Musical Genre

CHRISTIAN MATIJAS-MECCA

Exploring Musical Genres
James E. Perone, Series Editor

BLOOMSBURY ACADEMIC
NEW YORK • LONDON • OXFORD • NEW DELHI • SYDNEY

BLOOMSBURY ACADEMIC
Bloomsbury Publishing Inc
1385 Broadway, New York, NY 10018, USA
50 Bedford Square, London, WC1B 3DP, UK
29 Earlsfort Terrace, Dublin 2, Ireland

BLOOMSBURY, BLOOMSBURY ACADEMIC and the Diana logo
are trademarks of Bloomsbury Publishing Plc

First published in the United States of America by ABC-CLIO 2020
Paperback edition published by Bloomsbury Academic 2024

Copyright © Bloomsbury Publishing Inc, 2024

Cover photo: Cream, Ginger Baker, Jack Bruce, and Eric Clapton, UK, October 1967.
(Pictorial Press Ltd./Alamy Stock Photo)

All rights reserved. No part of this publication may be reproduced or
transmitted in any form or by any means, electronic or mechanical,
including photocopying, recording, or any information storage or retrieval
system, without prior permission in writing from the publishers.

Bloomsbury Publishing Inc does not have any control over, or responsibility for,
any third-party websites referred to or in this book. All internet addresses given
in this book were correct at the time of going to press. The author and publisher
regret any inconvenience caused if addresses have changed or sites have
ceased to exist, but can accept no responsibility for any such changes.

Library of Congress Cataloging-in-Publication Data
Names: Matijas-Mecca, Christian, author.
Title: Listen to psychedelic rock! : exploring a musical genre / Christian Matijas-Mecca.
Description: Santa Barbara : Greenwood, 2020. | Series: Exploring musical genres |
Includes bibliographical references and index.
Identifiers: LCCN 2019059398 (print) | LCCN 2019059399 (ebook) |
ISBN 9781440861970 (hardcover) | ISBN 9781440861987 (ebook)
Subjects: LCSH: Psychedelic rock music—History and criticism.
Classification: LCC ML3534 .M4325 2020 (print) | LCC ML3534 (ebook) |
DDC 781.66—dc23
LC record available at https://lccn.loc.gov/2019059398
LC ebook record available at https://lccn.loc.gov/2019059399

ISBN: HB: 978-1-4408-6197-0
PB: 979-8-7651-2696-7
ePDF: 978-1-4408-6198-7
eBook: 979-8-2161-1198-6

Series: Exploring Musical Genres

To find out more about our authors and books visit www.bloomsbury.com
and sign up for our newsletters.

Contents

Series Foreword	vii
Preface	xi
1 Background	1
2 Must-Hear Music	27
3 Impact on Popular Culture	185
4 Legacy	193
Bibliography	205
Index	209

Series Foreword

Ask some music fans and they will tell you that genre labels are rubbish and that imposing them on artists and pieces of music diminish the diversity of the work of performers, songwriters, instrumental composers, and so on. Still, in the record stores of old, in descriptions of radio-station formats (on-air and Internet), and at various streaming audio and download sites today, we have seen and continue to see music categorized by genre. Some genre boundaries are at least somewhat artificial, and it is true that some artists and some pieces of music transcend boundaries. But categorizing music by genre is a convenient way of keeping track of the thousands upon thousands of musical works available for listeners' enjoyment; it's analogous to the difference between having all your documents on your computer's home screen versus organizing them into folders. So Greenwood's Exploring Musical Genres series is a genre- and performance-group-based collection of books and e-books. The publications in this series will provide listeners with background information on the genre; critical analysis of important examples of musical pieces, artists, and events from the genre; discussion of must-hear music from the genre; analysis of the genre's impact on the popular culture of its time and on later popular culture trends; and analysis of the enduring legacy of the genre today and its impact on later musicians and their songs, instrumental works, and recordings. Each volume will also contain a bibliography of references for further reading.

We view the volumes in the Exploring Musical Genres series as a go-to resource for serious music fans, the more casual listener, and everyone in between. The authors in the series are scholars who probe into the details of the genre and its practitioners: the singers, instrumentalists, composers, and lyricists of the pieces of music that we love. Although the authors' scholarship brings a high degree of insight and perceptive analysis to the reader's understanding of the various musical genres, the authors approach their subjects with the idea of appealing to the lay reader, the music nonspecialist. As a result, the authors may provide critical analysis using some high-level scholarly tools; however, they avoid any unnecessary and unexplained jargon or technical terms or concepts. These are scholarly volumes written for the enjoyment of virtually any music fan.

Every volume has its length parameters, and an author cannot include every piece of music from within a particular genre. Part of the challenge, but also part of the fun, is that readers might agree with some of the choices of "must-hear music" and disagree with others. So while your favorite example of, say, grunge music might not be included, the author's choices might help you to open up your ears to new, exciting, and ultimately intriguing possibilities.

By and large, these studies focus on music from the sound-recording era: roughly the 20th century through the present. American guitarist, composer, and singer-songwriter Frank Zappa once wrote,

> On a record, the overall timbre of the piece (determined by equalization of individual parts and their proportions in the mix) tells you, in a subtle way, *WHAT* the song is about. The orchestration provides *important information* about what the composition *IS* and, in some instances, assumes a greater importance than *the composition itself*. [Italics and capitalizations from the original]. (Zappa with Occhiogrosso 1989, 188)

The gist of Zappa's argument is that *everything* that the listener experiences (to use Zappa's system of emphasizing words)—including the arrangement, recording mix and balance, lyrics, melodies, harmonies, instrumentation, and so on—makes up a musical composition. To put it another way, during the sound-recording era, and especially after the middle of the 20th century, we have tended to understand the idea of a piece of music—particularly in the realm of popular music—as being the same as the most definitive recording of that piece of music. And this is where Zappa's emphasis on the arrangement and recording's production comes into play. As a result, a writer delving into, say, new-wave rock will examine and analyze the B-52s' version of "Rock Lobster" and not just the words, melodies, and chords that any band could sing and play and still label the result "Rock Lobster." To use Zappa's graphic way of highlighting particular words, the B-52s' recording *IS* the piece.

Although they have expressed it in other ways, other writers, such as Theodore Gracyk (1996, 18) and Albin Zak III (2001) concur with Zappa's equating of the piece with the studio recording of the piece.

In the case of musical genres not as susceptible to being tied to a particular recording—generally because of the fact that they are genres often experienced live, such as classical music or Broadway musicals—the authors will still make recommendations of particular recordings (we don't all have ready access to a live performance of Wolfgang Amadeus Mozart's *Symphony No. 40* any time we'd like to experience the piece), but they will focus their analyses on the more general, the notes-on-the-page, the expected general aural experience that one is likely to find in any good performance or recorded version.

Maybe you think that all you really want to do is just listen to the music. Won't reading about a genre decrease your enjoyment of it? My hope is that you'll find that reading this book will open up new possibilities for understanding your favorite musical genre, and that by knowing a little more about it, you'll be able to listen with proverbial new ears and gain even more pleasure from your listening experience. Yes, the authors in the series will bring you biographical detail, the history of the genres, and critical analysis on various musical works that they consider to be the best, the most representative, and the most influential pieces in the genre. However, ultimately the goal is to enhance the listening experience. That, by the way, is why these volumes have an exclamation mark in their titles. So please enjoy both reading and listening!

James E. Perone, Series Editor

REFERENCES

Gracyk, Theodore. 1996. *Rhythm and Noise: An Aesthetics of Rock*. Durham, NC: Duke University Press.

Zak III, Albin. 2001. *The Poetics of Rock: Cutting Tracks, Making Records*. Berkeley: University of California Press.

Zappa, Frank, with Peter Occhiogrosso. 1989. *The Real Frank Zappa Book*. New York: Poseidon Press.

Preface

Psychedelic music is often remembered for both its visual and musical imagery. The images and sounds of *Sgt. Pepper's Lonely Hearts Club Band*, Jimi Hendrix, the Be-In at San Francisco's Golden Gate Park, Pink Floyd, Woodstock, or any number of bands, records, pictures, posters, concerts, or movies have been unearthed for analysis on the radio, in documentaries, in magazines, or (as with this volume) in books. In most instances, the topic will be shoehorned into the single year of 1967, while more generous commentators have expanded the era to include the twelve months on either side of that extraordinary year. Psychedelia is a far more complex genre of music than can be contained into a single collage of aural or visual images, with very distinct styles and influences that are specific to the geographic locations from which these artworks emerged. This volume will position the movement in four geographic regions, each of which has a long tradition of music making in a variety of genres: London, San Francisco, Los Angeles, and New York. Psychedelia did flourish in other cities in the Southern and Midwestern United States (Austin, Texas; Chicago, Illinois; and Detroit, Michigan), but the four above-named cities provided the cultural flashpoint for a majority of the artists we recognize as *psychedelic* or *acid* rock.

Like all rock and roll, psychedelic music has its origins in African American music, through its evolution from rhythm and blues, rock and roll, garage rock, and beat music. This is often overlooked because African American music has evolved at such a rapid pace that new styles are created and refined and then emerge but inevitably move forward before the marketplace can effectively monetize any one subgenre. African American artists were central contributors to psychedelia, such as Jimi Hendrix, the Los Angeles–based Love, Sly Stone, and Tom Wilson, and these same artists were rapidly moving through psychedelia en route to a style that was further out than anything the mainstream market could imagine. Motown's the Temptations were at the forefront of the psychedelic soul sound, and lesser-known artists on Gordy's labels left samples of this genre on record. Artists such as Sly and the Family Stone and, on the more extreme end, George Clinton's Parliament-Funkadelic merged psychedelia, soul, funk, and every imaginable kind of music into entirely original styles that could not be replicated by other artists. In England, Pink Floyd started off as an average R & B cover band before branching off into their own sonic world, and all three members of Cream, the original supergroup, were aficionados of authentic American blues. The more commercial forms of psychedelia, as performed by the Byrds, the Mamas and the Papas, and other folk-rock outfits, has its origin in the Greenwich Village folk music scene of the early 1960s.

This book is not a list of *The Fifty-Some Most Important Psychedelic Albums You Must Hear before You Die* or a similarly structured "Best of . . ." list. Instead, this volume will discuss many classic psychedelic artists, such as Jimi Hendrix, Jefferson Airplane, Vanilla Fudge, and the Doors, and will also include some less frequently referenced contributors who helped to provide an entrée into psychedelia, or at the very least the image of psychedelia as it has been passed down to fans in the early twenty-first century. Garage rock bands are included here, as are bands from a less widely known transitional period, many of them one- or two-hit wonders, who are now described as being part of the freakbeat scene (a 1980s definition for English beat music that served as a sonic appetizer just prior to the arrival of full-blown psychedelia). Records by the Beach Boys and Bob Dylan are included because their work in 1966 laid a foundation for psychedelia that enabled it to be more than a monothematic commercial genre.

The concluding essays will consider the influence psychedelia had on popular culture and will discuss selected artists who contributed to the neo-psychedelic movement in the late 1970s and early 1980s. Just as the original psychedelic movement absorbed some primary musical genres (rock and roll, rhythm and blues, folk), digested them, and used their numerous musical by-products to inform everything that followed in its wake, every wave of neo-psychedelia from the late 1970s to the present day has borrowed the structural and thematic tropes from the original artists but has also absorbed numerous global music styles and timbres. What followed the first psychedelic movement has been categorized as progressive rock, heavy metal, sunshine pop, funk, glam, ambient, and punk. The artists of the neo-psychedelic movement in the late 1970s to early 1980s also laid the groundwork for the explosive Britpop sounds of the 1990s. This, in combination with the DIY recording, production, and marketing model that evolved contemporaneously with the increased affordability of computer hardware, created countless artists who would emerge in the twenty-first century and whose work cannot be defined within a single genre.

This book seeks to provide an introduction to larger experiences around the history that defines psychedelic music. Included are essays on the records and artists who created an extraordinary body of work between 1966 and 1970 as well as artists who might not be considered psychedelic but contributed to the experimental and creative ragout that gave birth to the psychedelic movement. While a number of classic albums and records are discussed in this volume, less expected entries on the Who, Parliament, Deep Purple, the Yardbirds, and other artists, whose work either laid the foundation for psychedelic music or who may have provided the exit door from psychedelia en route to successive genres of popular music, have also been included here. There are a few artists who have been excluded from this list (and may not have been covered in the essay on the *Nuggets* compilation album), not to pass judgment on these artists but because they ultimately did not have a significant impact on the progression of the genre, despite their commercial successes. Although it may be unforgivable to some readers, I have chosen to exclude MC5 and the Stooges. They existed at the time of psychedelia's last breath, but their creative legacies provided a more direct pathway to punk rock.

I believe every record included in this book is worthy of anywhere from one to one hundred listenings, if only to experience how this music was not a brief or singular period in popular music history but a gateway (or "doorway," if one wishes to paraphrase Aldous Huxley) to other musical experiences and emotions.

I would like to thank Catherine M. Lafuente and her team at Greenwood for the invitation to author this volume in the Exploring Musical Genres series. A huge thank-you goes to James Perone, the series editor, who was willing to take me on for a second book. I was fortunate to have been invited to author a volume on Brian Wilson and now this volume on psychedelic music. I have been passionately obsessed with this music for longer than I can remember. So, thank you to both Praeger and Greenwood for making this possible.

I would like to thank my partner, Karen Fournier, the only music theorist who possessed PiL's *Metal Box* from its year of release, while I only could manage the first pressing of its standardized model,

Second Edition. My felines, also known as the "four neat guys," who once more tempered the hours of loneliness required to write this book, and were significant contributors (and distractions) to the creation of the volume. I also want to offer a significant thank-you to various members of the Wednesday film club (who will remain anonymous—"I will not name names"), the majority of whom lived through the original psychedelic era and were at Harvard, or were present at the first gathering of Students for a Democratic Society, or were in Chicago in the summer of 1968 and were involved in numerous events that are now considered a part of our history. All who shared their memories of the era helped me to frame the larger tenor of the period.

CHAPTER 1

Background

The Moody Blues' Ray Thomas was three decades premature in singing "Timothy Leary's dead . . ." in the opening verse of "Legend of a Mind," the fifth track on the band's 1968 follow-up to *Days of Future Passed* and their most psychedelic album, *In Search of the Lost Chord*. Thomas name checks Leary, the self-styled godfather of the psychedelic movement, who unfortunately has been included in most discussions about hallucinogenic drugs and the counterculture movements of the 1960s. While serving as an adjunct professor of psychology at Harvard University, Leary pursued theories that promoted and supported his beliefs in the therapeutic potential of psychedelic drugs. Contrary to apocryphal assumptions, Leary never was a tenured professor but a contract lecturer; and when he ran afoul of the university administration, it was not difficult for Harvard to fire him in 1963. His dismissal and the eventual, but unrelated, outlawing of LSD and other psychedelics turned him into an intellectual paterfamilias of 1960s counterculture and may have resulted in Harvard's decision to adopt a more conservative approach toward the field and to tamp down on more progressive approaches to psychiatry. Leary's co-researcher and psychedelic comrade-in-arms Richard Alpert also was fired from Harvard in 1963 and together with Ralph Metzner they decamped to Millbrook, New York where they, with financial support from sibling heirs to the Mellon fortune, founded the *International Foundation for Internal Freedom (IFIF)*. Richard Alpert would restyle himself as spiritual teacher and author Baba Ram Das in 1967 following a visit to India. His brand of hucksterism was less abrasive than Leary's and allowed him to sell his spiritual wares to a wider and more accepting market. Leary meanwhile would retain his outlaw status until his death in 1996.

2 Listen to Psychedelic Rock!

For the music, fashion, and youth culture of the 1960s, psychedelic music is just one soundtrack that accompanied the cultural upheaval of the period. The relaxing of sexual mores and the increasing experimentation with drugs, most notably marijuana and LSD, were bellwethers of change in the 1960s and beyond. Beyond the convenience of tying psychedelia to the counter- or youth culture, psychedelic music is far removed from the world Leary and his followers sought to shape for public consumption. The IFIF published *The Psychedelic Review* which appeared over eleven volumes between 1963 and 1971. In these journals, Leary, Metzner, and a collection of other writers attempted to defend their alternative reality and put an intellectual spin to their pharmacologically driven activities. Their highly subjective writings (selected essays have been collected into a single volume titled *The Psychedelic Reader*) attempted to provide a moral and ethical foundation for others who wanted to believe in the long-term value of these substances. Ultimately, this is their only contribution to the much larger creative and social movement of psychedelia.

Author and counterculture figure Ken Kesey is another notable personality of the period. The author of *One Flew over the Cuckoo's Nest* (1962) had participated in government-sanctioned experiments of LSD, and he became an enthusiastic proponent of the drug. Kesey and his circle, known as the Merry Pranksters, dropped copious amounts of psychedelics while they traveled around the United States and Mexico in their psychedelic bus. Their exploits were recorded by Tom Wolfe in his book *The Electric Kool-Aid Acid Test* (1968). LSD was still legal, and the travels of the Merry Pranksters led to Kesey's hosting "acid tests," where orange Kool-Aid was spiked with LSD and consumed by those in attendance. The Grateful Dead and Jefferson Airplane were participants in the early acid tests, and they also participated in Kesey's mixed-media event, the Trips Festival, held at San Francisco's Longshoreman's Hall in January 1966. These events incorporated various media and extraordinary light shows, and the graphic arts that featured in these shows became a central visual motif for "acid," or psychedelic, rock. The phrase "drinking the Kool-Aid" absorbed more sinister connotations a dozen years later when Jim Jones instructed his followers in the *Peoples Temple of the Disciples of Christ* to drink cyanide laced grape Kool-Aid as part of a mass suicide at their jungle commune in Jonestown, Guyana. Jim Jones founded The Peoples Temple in Indianapolis during the mid-1950s but moved his temple to Northern California not long after the Summer of Love. Jones' mix of traditional Christianity with socialist principles and racial equality became a magnet for people of all social classes who were looking for answers in the new era of mystical spirituality. While Jones would acquire legitimate support from certain left-leaning politicians throughout the 1970s, the Peoples Temple would slowly become recognized as a cult and prompted Jones to move his temple to Guyana.

Media-savvy personalities inevitably become talking points to demonstrate their impact or value to a particular social movement. For the period during which time psychedelic music came to its flowering maturity, certain personality types could negotiate their media placement to generate maximum impact for their message. The quest for personal enlightenment was mixed into the organic development of psychedelic music, and, for some, they are inseparable from each other. Elements of the movement were sucked into the abyss of pop psychology, inner peace, or spoiled political agendas, but thankfully some people simply could knock it (or someone) out when necessary.

Abbie Hoffman, another self-appointed counterculture spokesperson, political activist, and anarchist, ran afoul of Pete Townshend, the Who's guitarist, in a legendary exchange at Woodstock at 5:00 a.m. on Sunday, August 17, 1969. The show order had been delayed, and when the Who took the stage at 5:00 a.m., following Sly and the Family Stone and ahead of Jefferson Airplane. Hoffman sorely misjudged the tenor of the moment and the artists onstage, whose time he attempted to hijack. The event was not captured on film, but an audio track of the event conveys the intensity and importance of this exchange.

As a member of the Chicago Eight (or Chicago Seven, depending on whose narrative you choose to study), Hoffman possessed rather high opinions on the value of his beliefs. During a brief break in the Who's set, Hoffman went on stage to make his own political statement, decrying John Sinclair's conviction of ten years in prison for selling two joints to undercover cops. Townshend never was one to suffer fools, and upon realizing that Hoffman had interrupted their set, he removed Hoffman from the stage accompanied by a wave of expletives. Hoffman later claimed that he willingly left the stage, and Townshend denied attacking him; however, witnesses claim Townshend whacked Hoffman in the back of the head with his guitar and sent him tumbling off the stage. Townshend agreed with Hoffman's message, but he believed the Who's set was no place for an outsider to make a statement.

Hoffman, like Leary, may be viewed as an important figure in the psychedelic or counterculture movements, but it is best to leave the legacies of Leary, Kesey, Hoffman, and several other figures outside of the musical/social movements of psychedelia. All three men were expert self-promoters, and history has allowed their self-authored narratives to stand, despite truths to the contrary.

Influential musicians were always a draw for agitators who wanted their message to reach audiences beyond their immediate sphere. While Leary would, after 1970, become a curio in the musical world, other personalities would continue to cross the creative/social lines of the post-psychedelic counterculture. The White Panther Party was closely aligned with Detroit's MC5 through their "manager" John Sinclair, who was also one of the party's founders. This connection was a logical continuation from the band's sympathies for the Marxist leanings of the Black Panther Party and their interests in the Beat poets. The organic symbiosis of MC5, the White Panthers, and other political elements was less an intrusion of one voice onto another but instead a perpetually hazy area of creativity, political unrest, and Midwestern counterculture. After John Lennon and Yoko Ono moved to New York City in 1971, they were set upon by radicals in Lower Manhattan, most notably Abbie Hoffman's Chicago Eight coconspirator, Jerry Rubin. Like Hoffman, Rubin knew how to access the influence that could be wielded by pop musicians. Lennon and Ono even took up John Sinclair's cause in 1972, but Lennon eventually withdrew from overt political activities when it became apparent that his application for permanent residence was being blocked by the Nixon administration through the FBI and Nixon's attorney general, John Mitchell.

The social, political, and musical movements of the 1960s did not emerge from the ether but were the culmination of events that began to gather momentum soon after the end of World War II. In the decade prior to psychedelia, the poets and writers of the Beat Generation were at the peak of their influence and existed concurrently with the revival of folk music, which had emerged as a radical form of modernism that was ultimately pushed aside by the arrival of rock and roll and beat music. Many of that generation on both sides of the Atlantic adopted a new worldview that, subconsciously or not, was inspired by the events of the fifteen years that preceded their emergence onto the center of the social stage.

Lsyergsäure-diäthylamid, from which the initialism LSD is derived, was synthesized in 1938 by Swiss chemist Albert Hoffmann. It is this drug that is often at the center of any definition of *psychedelic*. Hoffman's accidental ingestion of the substance enabled him to discover properties of the chemical that we use to describe a "psychedelic" experience. A heightened sensory awareness to one's surroundings and a sense of physical/spiritual disembodiment are just two of the emotional/

physical states one could feel when under the influence of LSD. The compound was introduced as a psychiatric drug in the late 1940s, and by the 1950s, the nascent Central Intelligence Agency (CIA) had begun to test the drug on human subjects, often without their consent or knowledge. Project MKUltra was a component of the CIA's Cold War–era agenda to develop a method of mind control using LSD.

Although military studies of the drug were scaled back in the 1960s, the youth counterculture used the still legal substance as a recreational drug, and for some it served as a gateway to a new plateau of awareness and spirituality. While it was eventually banned in the United States in late 1966, LSD and a variety of psychotropic drugs were ultimately outlawed globally in a 1971 United Nations treaty, the Convention on Psychotropic Substances, which was signed by over 183 member states. Though LSD was found to possess no addictive properties, it was singled out as the "BIG" drug, a gateway to all other drugs. Misinformation and fear were the goal, and governments across the globe enabled, with little difficulty, a heightened and paranoid sensibility throughout the general, or straight population.

While it is convenient for us to consider the years of 1966–1968 as a golden era for psychedelic music, it is more appropriate to look at the years 1963–1970 as a significant weigh station within the post–World War II era of Western history, and any discussion of psychedelic music should include various social movements of the 1960s to better understand their influence on psychedelic music. A cultural revolution that began in 1963 continued with President Lyndon Johnson's signing of the Civil Rights Act of 1964 and would, before the end of the decade, incorporate the anti-war movement and its protests of the war in Vietnam and Cambodia. These seismic events provided the momentum needed to support the emergence of the gay rights movement in the wake of the Stonewall riots, the second-wave feminist movement, the Chicano movement, and larger global issues that we group as the environmental movement.

The year 1963 was a watershed moment when the generation born in the 1940s was at the forefront of a new social revolution and movement that would unfold and evolve throughout the decade. While many young people felt energized and inspired with a belief that they could change the world, an equal, if not greater, number of youths, especially women, likely experienced something quite different. Betty Friedan's publication of *The Feminine Mystique* in 1963 was concurrent with the increasing availability of birth control, which may have helped to fuel the sexual revolution, despite access to oral contraception not being guaranteed for all women. State and regional laws varied on this issue, and in some areas, only married or engaged women were provided access to birth control. Young single women were not the immediate beneficiaries of the pill, but the relaxing of sexual mores and acceptance of an emerging drug culture, where smoking marijuana or taking LSD was seen by many to be completely normal, became the accepted companions to the massive social changes that occurred throughout the decade. These changes were accompanied by new styles of popular music that would eventually explode into an even larger panoply of musical genres, and psychedelia provided a doorway to these changes. Psychedelic music was not a single movement that existed from 1966 to 1968 but a transitional period that absorbed everything that came before and transformed everything that followed in its wake.

Social change is just one subject to consider when choosing to study the popular music of the 1960s, and it was bracketed by a series of tragic assassinations that impacted a generation that thought it could change the world. Noted feminist scholar Abigail Stewart described this period as "a time in which things were constantly falling apart and the center did not hold." For all the optimism that was generated in the first half of the decade, it was methodically chipped away through the tragic killings of leading social figures, the horrific killings of celebrities and public figures, impromptu wartime public executions of persons held in custody (or civilians who were simply in the path of an unconventional war), and a widening division between the country's youth and the establishment. In the one hundred years preceding the November 22, 1963, assassination of President John Fitzgerald Kennedy, nations and empires both endured and collapsed in response to the murder of its leaders. The assassination of Kennedy's accused killer, Lee Harvey Oswald, just two days after Kennedy's assassination, was the first live television broadcast of a public execution. This may have primed, but could not have prepared, Americans for the tragic assassinations of many of that generation's leaders. The February 1968 television broadcast of the impromptu street side assassination of Viet Cong guerrilla Nguyen Van Lem may have been as shocking as the public execution of Lee Harvey Oswald four-and-a-half years earlier, but with the killings of Malcolm X in February 1965, Martin Luther King Jr. in April 1968, and Robert F. Kennedy in June 1968, the optimism that had driven so much of that decade was reduced to a nearly silent but angered crawl. Seemingly ordinary people could carry out heinous acts upon our leaders and public figures, and the moral center that once defined society's "acceptable" acts was no longer so obvious. The absence of an acceptable center in our society attempted to right itself in the post-Watergate years. However, since the Columbine school shooting in 1999, over a quarter million school students have endured shootings on campuses that once were presumed to be their safe havens, while the country has absorbed and found ways to cope with the over two thousand mass shootings that have occurred since Columbine.

As the 1960s drew to a close, music fans helped to provide both the market and the rise of the festival show. Pop music had always been an active resource in the marketing of package tours, where multiple artists were bundled into a "package" that was then sold to concert promoters. The benefit of paying a single fee to acquire multiple musical acts was attractive to promoters, and package tours would play a stream of theatre dates (if in Britain) or dance hall or auditorium dates (in the United States). The "day the music died," the morning of February 3, 1958, when Buddy Holly, Ritchie Valens, and J. P. Richardson, "the Big Bopper," died in a plane crash outside Clear Lake, Iowa, followed the eleventh date of a twenty-four date package tour named Winter Dance Party. Package tours were standard fare in popular music, but with the stratospheric rise of superstar acts such as the Beatles and the Rolling Stones, tours began to focus on single star acts with a couple of opening acts as a warm-up for the star attraction.

Beginning in late 1965 and into the early days of the psychedelic movement, specific locations and venues became known for their presentations of groundbreaking psychedelic artists. In San Francisco, the Avalon Ballroom, the Matrix, and the Fillmore (later the Fillmore West) presented many of the leading psychedelic bands. Chet Helms and his Family Dog Productions managed the Avalon. Jefferson Airplane founder Marty Balin had helped to organize the Matrix, where his group started as the house band. And the Fillmore was the brainchild of Bill Graham, who would go on to become one of the major concert presenters and artist managers of the late 1960s and 1970s.

In England, Liverpool, Manchester, and Birmingham had clubs where the latest acts could perform, but London would provide both the infrastructure and cultural community needed to promote the development of psychedelic music. The Roundhouse and the UFO Club are the two most important venues in the emergence of psychedelia. In 2020, the Roundhouse is a Grade II–listed concert venue, but beginning on October 15, 1966, with the *All-Night Rave* that featured Pink Floyd and the Soft Machine, it would host legendary concerts by the Rolling Stones, Led Zeppelin, Jimi Hendrix, David Bowie, the Doors, the Yardbirds, the Incredible String Band, and Jefferson Airplane. In the mid to late 1970s, it hosted shows by punk rock groups, including the Ramones, the Clash,

Patti Smith, the Stranglers, Ultravox, and others. The venue's October 1966 opening supported the launch of the underground newspaper *International Times* and was the first use of that space in over a dozen years and its first use as a music venue. The former railway engine shed/gin warehouse had devolved into a decrepit, filthy building with two toilets (that flooded early on that opening evening), and had a single entry/exit passage that consisted of one narrow staircase. As the venue became a home for major rock artists, the broken-down building reemerged as a functional facility and ultimately as a cultural landmark. Pink Floyd ended 1966 with a show at the Roundhouse that was billed as Psychedelicamania, where they, along with the Move, supported the Who.

The UFO Club opened on December 23, 1966, and while smaller in size, it was of equal cultural importance to the Roundhouse. Its creation came from necessity when the London Free School faced ongoing financial difficulties and was limited in terms of the audiences they could attract at All Saints Hall (another early psychedelic venue). John "Hoppy" Hopkins and Joe Boyd started the UFO on Friday nights in the basement of an Irish dance hall, the Blarney Club, on Tottenham Court Road in London's West End. The club had a short run and was closed by October 1967, having been banished from the Irish dance hall as a likely response to a *News of the World* expose that claimed drug taking had occurred in the club. By mid-1967, psychedelia in England ceased to be the provenance of the underground and was now integrated into the mainstream.

These changes in the presentation of live music, both in England and the United States, may have helped launch the concept of the festival concert. In England, this would emerge as the Hyde Park free concerts that, between 1968 and 1970, presented twelve separate concert events featuring between four and eight bands/artists per concert. Not only were the top psychedelic artists presented at Hyde Park, but English blues bands, early hard rock groups, and, in the final years, progressive rock acts headlined these shows. These concerts drew tens of thousands of listeners and were, for the most part, uneventful in terms of any issues with the thousands of audience members who attended these events. In the United States, this concept had to be different. Everything in the United States had to be bigger (a cultural phenomenon we continue to observe in nearly every aspect of life in the United States), and in 1969, with the decade coming to a close, we have the presentation of no less than four major music festivals that presented many of the major artists of the period.

The Atlanta International Pop Festival on July 4–5, 1969, is believed to have drawn anywhere between 150,000 and 600,000 attendees and was followed by Woodstock, the 400,000-strong festival that was the highlight for the counterculture and psychedelic movement at the end of the 1960s. Woodstock, on August 15–18, 1969, was followed by the Texas International Pop Festival on August 30–September 1, 1969, which drew between 120,000 and 150,000 attendees. Many artists who appeared at Woodstock were likely to have appeared at either the Atlanta or Texas music festivals.

The optimistic streak engendered by concert festivals that hosted, with relatively few problems, one hundred thousand–plus attendees was put to rest with the daylong violence and tragic murder of an audience member at the Altamont Free Concert on December 6, 1969. This show, what was thought of as a "Woodstock West," featured Santana; Jefferson Airplane; the Flying Burrito Brothers; Crosby, Stills, Nash & Young; the Grateful Dead, and the Rolling Stones. The Dead pulled out of performing, supposedly in response to the violence that had begun brewing early in the festivities. A documentary concert film recorded by Albert and David Maysles primarily focuses on the Stones and the murder that occurred at the height of their set, but many of San Francisco's finest artists appeared at this concert. The tenor of Altamont was far removed from the dozens of concerts that occurred at the Avalon, Fillmore, and the Matrix and was the violent conclusion to a scene that began barely four years earlier with the Be-In in Golden Gate Park and Ken Kesey's Trips Festival.

Amid these legacy-laden festivals and events, one musical event from that year is largely unrecognized. The third annual Harlem Culture Festival took place over six Sunday afternoons between June and August 1969 in what is now known as Marcus Garvey Park and would, in retrospect, be referred to as the "Black Woodstock." It was cosponsored by the New York City Parks Department and beverage concern Maxwell House. The total attendance over the six free concerts totaled close to three hundred thousand people. The artists who appeared at that year's festival covered a range of genres, including gospel (Edwin Hawkins), blues (B. B. King), jazz (Max Roach), pop (the 5th Dimension), Motown (Gladys Knight and the Pips and Stevie Wonder), in addition to Nina Simone, the Last Poets, Mahalia Jackson, and Sly and the Family Stone (who also appeared at Woodstock). New York City mayor John Lindsay was a smiling, friendly, and active presence at the event. The Black Panthers helped to provide security, and all went off without a problem. This was quite the opposite of what would happen a few months later at Altamont, where the Hells Angels would provide security, punching Marty Balin of Jefferson Airplane and killing a black member of the audience. The events in Harlem were filmed, though the footage has never been seen. These concerts were enjoyed by many of Harlem's residents, and there were no instances of violence. This would serve as an inspiration for Brooklyn's Afropunk festivals, now in their fifteenth year.

The peaceful beauty of the psychedelic movement evolved throughout the first half of 1969, but the social and civil unrest of the era helped to shed much of psychedelia's superficial representation of peace, love, and freedom. The teens of 1967 were the young adults of 1969, and the counterculture movement was not a warm or welcomed subgroup within the larger social makeup. The brutal Tate-LaBianca murders of August 8–9, 1969, brought the era to a close for many people. The horrific and gruesome murders of Sharon Tate, a pregnant twenty-six-year-old actor and wife of filmmaker Roman Polanski, and her three houseguests were followed by the equally violent murders of businessman Leno LaBianca and his wife, Rosemary, and went unsolved for months. Once members of a commune-like group of misguided youths, who collectively were known as "the Manson Family," were charged with these murders, society could no longer trust itself to identify the "middle" in daily life. Again, seemingly normal, however alternative in their views, people could commit heinous and violent crimes and show no remorse for their acts. That generation had watched its leaders be killed and would have the daily carnage of the war in Southeast Asia broadcast into their living rooms every night. Was this the price society would pay for accepting an alternative psychedelic world?

The widening gap between the youth culture and the mainstream and the already crumbling relationship between youth and the government would be further cleaved and embalmed in response to the Kent State Massacre of May 4, 1970, when National Guard troops opened fire on unarmed college students who were protesting the U.S. bombing of Cambodia. Society had become desensitized to this level of public murder, and the music that spoke of peace and love and whose goal was to inspire feelings of happiness and euphoria could no longer sustain this empty message. Between 1968 and 1971, we see the end of psychedelia, and emanating from its core is a music that speaks throughout the 1970s to both to a hardened realism and a desire for escapist pleasures. Many of the musical artists who were active in the psychedelic scene would go on to participate in shaping the many genres of music that emerged from the gases of a vanishing movement. Hard rock, progressive rock, glam, electronica, sunshine pop, funk, hard funk, space funk, blues rock, neo-psychedelia, and even the singer-songwriters who defined what we now call the Laurel Canyon sound were the inheritors of the musical world left in the wake of psychedelia.

ELVIS, BOB, AND THE BEATLES

If psychedelic music is the path through which numerous other genres of music came to life, what paved the road toward psychedelia? Elvis Presley, Bob Dylan, and the Beatles are the inescapable and overarching influences who defined popular music in the mid–twentieth century and ultimately led musicians to create what would become psychedelic music. Their work was the most eclectic and entirely original music of their generation, and each of these artists was responsible for helping to chart the course of twentieth-century music.

Elvis Presley did not invent rock and roll, but he presented a musical form that was shaped and burnished by his mixture of country, gospel, and black rhythm and blues. In presenting it to white America, he unleashed a raw sexuality that had never been so publicly expressed by a white artist. In his first appearances on American TV in 1956, he displayed his pelvic virtuosity with a raw magnetism, but it was his appearance on the Ed Sullivan television show in 1957 that attempted to neutralize and rein in the singer from Tupelo, Mississippi. The cameras filmed Elvis from the waist up because censors considered his physical gyrations to be too sexual and unsuitable for television broadcast.

Aside from his magnetic live performances, the extraordinary records Elvis created until the early 1960s influenced musicians in the United States and England in profound and far-reaching ways. Despite his becoming something of a caricature (inspiring countless impersonators with drag-like fascination) in his later years, Elvis's work helped to shape the development of popular music on both sides of the Atlantic.

Bob Dylan, a Jewish-American guitarist and singer from Hibbing, Minnesota, relocated to Greenwich Village and emerged as a devout folk musician. In July 1965, he made his now legendary appearance at the Newport Folk Festival, where to the horror of devout folkies, he plugged in and went electric. To the present day, he defies classification, and his extraordinary body of work has no equal in the field. The raw sincerity in his performances, his narrative skills, and his powerful social commentary have influenced folk, country, and rock music artists. His songwriting, prolific beyond description, spoke both to the crises and the pleasures of the day, and his verses succinctly captured the hearts of his listeners while also reflecting the rising tensions that would widen the gulf between the younger generation and the establishment.

When he began his musical apprenticeship in Hibbing, Dylan was influenced by Hank Williams, Johnny Cash, Little Richard, and the many artists he listened to on the nighttime broadcasts from Nashville's WSM and WLAC radio stations. From these artists, he learned not only how to play but also how to compose. The Saturday night broadcasts of the Grand Ole Opry were the musical diet that shaped his aesthetic, one that defies categorization now just as much as it did over six decades ago. He set out to convey the emotional and spiritual voice he heard in these artists and began to do so through the rich tradition of American folk music. He sustained the voice of American music that had been fueled by one of this country's musical giants, Woody Guthrie.

Generations of popular music artists have performed Dylan's songs more than any other American composer of his generation. He followed no trends, though his deceptive, chameleon-like artistry would inspire numerous trends among a variety of artists. Although his own performances are moving and memorable for his core fan base, many artists who covered his songs have created iconic versions that in many cases are better known than Dylan's original recordings. His first self-titled album was released in 1962, two years after Elvis had returned to civilian life following his stint in the army, a period when rock and roll had effectively been whitewashed to remove any trace of "blackness." Brill Building songwriters could sustain the energy and drive of popular music for the young adult and teen markets, but Bob Dylan created the first mature music for his generation.

Throughout his career, Dylan married multiple styles of music in a completely original manner, and despite the absence of a dulcet voice and his lack of instrumental virtuosity, the impact on musicians who followed in his wake cannot be defined in a single statement. His performances were punk just as, more than a dozen years later, Patti Smith, the Sex Pistols, the Clash, the Ramones, and others were punk. The raw individuality and expressive qualities of his songs enabled countless musicians to find their own voice. His work reflects his individuality, and his genius has remained a creative force for over five decades.

The Beatles were originally influenced by their homegrown skiffle and early American rock and roll artists such as Elvis Presley, in addition to a rich collection of blues and early rock and roll artists, but within their first year as recording artists, they, like Dylan, forged a completely original voice that copied no one but influenced everyone who followed in their wake. The Beatles' extraordinary success changed the trajectory of popular music for the third time in the decade that began with Elvis's "Hound Dog" in 1956, and their music had an impact on the aspirations and dreams of an entire generation. They did not invent beat music, but all beat music owed a debt to their work. They did not invent psychedelic rock, but their 1967 album *Sgt. Pepper's Lonely Hearts Club Band* became the standard by which other artists would have their work compared. Their multilayered successes enabled them to experiment and venture into new sonic territories without concern for commercial acceptance.

Although 1967 has been described as the Summer of Love, psychedelia can trace its roots much further back than that particular year. One year prior, an array of album releases signaled the arrival of a new aesthetic completely removed from the two-and-a-half-minute pop single that had ruled AM radio. Simon & Garfunkel, a very unpsychedelic act, saw the 1965 rerelease of "The Sound of Silence" become a massive hit. The song had been released in its wholly acoustic form a year prior and had vanished without a trace, after which the duo decided to part ways following the lukewarm reception of their 1964 Columbia Records debut, *Wednesday Morning, 3 A.M.* Paul Simon went to England and had the benefit of being present at the earliest days of the psychedelic movement with the Syd Barrett–led Pink Floyd, Soft Machine, and others. While the nonstarter of a career with Art Garfunkel had prompted him to pursue solo success in England, Columbia staff producer Tom Wilson (a figure who will show up in entries on Bob Dylan, Frank Zappa, and the Velvet Underground) took the original acoustic recording of "The Sound of Silence," enhanced it with an orchestration that he overdubbed on the original recording, and created the classic hit that is known to this day. Wilson had previously attempted to overdub electric instrumental arrangements over acoustic recordings, and Simon & Garfunkel were not the first recipients of this treatment. He tried this on four of Dylan's acoustic songs, to Dylan's very vocal displeasure. This may have been the final crack in their working relationship, which had already progressed into irreparable territory. Wilson's arrangement of Simon & Garfunkel's "The Sound of Silence" was released by Columbia without the duo's knowledge.

Tom Wilson was the first African American staff producer at Columbia Records. A Texan with an Ivy League education and a background in jazz, Wilson was the producer who helped to launch folk rock and had a hand in producing Dylan's records, beginning with a handful of tracks on *The Freewheelin' Bob Dylan* (1963). He shepherded Dylan's sound into the electric world he introduced at the Newport Folk Festival and enabled it to explode onto vinyl on *Bringing It All Back Home* (1965). One year and two albums later, Dylan released the second mature album of the rock era, the Bob Johnston–produced *Blonde on Blonde* (June 1966). Although it was preceded by the Beatles' *Rubber Soul* (December 1965), *Blonde on Blonde* announced to the world that popular music had matured and would change how we experienced music. Psychedelic music was built upon a stunning trio of albums released over a four-month period in the summer of 1966. The Beach Boys' *Pet Sounds* (May 1966), Bob Dylan's *Blonde on Blonde* (June 1966), and the Beatles' *Revolver* (August 1966) declared their independence from pop or rock music and over the remainder of the decade this trio of albums raised the bar and set a standard of creativity and originality that enabled psychedelic artists to expand their sonic and compositional boundaries to create sounds and colors that were entirely new.

Although psychedelic music is not tied to any city or country, the essays contained here place London, San Francisco, Los Angeles, and New York City as the epicenters of psychedelic, or acid, rock. In each location, it was an entirely different creative experience, and each provided a different exit route in the creation of new styles of rock music. Psychedelia in San Francisco was based on an amalgam of genres that could include elements of blues, folk, pop, roots, and country, but at its core, it remained a relatively conventional form of music that represented, among other things, a rejection of the suburban middle-class values and societal expectations of postwar consumer expansionism. The neighborhood at the intersection of Haight and Ashbury is where psychedelic music and the counterculture for whom it was created had both a physical and spiritual home and where people from across the globe would come in search of this "other" world. The visual representation of psychedelia in the art posters that advertised the dozens of musical, cultural, and social events were brilliantly conceived by the many artists and designers who called Haight-Ashbury their home.

In Los Angeles, psychedelia was informed by the music emanating from clubs on the Sunset Strip as well as the underground culture where movies and literature both promoted the benefits of drugs and warned people of the tragic damages that could occur if one succumbed to them. The generous amounts of money that pass through an entertainment capital such as Los Angeles meant that LSD and other substances were not just for the youth but could also be for "straight" society. Los Angeles has long fostered a tragic-comedic obsession with youth and beauty, so drug use and the loosening of sexual mores was not exclusive to the baby boom generation. People in the third and fourth decades of their lives could be participants in these seismic cultural shifts that might otherwise be exclusive to young people in any other city.

If psychedelic music in San Francisco could trace its conventional roots through folk and blues, the psychedelic music scene in Los Angeles added to this a willingness to embrace a certain anarchy of thought. The city could birth the kaleidoscopic tumbling of pop, blues, and jazz in the music of Love or the Doors but could also produce the hitherto unheard sounds created by Frank Zappa and the Mothers of Invention. Concurrent with this, a folk-rock scene had emerged in Los Angeles thanks to the many artists who moved west from Greenwich Village, which had long been a home base for folk music, jazz, and stand-up comedy. In Los Angeles, such groups as the Byrds and the Mamas and the Papas were among the most significant challengers to the sound of the Merseybeat and British Invasion that had swallowed the aesthetic preferences of young Americans throughout 1964–1965. In the aftermath of Los Angeles's psychedelic period, artists from the Topanga Canyon and Laurel Canyon region north of Hollywood created a new minimalist singer-songwriter aesthetic that was a response to the overextended aural palate of the psychedelic bands that dominated the city in 1966–1967.

In both the United States and England, popular music in the 1960s served the roles of anti-parent and anti-authority and was an emotionally liberating form of expression for kids who came of age with their own styles of clothing and language that served as signifiers for various subcultures. Once the major record labels caught on to the myriad youth-driven styles and preferences, they signed acts and "created" a commercially profitable scene that was tailored to market, by which time new forms of music had risen to take their place, staying one step ahead of the record companies. In nearly every instance, black American music, at first jazz and then rhythm and blues, served as the flashpoint from which newer forms of popular music could emerge. Psychedelic music emerged from black American music as all the early psychedelic bands began as white-fronted R & B bands, and with their own signifiers of dress and speech, they would become as influential a subculture as rock and roll or jazz.

LONDON

English popular music evolved more rapidly than its American counterpart. Bands could be somewhat ephemeral, making a single or two and then vanishing only for half of its members to reemerge with a couple of new faces to form an entirely different group. Although the British Invasion had an enormous impact on American popular music, the impact in its home country was perhaps greater. Bands could not rely on approximating a sound similar to the Beatles, so they continued to absorb the same influences, American R & B, soul music, and classic rock and roll, and came out with something that had even greater impact and originality. In the United States, the term *garage rock* has a slightly different connotation, but in Britain, a DIY variety of beat music that was faster, tighter, and more exciting was also referred to as "garage rock" for its raw and immediate sound.

In the 1980s, the more descriptive term *freakbeat* was coined to describe this music, and it is a substantial genre that flowered just prior to the dawn of the psychedelic movement and has its origins in the mod movement as well as in the straight rock and roll of the period. The fashions and trends of the period meant that these bands had a distinct style and look that featured new hairstyles, stylishly sharp clothes, and fantastically good music. In many ways, the mod revival of the 1980s owed a greater debt to the freakbeat scene than it did to the straight-up mod stylings of the Who or Small Faces.

This music is available today in part because so much of it was released on the major labels in England. In the United States, garage rock was often dependent on independent and niche labels, which made distribution and sales a challenge for any outfit. In England, labels such as Decca, EMI (Columbia and Parlophone), Pye, and others released many of these records, giving the majors a stake in the continually evolving sound of popular music. Bands such as the Attack, the Syn (with a pre-Yes Chris Squire), Mark Four, Episode Six (featuring Ian Gillan and Roger Glover, pre–Deep Purple), the Arthur Brown Set (before he transformed into the Crazy World of Arthur Brown), John's Children (featuring a young Mark Bolan), the Syndicats, the Rockin' Vickers, and the In Crowd were some of the most notable groups from this period. Also included are more familiar bands who typically are grouped into discussions on mod music: the Spencer Davis Group, the Small Faces, and female singers in the vein of Sandie Shaw. This music was not a pastiche of Beatles and Rolling Stones rock but bold steps toward psychedelia.

In England, psychedelia was an outgrowth of various youth cultures, where dress, style, and attitude were paramount, and they evolved as an entirely distinct experience that had few, if any, shared elements with its companion movements in the United States. English psychedelia was birthed through the literary, cultural, and social movements that coalesced in the early part of the decade, and as an entirely original genre, it remained quite distinct from its American version. English bands, like their American counterparts, were influenced by black American rhythm and blues, protest, and folk music; however, English artists also strove for a level of authenticity in their performances of black American music that was missing from most stateside rock groups.

The generation of musicians who pioneered the psychedelic movement in Britain came from backgrounds that were different from those of their American peers, and this was reflected in their diverse musical styles. Storm Thorgerson, one-half of the Hipgnosis art and design team who would go on to design the artwork for the majority of Pink Floyd's albums and for albums by dozens of other artists through to the new millennium, recognized that the psychedelic movement in England was multilayered and simply not a youthful rejection of middle-class suburban life. He describes the movement in John Cavanaugh's *The Piper at the Gates of Dawn* (2003): "People in Haight Ashbury probably thought that San Francisco was the centre of the world. . . . They may have had the Grateful Dead, they may have had Jefferson Airplane and they may even have had Captain Beefheart. . . . But they were wrong, of course" (37). Psychedelia in England was developed by a generation who lived through postwar Britain, with its ration books and privations, and likely would have accepted the empire of their forefathers was finished. Their society would have to evolve, and they would shape it through a reconstruction of culture and art.

The flourishing of the English fashion industry in the 1960s, innovations in retail, and the iconic models and photographers whose images documented this societal transformation accompanied the emergence of psychedelic music. All these sources informed and influenced each other, partly because of their shared generational standing among the creative class in mid-1960s Britain. Military conscription ended in the United Kingdom in 1960, which enabled a new generation of young people to pursue goals that were not available in their parents' generation, whether it was attending one of the newly opened colleges that dotted the nation or through the more direct pursuits of creating art. Designers such as Mary Quant and Ossie Clark, photographer David Bailey, and models Jean Shrimpton and Twiggy were part of a burgeoning culture that had its mythical home in Carnaby Street, an otherwise small and unassuming side road in the Soho area of London. Musical artists such as Lennon and McCartney, Ray and Dave Davies, Jagger and Richards, Clapton, Page, Donovan, Townshend and Daltrey, Dusty Springfield, John Barry, a quartet of university-educated satirists known as *Beyond the Fringe*, and countless others created the soundtrack for a cultural explosion that enabled an entirely original form of psychedelic music to flourish in England.

The generation who came of age in the early 1960s coalesced around organizations such as the Campaign for Nuclear Disarmament (CND) and continued their demands for social change. The British Invasion and Swinging London are two consecutive and interrelated chapters in the narrative of Britain's postcolonial reemergence, and they experienced a somewhat earlier, when compared to the United States, gestational period for psychedelia in England. Its own source(s) of inspiration were distinct from the parallel movements in the United States.

In Britain, psychedelic music was constructed on a collection of numerous bands who played an entirely fresh style of music. They may have begun a year or so earlier by playing a diverse range of pop and American rhythm and blues, but the rapidly exploding scene enabled them to create hitherto unheard-of styles of pop music. The social movement was led by an intellectual and artistic elite who were swept up by societal changes and social progress in areas such as women's rights and the abolition of archaic laws on divorce, obscenity, abortion, and homosexuality. An event that could be considered the birth of the psychedelic movement in Britain is the International Poetry Festival at the Albert Hall on June 11, 1965, organized by Warhol associate Barbara Rubin; it featured Allen Ginsberg, Lawrence Ferlinghetti, and nearly two dozen other poets along with New York scene makers such as Andy Warhol. It was expected to draw a few hundred, but the crowd was reported to have been near seven thousand. Peter Whitehead recorded the event for a short film titled *Wholly Communion*, and while psychedelia may have been about peace and love, it also carried a good dose of social anarchy.

London's Indica Bookshop figured into the lives of numerous artists of this era, and many of the intersectional connections that gave birth to psychedelia came through the Indica. The bookstore was started with funding from Peter Asher (of Peter and Gordon, and brother to Jane Asher, who, at the time, was dating Paul McCartney, who also helped to fund the shop), who was friends with future Pink Floyd managers Peter Jenner and Andrew King. The Indica was also supported by Barry Miles (the author of one of the earliest Pink Floyd biographies) and John Dunbar (Marianne Faithful's first husband). The psychedelic counterculture in England was made possible in part by the resources and connections of both pop stars and young people of means who believed in the changes represented by the movement.

Many of these same people also contributed to the founding of the London Free School in the Notting Hill area of London that was spearheaded by John "Hoppy" Hopkins, who sought to bring alternative education to the masses. Hoppy and Miles started the alternative press for this emerging community with the *International Times*, and along with Elektra Records' U.K. representative, Joe Boyd, they founded the UFO Club, which would become one of the cultural playgrounds for the movement. The UFO Club was for a moment that magical place where the Beatles, Pete Townshend, and any number of then current pop stars could come to observe and absorb the scene and not be set upon by fans. It was at the UFO Club where Jimi Hendrix could sit in with the Soft Machine; the Crazy World of Arthur Brown made their early appearances here, and Pink Floyd refined their sound over the course of many performances. In his book *Inside Out: A Personal History of Pink Floyd* (2017), Pink Floyd drummer Nick Mason recalls the period:

> Jobs were relatively plentiful and long-term careers easily available. . . . The only real downside to all of this was not to appear for another thirteen years. In the brave new, and very middle-class alternative world, mainstream politics were rather neglected. But [by] the time anyone realized, it was too late. The wallflowers, who had been left out of all the fun in the Sixties, got their own back during the 1980s by gaining control of the country and vandalising the health service, education, libraries, and any other cultural institutions they could get their hands on. (45)

In the late 1960s, the Notting Hill area of London was a diverse and multicultural neighborhood within London, and this cultural melting pot helped to give birth to an alternative, or underground, scene. The wartime babies who came of age in the 1960s grew up in an England they would recall as being drab and colorless with the aftereffects of the war (food rations and fuel and housing shortages) that took decades to rectify. Psychedelia was antidrab, and everything about the movement was awash in color.

While bands and musicians such as Pink Floyd, Cream, Jimi Hendrix, and others were the major recording artists of the psychedelic period, record companies did their best to cash in on this new genre through superficial makeovers on groups already working the club circuit. In *Inside Out*, Mason described the commercialization of psychedelic culture: "most of them were R & B bands who had cheerfully swapped their Cecil Gee suits for loon pants, acquired crops of permed hair and adopted a flower power name, but still carried on playing the same old Chuck Berry riffs" (117). While generally true, most of these bands, if signed to a label, would make a single or two and, in rare instances, an album. But because they were shoehorned into a particular look, sound, and style that was structured to fit the prevailing winds of the moment, they did not have the creativity to move beyond a superficial representation to create anything truly influential or lasting. Despite these manufactured wonders, the psychedelic scene in England that followed in the wake of Liverpool's Merseybeat and Birmingham's Brumbeat scenes was sincere and stocked with some of the most creative music ever heard in popular music. It was a scene quite distinct from the movements taking place on both coasts of the United States and was more open to accepting the rapidly shifting tastes and influences of the era.

SAN FRANCISCO TO LOS ANGELES

While England ended mandatory conscription in 1960, the United States' need to deploy and maintain a military presence in Vietnam, in post–World War II Europe, and across vast areas of the globe required a military draft to provide the number of soldiers and officers needed to fill those roles. The final iteration of the Selective Service Act, or in the vernacular of the era "the draft,'" (The Selective Service Act of 1948 was expanded and amended numerous times until 1971, and was suspended in 1973), enabled the federal government to draft men between the ages of eighteen and twenty-five for military service. For a young person in the United States, if you were academically successful at the age of seventeen, you might have an opportunity to attend college. For the poorer and less privileged classes, academic pursuits beyond secondary school were less attainable, so whether justified for economic or academic reasons, it was all but guaranteed that young men from the lower-middle and lower economic classes would form the core of the nation's standing army. The minimum age for voting was twenty-one, so rebellion among teens and twenty-somethings in the United States required other outlets, as they had no voice in the society that predetermined their lives. Psychedelic music in the United States spoke to this rebellion through its dynamic volume and its rejection of middle-class signifiers such as clothing, personal appearance, and life choices. It was also infused with a return to core musical forms, such as blues, folk, and pre–British Invasion American rock and roll. The psychedelic movement in the United States was a wake-up call for the generation that was raised in the modern and comfortable world of the 1950s but was floored by the impact of the British Invasion.

In the United States, because many bands were influenced by the British Invasion, psychedelia lacked a sense of stylistic cohesion and would emerge from a variety of musical genres, mostly R & B based but also equally influenced by garage rock, folk, or pop music. Garage rock in the United States collected many bands that would later be, for the sake of simplicity, attached to the developing "psychedelic" sound. Bands such as the Beau Brummels, Sopwith Camel, Music Machine, and, later, the Electric Prunes, the Vagrants, the 13th Floor Elevators, the Chocolate Watchband, and the Seeds all fall into the camp of garage rock. Their prepsychedelic sound was not a challenge to true pioneers such as Jefferson Airplane or the Grateful Dead, but their sound is identifiable and immediately placed between the periods of folk-rock and psychedelic, or acid, rock.

For many, San Francisco was the psychedelic plumb line for North America. It was the home of Jefferson Airplane, the Grateful Dead, Quicksilver Messenger Service, Big Brother and the Holding Company, and numerous other bands. It hosted Ken Kesey and his Merry Pranksters, and the Haight-Ashbury neighborhood was its spiritual center. South Carolina–born John Phillips was Greenwich Village–practiced in the art of folk music and marketed in Los Angeles as the leader of the Mamas and the Papas. He authored one of the most effective marketing tools for the Bay Area, "If You're Going to San Francisco (Be Sure to Wear Some Flowers in Your Hair)." Sung by Scott Mackenzie (a former bandmate of Phillips) and released mere weeks ahead of the Monterey Pop Festival, this song made San Francisco the holy land of the psychedelic movement despite that not one of its creators was from San Francisco.

The neighborhood anchored at the intersection of Haight and Ashbury became ground zero for this new movement. While LSD was still legal and rents in the once posh and affluent district were affordable, this area was home to the new counterculture, and how Liverpool represented some magical land in the aftermath of Beatlemania, Haight-Ashbury would be the home of psychedelia. Free concerts in Golden Gate Park and the Trips Festival, a multimedia festival first launched in January 1966 at Longshoreman's Hall, was the inauguration of acid rock and could not have occurred in Southern California, primarily because Los Angeles lacked a community that was geographically fixed along the lines of Haight-Ashbury.

The legends about San Francisco were rich, romantic, and had the ability to cross the globe. Eric Burdon of the Animals (Newcastle upon Tyne's first significant contribution to popular music), upon the demise of the original Animals, formed another group and relocated to San Francisco as the newly psychedelic Eric Burdon & the Animals. When bands like Pink Floyd came to the United States, they expected San Francisco to be a mind-blowing experience; however, they reported that, while the visuals and marketing was good, the music was not far removed from the blues and not nearly as experimental as what was being created in London. The image, culture, and presentation of San Francisco as a center of psychedelic music is important to acknowledge, but the fairly straightforward music included everything from folk to acid and was generally a looser and less structured sound than what was being created in London, New York, or Los Angeles. San Francisco also became a home for psychedelic bands who moved to the Bay Area from elsewhere in the country and would take on the aura of being Northern California bands.

Los Angeles and San Francisco have contested each other for the right to claim "best in state" for the better part of the last two centuries. The California gold rush in the mid–nineteenth century began in Northern California and enabled San Francisco to become California's cultured and jeweled city at the dawn of the twentieth century; while at the end of the nineteenth century, the oil boom in Southern California made California the largest oil-producing state in the country. Oil money did not immediately transform Los Angeles in the way the gold rush transformed San Francisco because Southern California is a sprawling geographic landmass that was connected by a series of historic ranchos that covered thousands of acres of land in the lower third of the state, making the region slow to coalesce around a central city.

Still, the discovery of oil enabled Los Angeles to evolve over the course of a few decades from something of a hardened Wild West town into an emerging, if somewhat unremarkable, metropolitan center. The men who ran the railroads, the oil fields, and the all-important water rights acquired enormous wealth for themselves and their heirs and created a city that was open for business. Where San Francisco invested in the development of cultural resources and an educational system for its diverse citizenry, Los Angeles built a patchwork of towns on the entrepreneurial backs of land speculators and actively sustained a level of institutional racism that ran through its businesses, housing, and resources. Mexicans had to live east of the Los Angeles River, and blacks lived south and west of the city on some of the most barren and unfriendly land in the region. When Jewish filmmakers wanted to relocate from New York to Los Angeles for the abundant sunshine that would enable them to work out-of-doors all year round, they could not set up shop in the central part of the city but were offered acres and acres of orchards located beyond the Cahuenga Pass that ran north and west from downtown. And from that bit of "not in our backyard" civic mindedness, Hollywood was born.

In addition to show business and popular music, Southern California was also the home for countless surfing towns. Lacking a "scene" or a community in the way San Francisco's hippie community was built around the Haight, popular music in Los Angeles emerged from numerous isolated pockets across the region. The focus on presentation and show business meant that bands who sought some modicum of success played the roles needed to achieve this. From this sunny and optimistic landscape came an early form of sunshine pop. This did not exactly replicate the British Invasion bands, but groups such as the Association set a model that certainly was not experimental; their music had accessible hooks and melodies that made it appealing and radio friendly. The electrified folk-rock of the Byrds, the polished folk/pop of the Mamas and the Papas, and the slightly harder-edged sound of Buffalo Springfield were the more mainstream alternative sound to groups like the Doors or Love.

Just as the British Invasion was taking hold in North America, Los Angeles became a hotbed of new clubs on and around the Sunset Strip in West Hollywood. Clubs such as Fred C. Dobbs, the Trip, Bito Lido's, Brave New World, the London Fog, the Whisky a Go Go, Pandora's Box, the Sea Witch, and the Unicorn played host to every kind of band that sought to make a name in the city. These clubs were filled with folk groups and pop bands who were making their own wild and loud music. Arthur Lee and Love, along with the Doors, would become two of the biggest names in psychedelic rock to emerge from this scene. Despite the very original sounds that emanated from the Sunset Strip, San Francisco remained the psychedelic capital of the West Coast.

The intellectual and creative soul of the state was in the north with the founding of the University of California. The first professional symphony orchestra and first professional opera company west of the Mississippi were in San Francisco. Student radicalism flourished in Berkeley in the postwar years, and a multicultural tolerance of different ideas and forms of expression made San Francisco a town where psychedelia could develop in a way that no other city in the United States could ever hope to experience. Los Angeles, the entrepreneurial soul of California and the film and entertainment capital of the world, contributed a different dialect of psychedelia. The bands Jefferson Airplane and the Grateful Dead are most often the go-to names when describing the San Francisco sound, but the history and its players are a richer and more complex collection of participants than might be assumed on first consideration.

The postwar years in the Bay Area brought some of the greatest jazz players to the city. Folk music and jazz were a constant presence in the region, but the expanding youth culture of the late 1950s lacked a voice in popular music of the sort found both in New York and Los Angeles. The British Invasion sparked the growth of new pop music groups from the Bay Area. The Beau Brummels, a British Invasion–flavored pop band, was the first San Francisco rock group to make a mark on the Billboard charts in 1965. With clever hooks not unlike those produced by the British pop band the Zombies, their records fared well both in sales and on radio in 1965–1966 (they also "appeared" on the animated television show *The Flintstones* as the Beau Brummelstones). Their first two albums on the San Francisco–based Autumn record label were produced by Sylvester "Sly Stone" Stewart (who later, with Sly and the Family Stone, contributed to the region's psychedelic and funk movements). The sound of the Beau Brummels and bands such as Sopwith Camel could not be sustained after 1966 with the arrival of more progressive groups, such as Jefferson Airplane, the Warlocks (the soon-to-be Grateful Dead), Quicksilver Messenger Service, and Big Brother and the Holding Company.

Monterey, a scenic town south of San Francisco, hosted the groundbreaking Monterey Pop Festival on June 16–18, 1967, and introduced many of the leading musical acts of the period. If the Trips Festival was the formal launch of acid rock, then Monterey was the official coming out of psychedelia for the entire country. Big Brother and the Holding Company (with Janis Joplin), Quicksilver Messenger Service, the Grateful Dead, and Jefferson Airplane appeared alongside Simon & Garfunkel, Lou Rawls, Booker T. & the M.G.'s, Otis Redding, Ravi Shankar, the Who, the Byrds, Hugh Masekela, Jimi Hendrix, and many others. With Monterey, it was abundantly clear that San Francisco was a major voice in popular music, and its cultural, social, and economic capital would not fade away, as had long been the hope of older generations who could not and would not understand the world that had changed before them.

NEW YORK

For the better part of the twentieth-century, New York was the entertainment capital of North America. It is the home of Broadway and the musical, in addition to the early days of television and the business of music, whether it was live, recorded, or published. The Brill Building is both the name of the building at 1619 Broadway and the general name for New York's Tin Pan Alley, which flourished in two locations at 1619 Broadway and 1650 Broadway, and was the pulsating, beating heart of popular music in the United States. The big band era flourished at these addresses in the 1940s, where writers and performers created the era's most iconic compositions, and in the following decade, it developed into the number one source of popular music in the 1950s.

Vocal groups still reigned in New York. The Drifters, Little Anthony & the Imperials, the Tokens, the Impalas, the Four Seasons, and countless others were the soul of New York's popular music scene from the advent of rock and roll into the 1960s. The list of songwriters and artists who came from the Brill Building is beyond the scope of this book, but it is important to recognize how much cultural influence was wielded by the businessmen and artists who churned thousands of hit records and published countless songs from the 1940s to the mid-1960s at the north end of Times Square.

When the focus of popular music began to shift to the West Coast, the music scene in New York had to adjust to these changes. Folk music had been a powerful movement, with its resident footprint based in Greenwich Village. Many artists who started there (Bob Dylan, Joan Baez, Arlo Guthrie, Peter Yarrow) went on to emerge as major figures in their field. Live music remained the life blood of the city, and the business end—record production, music publishing, and promotion—would remain in Manhattan, even as West Coast offices sprung up in Los Angeles. Groups such as the Young Rascals and Vanilla Fudge represented the diversity of garage and psychedelic music coming from the New York and New Jersey area. The Velvet Underground was the most extraordinary and radical group (whose records were commercially available to record buyers) to come out of Manhattan in the 1960s, and the anarchy and decadence the band embodied became a flashpoint for glam, punk, and, ultimately, rap music. In a perverse twist of events, Frank Zappa and the Mothers of Invention played extended residencies in Greenwich Village in the years around their first three albums. This Los Angeles group created some of its best early work as an East Coast band. There were no rules, and everything was acceptable in the art rock world.

It would be a few years after the end of the psychedelic movement before New York once more began to re-shape popular music. During this brief period from 1966 to 1970, when Los Angeles and San Francisco were the centers for psychedelic and popular music in the United States, New York redefined its own musically creative voice. By the mid-1970s, this part of the country was home to many of the biggest-selling artists in both rock music and rap music, and entirely new cyclical models of popular music exploded onto mainstream culture.

CHAPTER 2

Must-Hear Music

THE BEACH BOYS: "GOOD VIBRATIONS" (OCTOBER 1966)

The Beach Boys are seldom thought of as a contributor to the psychedelic movement, but under Brian Wilson's creative direction, they produced two psychedelic masterpieces, though fans would have to wait until 2004 before they could experience the second of the two works in its official construction. In May 1966, they released the LP *Pet Sounds*, an album now recognized across the pop music world, along with the Beatles' *Sgt. Pepper's Lonely Hearts Club Band*, as one of the most important albums in popular music. The instrumental tracks for the album had minimal involvement from the Beach Boys and were executed by the famous Los Angeles–based session musicians the Wrecking Crew. At this time, the Beach Boys were a constant touring concern, so instead of relying on them to realize the increasingly difficult music he was creating, Wilson began to use session musicians for the majority of his sessions in 1964. When it came time to record *Pet Sounds*, both Wilson and his studio players had achieved a natural symbiosis in the studio. After the Beach Boys returned from tour, they added the complex and rich vocal parts to the already completed instrumental tracks.

Pet Sounds was recorded over a nine-month period, from the summer of 1965 to the spring of the following year. Throughout this period, Wilson worked on a number of other projects and released an additional album (*Beach Boys' Party!*) in the time it took to record *Pet Sounds*. Initially, the album was not a hit when first released in the United States, though it was considered a masterpiece in the United Kingdom and was seen as a game changer—the new bar of creative excellence that other bands would strive to achieve. Lennon and McCartney, Mick Jagger,

Andrew Loog Oldham, Keith Moon, Pete Townshend, Eric Clapton, and others of the British pop cognoscenti treated this album as the next word in popular music. The marketing team at Capitol Records failed to see the value of the album and did not promote the work in the domestic market as they did nearly every other Beach Boys record.

Bob Dylan is not an artist who was influenced by any other pop musician of his generation, but *Blonde on Blonde*, released barely two months after *Pet Sounds*, and the Beatles' *Revolver*, released two months after *Blonde on Blonde*, comprise the triptych of long-playing albums upon which the psychedelic movement would be constructed. All three albums would alter the landscape of popular music and were the first artworks of the rock era.

In October 1966, two months after *Revolver*, the Beach Boys released the first psychedelic masterpiece in a three-minute, thirty-eight second single, "Good Vibrations." Brian Wilson willingly admitted this song was the first of his compositions created in response to an LSD trip. The song is unlike any other work of the period. The instrumental colors are so perfectly blended that you don't hear individual instruments as much as you experience a tapestry of sound. It was a hit single both in England and the United States, where it became the band's first No. 1 single.

Like *Pet Sounds*, "Good Vibrations" was created over an extended period of time and was considered to be the most expensive single ever produced. Brian began work on the song in February 1966, while he was in the final stages of recording the *Pet Sounds* album. While work continued on "Good Vibrations," he began work on his next project, tentatively titled *Dumb Angel*. This ambitious project would develop into *SMiLE* and become the undoing of Brian Wilson's creative leadership of the Beach Boys.

The Beach Boys generated so much cash for Capitol Records that they were willing to extend their patience in waiting for whatever Brian Wilson was creating, including his process in completing "Good Vibrations." The path to this song was perhaps the most difficult Wilson had faced up to that point in his career. He began the single with a set of lyrics from his *Pet Sounds* collaborator, Tony Asher, but before the single was released, he had worked through three lyricists. He put aside Asher's lyrics and asked his *SMiLE* collaborator, Van Dyke Parks, to work on the song, but in the end, the single featured the core of Asher's lyrics layered with a completely new set created with his cousin and bandmate, Mike Love.

Wilson recorded idea upon idea, discarded them, recorded more ideas, and discarded them. He originally described "Good Vibrations" as an

R & B track, and for a period of time, he considered giving the song to a soul or R & B artist when his frustrations, exacerbated by his bandmates, became overwhelming. While Brian was in the early stages of the *Dumb Angel/SMiLE* project with collaborator Van Dyke Parks, it was Parks, along with Brother Records' business associate David Anderle, who encouraged Wilson to forge on with the song while still creating *SMiLE*.

Wilson's extraordinary and innate musicianship was seldom limited by his rudimentary music training, but with "Good Vibrations" and *SMiLE*, the lack of formal training required him to laboriously construct section upon section. He had difficulty shaping this song into the traditional model of verse-chorus-verse-chorus-bridge-verse-chorus. He decided to create the song with a series of individual melodic/harmonic/timbral sections that would be fitted together, an approach that can be described as a modular method of composition. This was not a collage technique, but one where all modules had equal value and could be arranged into whatever order the composer believed they should be placed. Wilson discovered that when he placed the selected modules into a specific sequence, he still managed to create a song that felt like a traditional pop song, even if it sounded nothing like any song that had come before.

Throughout the summer of 1966, Brian kept coming to what he felt was the "final" version of the song. He was already deep into recording *SMiLE*, and he put the song on the shelf for part of the summer. When he came back to it in the late summer, the song took its final form, with Mike Love's lyrics against a most extraordinary instrumental track, one that featured the theremin. Although "Good Vibrations" was, at the time, the most complex single ever created, it became a standard in the Beach Boys' live show as well as in Brian Wilson's solo live shows. When Brian finally let the song go to press for an October 1966 release, it was coupled with the gorgeous instrumental from *Pet Sounds*, "Let's Go Away for Awhile."

Thirteen days after its release, the band gave its first live performance of the song in two concerts at the University of Michigan, recordings that are now available on most streaming sites. In both performances, we hear a simplified and stripped version of his symphonic masterpiece, and its impact is still without question. The surreal lyrics and complex layering of instrumental textures, whether in its minimalist live performance or in the extraordinary studio version, are unlike any other song that had been released to that time. Mike Love learned to play the theremin for concert performances using a Moog-designed theremin rather than the more difficult to master Leon Theremin–designed instrument.

In many recordings of the live performances from late 1966 to early 1967, Mike Love introduces the song by referring to it as the most "nerve-wracking experience." Mike was the consummate showman and seldom played an instrument on stage (when he did, it was a rudimentary saxophone part), so when faced with having to play the theremin, it surely was reason enough to be nervous.

The studio version is available in a number of mixes, both in mono and in stereo, and on *Brian Wilson Presents SMiLE* (*BWPS*), where it appears with the earlier, and ultimately incomplete, Tony Asher lyrics, upon which Mike Love completed the song. But in the official version of the song, it is clear from the song's opening that despite any developments in the then-emerging psychedelic scene, no song of this type had ever been heard from any artist. The lyrics, from "I love the colorful clothes she wears" to "on the wind that lifts her perfume through the air," are pure acid-spiced imagination, even though they were composed by the one "drug-free" member of the band, Mike Love. He captured Brian's childhood recollections and LSD experiences, through which he composed one of his finest lyric narratives. Brian has claimed, both at the time of its composition and in subsequent years, that his concept of "good vibrations" was based on his mother telling him as a child that animals could sense a person's vibrations. As Brian became more introspective in his songwriting and began using marijuana and LSD as tools with which he could unlock his imagination, the idea of vibrations developed into a song.

The song is one of the Beach Boys' and Brian Wilson's greatest moments, and though they would soon fall out of favor among a new generation of musicians and with the commercial marketplace, "Good Vibrations" stands as one of the greatest singles of the period.

THE BEACH BOYS: *SMiLE/SMILEY SMILE* (PROJECTED FOR WINTER 1967/SEPTEMBER 1967)

SMiLE/Smiley Smile is the most unusual entry in this volume because of its fractured gestation, its multiple versions, and its formal realization that occurred three decades after it was first announced. *SMiLE* began as a Brian Wilson project for the Beach Boys titled *Dumb Angel* and was supposed to be the long player to follow *Pet Sounds* as well as the full-length realization of the compositional techniques Brian Wilson perfected in miniature form on the single "Good Vibrations." Subtitled "A Teenage Symphony to God," it was anticipated that this work would expand on Wilson's worldview in the wake of disclosing his belief in "vibrations" and would focus on the healing properties of laughter, topics very dear to the emerging generation of youth, who looked to contradict the cultural expectations of their parents' generation.

The process of composing and recording *SMiLE* took an extraordinary toll on its emotionally sensitive composer, and its release was cancelled following a year of anticipation both from Capitol Records and the band's still loyal fans. Wilson needed to silence any hope of its release and declared on multiple occasions that he had destroyed the master tapes. A few of the songs began to appear, in their all-but-completed form, on Beach Boys albums from 1969 to 1972, but Wilson still insisted that the album tapes had been destroyed. Ultimately, his opus was released in its intended form, reconstructed from the nearly completed 1966–1967 master tapes by Brian Wilson and his four-year-old touring band, and released in September 2004 as *Brian Wilson Presents SMiLE* (*BWPS*). A Beach Boys version of the work, constructed from the many hours of session tapes from the 1966 to 1967 recordings, was released in October 2011 as *The SMiLE Sessions*. This was a curated work, reconstructed from multiple source materials by Alan Boyd and Mark Linett, under Brian Wilson's supervision, that offered a complete (or as near to complete as possible) version of the work as recorded by the Beach Boys in 1966–1967. *BWPS* was presented as a completed work, with the final, unresolved sections tied together with Van Dyke Parks's original (but unrecorded in 1967) lyrics. *The SMiLE Sessions* was constructed from the materials Brian and Beach Boys recorded between May 1966 and June 1967 and resulted in a running order that was slightly different from *BWPS*. The inclusion of *SMiLE* in this volume requires that all three versions of the work, *BWPS, The SMiLE Sessions, and Smiley Smile*, are discussed as equal contributors to psychedelia.

While multiple narratives maintain that *SMiLE* was scrapped in May 1967, it is true that the Beach Boys released *Smiley Smile* in its place, a stripped-down alternative collection with songs and fragments derived from *SMiLE* that ended up as an early example of a "stoner" album. The scrapping of *SMiLE* has become a commonplace component of the Wilson narrative simply because a May 1967 press release from Derek Taylor (who was the Beach Boys' PR agent for a brief tenure), published in the U.K. magazine *Disc and Echo*, declared that Brian had "scrapped" the entire project. But with Taylor back in the United Kingdom and Brian in Los Angeles, it is possible that Brian knew nothing about Taylor's definitive proclamation. Wilson was in the studio a few days after Taylor's article appeared in the United Kingdom, recording "Love to Say Da Da," "Cool, Cool Water," and "You're with Me Tonight."

May–June 1967 was a period of great stress for Brian and for the Beach Boys, and this clearly played into Brian's decision-making just as the Summer of Love was about to dawn. Carl Wilson was detained by the FBI for his refusal to report for his draft call-up and standing as a conscientious objector. That same spring, although the band won World's Top Vocal Group from Britain's New Musical Express, they were savaged in the British press for their underwhelming live performances, which had been hamstrung when Musician's Union rules prevented the band from working with the supplemental musicians that had helped the band reproduce Brian's increasingly elaborate arrangements. Reduced to a five-piece, their performances were roundly criticized in the press. These events may have precipitated Brian's decision to pull the Beach Boys from their scheduled headline slot on the Saturday night bill of the Monterey Pop Festival. The story behind their decision to withdraw from the festival continues to develop in numerous narratives, but with Brian having lost focus in the studio on *SMiLE*, the dodgy U.K. concert appearances, Carl's draft issues, and the no-show at Monterey Pop, making an abrupt change in direction may have seemed to Brian to be his best decision in the moment. So, exit *SMiLE* and enter *Smiley Smile*.

Brian Wilson was at the top of his creative game in 1965–1966, and with the release of *Pet Sounds*, his most personal album, he faced resistance from select bandmates and certain managers within Capitol Records. Although the album was not heralded as his magnum opus, he still managed to forge ahead with the brilliant single "Good Vibrations." The increasing complexity of the vocal work on *Pet Sounds* was a source of frustration for certain members of the group, but they still managed to deliver some of their most subtle and beautiful vocal work. Despite the rapturous reception *Pet Sounds* received in England, its sales in the United States gave pause both to the band and to Capitol Records.

Because Brian had come off the road in 1964, it was expected that he would continue to write music for the Beach Boys, which could be understood as music they could play in concert. Every time they returned from tour, Brian had something new that was more complex and in a style that was unfamiliar when compared to their hits. Brian expected them to master his new works in the studio, and they also had to come up with a reasonable facsimile for concert performance.

The recording of "Good Vibrations" caused further tensions, partly due to the endless takes and retakes of the simplest vocal parts. Where the Beach Boys sang four-part vocals across all their albums with apparent ease, Brian had them singing in four parts that were broken down into short motifs that he could fit into the interchangeable instrumental modules he had created for "Good Vibrations." No longer content with text, wordless syllabic phrases, and articulated sounds, he expected the band to sing what amounted to sound effects in addition to the other techniques they had refined over the previous five years. All of these factors, coupled with Brian's increasing drug intake, attendant paranoia, and the increasing number of hangers-on who drifted in and around his home, left the band feeling both left out and protective of Brian, who they felt was being led in myriad directions that were not focused on the Beach Boys.

Between May 1966, when Brian laid the first tracks for "Heroes and Villains," the song destined to become the centerpiece for the new Beach Boys album, and May 1967, when work on *SMiLE*, already having slowed to a crawl, concluded with yet another compositional fragment, "I Love to Say Da Da," Brian's emotional and creative world began to unravel. The much-anticipated album that would have rivaled *Sgt. Pepper's Lonely Hearts Club Band* became nothing more than a legend. The Beach Boys had invested a great amount of money in recording the album, and the anticipation of the next "masterwork" was at the breaking point. To move forward, all rock music after mid-1967 would react, respond, or consciously ignore the immense influence the Beatles had thrust upon the field. How might the changes in popular music after 1967 have been more complex and enhanced if *SMiLE* had been released in spring 1967, followed by the Beatles' masterpiece? No one knows, because in place of *SMiLE*, the Beach Boys released one of the most unusual, and now recognized, four decades after its release, most influential, albums of their career, *Smiley Smile*.

Released in September 1967 on their short-lived Brother Records imprint, *Smiley Smile* appeared in place of the long-anticipated *SMiLE* and was their shortest album since 1965. It featured "Good Vibrations," in the same form as the single that had been released nearly a year earlier, with ten additional titles, including their newest single, "Heroes and Villains," which had previously been reworked into more shapes and configuration than perhaps any other song in Wilson's catalog, before or since. In this simplified iteration, listeners were given no indication of its centrality to the entire *SMiLE* project; it was a good but not outstanding slice of Wilson's creative voice.

Eight of the nine remaining tracks had originally been prepared for *SMiLE* in extraordinarily rich and elaborate arrangements that, in each instance, were longer and central to the through-composed form of Brian's original concept. "Vegetables" was a simple campfire sing-along reworking of "Vega-Tables." "Fall Breaks and Back to Winter (Woody

Woodpecker Symphony)" was a clever and unusual, if somewhat aimless, instrumental derived from a fragment of *SMiLE*'s most infamous work, "Fire" (also known as "Mrs. O'Leary's Cow"), which Brian would claim gave him reason to suspend the whole project. "Fall Breaks . . ." is such an innocent, almost simplistic work that it is hard to connect how it could have been birthed from such a sinister part of the *SMiLE* legacy. "She's Goin' Bald" is another campfire sing-along reworking of "He Gives Speeches," an otherwise humorous link for *SMiLE*. In "She's Goin' Bald," the idea is stretched into an absurd story about a girl who loses her hair, and it comes off more like a novelty cabaret song. "Little Pad," recorded under the influence of weed, was a redo of three semirelated works: "In Blue Hawaii," "Love to Say Da Da," and "Cool, Cool Water." All three were excellent works on their own merits but were transformed into a cut-and-splice stoner song.

"With Me Tonight" also had origins in the late sessions for *SMiLE* as "You're with Me Tonight," and was a charmingly simple finger-snapping shuffle. For *Smiley Smile*, Brian chilled the full, rich arrangement of the original into a peaceful doo-wop number. In its original arrangement, "Wind Chimes" was a complex and layered work with a bass and marimba rhythmic bed, but on *Smiley Smile*, it was reduced to a deconstructed timbral canvas that features a barely present lead vocal with an organ drone. "Gettin' Hungry" was a new work that focused on Brian's two great loves, women and food. It is a simple ostinato pattern for organ and bass with some humorous vocal licks. "Wonderful" was one of the most touching compositions on *SMiLE* and was reworked to a seemingly simpler version, but, in truth, it shows that Brian could make a deconstructed arrangement that was every bit as complex as his formal arrangements. The album's closer, "Whistle In," was one of the many fragments Brian recorded as one of the linking pieces for the original "Heroes and Villains."

Smiley Smile was described in the liner notes to the 1990 CD reissue as "do it yourself acid casualty doo-wop music," but this underestimates Wilson's conscious effort to create something completely different from his original concept. The album was not the Beach Boys' worst chart showing, but it opened a streak of underperforming albums that would not be reversed until 1972. In retrospect, its influence has been constructed as a reflection of Wilson's brilliance in a return toward simplicity in his music. The release of Bob Dylan's *John Wesley Harding* (December 1967) and the Beatles' *White Album* (November 1968) are two albums that critics often reference as proof that Brian Wilson was once again setting the trends, not responding to them. This is a comforting position to take when three decades stand between us and the time when *Smiley*

Smile was released. Beginning in the 1990s, its influence was felt in the genre's embrace of lo-fi music, and the album's truly unique qualities could be fully appreciated.

There are numerous articles and book chapters written about *SMiLE*, a majority of which attempt to use the album to demonstrate Brian Wilson's true genius as observed through his organically constructed masterpiece. Between 1967 and 1998, there were a number of attempts to bring *SMiLE* to completion, but it would have to wait until Brian was emotionally ready to face his own legacy and reclaim control of the work that had been bruised, bargained for, and ultimately taken away from its author. The album *BWPS* would never have come to any level of completion if not for the encouragement of his wife, Melinda, and members of his solo band, in particular Darian Sahanaja and Jeffrey Foskett, who handled the laborious task of taking Brian's complex arrangements and reconstructing them for the new recordings and for performance in concert. *BWPS* and the 2011 release of *The SMiLE Sessions* are both similar and different enough that we can decide for ourselves how important *SMiLE* could have been to the development of popular music in the wake of 1967.

THE BEATLES: *REVOLVER* (AUGUST 1966)

Two years of the Beatles' relatively brief history, 1963 and 1966, were loaded with so much creativity that most works created in those years dwarf many of the other extraordinary accomplishments they accrued throughout the seven years of their recording career. By 1963, they were in the second phase of their career. They were no longer a regional curio but recording artists with EMI, "The Greatest Recording Organisation in the World," as their brand proudly claimed. Their touring was largely contained within England, though they also appeared in Sweden, Ireland, Scotland, and Jersey. The year began with the band playing their last dates at the Cavern Club in addition to maintaining a herculean schedule on the regional cinema and dance hall circuit. They managed to record and release their first two albums and a wealth of singles. The year ended with the mass hysteria that now followed the Beatles wherever they appeared and that Fleet Street publicists coined as "Beatlemania." This was fandom beyond any description and would not subside until mid-decade.

The Beatles spent six years struggling as a bottom tier band in Liverpool's modest beat music scene in the late 1950s, then faced multiple punishing residencies in Hamburg, where they honed their craft and gelled as a musical unit, to the early 1960s, when they were loved in Liverpool but could not attract the attention of record companies in London. Manager Brian Epstein's tireless and unshakeable belief in the "boys" placed the Beatles at the forefront of a social and cultural revolution. By 1963, they were the biggest stars in England and would soon take over the world and redefine popular music.

Beatlemania became an international phenomenon, but in the madness of the hysteria, no one could hear their music over the screams. The years spent refining their sound were seemingly wasted, as the quality of the playing no longer mattered. No one could hear them in concert, they could not hear themselves, and they were soon tired of the entire experience. No other year in popular music would have such an impact upon any one group as the Beatles experienced in 1963.

The year 1966 marks the beginning of the Beatles' third era and the start of their period as studio artists. This model had never been tried by any popular music artist, but the years of fame and hysteria that had prevented them from living any normal semblance of a life, even by standards accorded to entertainers, enabled them to break the business model and create something new. This was the year they would quit performing live and become musical artists in the truest sense of the word. They gave one brief concert in England in 1966, having completed their last whistle-stop tour of the homeland at the end of 1965. North America had been saturated with the Beatles in 1964 and 1965, so the Beatles began their final world tour in the summer of 1966, traveling to Germany (for their first appearances since 1962), Japan, and the Philippines, the latter two being countries where Beatlemania already existed but where they had never performed in concert. They finished the summer with a final U.S. tour.

The summer of 1966 became the Beatles' worst tour experience, and despite the harrowing events that occurred in the Far East, they were able to dispose of their public image as lovable mop tops. In Japan, they faced threats and protests for performing in the Nippon Budokan Hall and were restricted to their suite of rooms in the Tokyo Hilton. The time in the Philippines was their most harrowing to date. The local press had taken a dislike to them, and a miscommunication led to their unintended no-show at a party hosted by the Philippine first lady, Imelda Marcos, for over four hundred of the Marcos' closest friends. The perceived snub of the Marcos family led to death threats and a narrow escape in which they were jostled and assaulted in the airport. They were prevented from leaving, ostensibly for an unpaid tax bill, but ultimately were allowed to depart after Brian Epstein posted a sizable bond for the taxes on their concert earnings, which the promoter had withheld from them. A brief return home separated the Far East tour from their last American tour, which would be remembered for John's "We're more popular than Jesus" quote, which was nothing more than a paraphrased statement taken out of context, that became the flashpoint for a public relations crisis in the United States. In the Deep South, radio stations hosted events where fans could bring their Beatles records to be burned.

The band survived that tour amid death threats in a couple of cities, but as can be heard in various recordings of concerts from that summer, it was the sloppiest and most intonationally challenged playing ever captured from them. Everyone still screamed, and no one could hear them—so what did it matter? Drowned out by thousands of screaming fans, the quality of their performances had long since devolved into sloppy, ragged playing that the Beatles cared little to improve. On August 29, 1966, the Beatles played their last official concert in San Francisco's Candlestick Park. The album they had released earlier that month, just prior to their final U.S. tour, *Revolver*, is one of the first truly psychedelic masterpieces and is the beginning of their third and final period.

Revolver is the album that even casual Beatles fans will regard as exceptional. It is a favorite of many fans, and it set the groundwork for everything they would do in their remaining two-and-a-half years as the Beatles. *Revolver* was released in August 1966 and served as the decisive statement that the touring Beatles no longer existed; the recording studio now was their canvas. Freed from the constraints of repetitive live performances, the group created new sonic landscapes that helped to usher "modern" popular music into sonic maturity that would soon become psychedelia. The Beatles had worked closely with producer George Martin to shape their legendary body of work, but now they began to rely on Martin more as well as a new collaborator, engineer Geoff Emerick, to push their ideas into reality. The result was fourteen tracks of the most perfect and wildly original songs they had ever created.

The Beatles seventh U.K. album featured songs that would never be heard as live artifacts. Although they introduced new timbres, such as the sitar on "Norwegian Wood" and a string quartet on "Yesterday," they generally maintained a traditional approach to the kinds of instruments they incorporated on their records. This all changed on *Revolver*. George Harrison hired Anil Bhagwat, one of London's top South Asian musicians, to play the tabla on "Love You To," and the Philharmonia Orchestra's Alan Civil performed the exquisite horn solo on McCartney's "For No One." The sole instruments on "Eleanor Rigby" were those of a string octet (or double string quartet). New sound effects that were created by playing tapes backward were used in "Tomorrow Never Knows," the album's final track. Lennon's experiments with the manipulation of audio tape was used on the single "Rain," a song that, along with its companion song "Paperback Writer," was recorded during the *Revolver* sessions but released earlier that year as a single.

The album featured three songs composed by George Harrison, whose development as a songwriter had expanded on every album. Just one year earlier, Harrison had contributed the wonderful "I Need You" and "You Like Me Too Much" on the British LP *Help*. Four months later, he contributed the fuzz guitar work on *Rubber Soul*'s "Think for Yourself" and a twelve-string Rickenbacker timbre on "If I Needed Someone." But on *Revolver*, he surpassed all expectations with the cutting political commentary of "Taxman." This song, the opening track on the album, began with studio chatter and became one of the most identifiable songs on the album (the Jam's Paul Weller copied this chord progression for their 1980 single "Start!"). He also contributed his first fully "Indian" tune, "Love You To," and the Carnaby Street–worthy rocker "I Want to Tell You." "I'm Only Sleeping" is the first acid song on the album, with effect treatments such as varispeed and tape loops that are used to create a dream state in audio form. "Here, There and Everywhere" is a song that was influenced by the Beach Boys' *Pet Sounds* album. "Yellow Submarine" was the Beatles' first inclusion of a children's song on an album and is one of the most elaborately produced songs on the album. This was a vehicle for Ringo to have a lead vocal, and the song served as the inspiration behind 1968's animated movie of the same name.

"She Said She Said" is the second of Lennon's acid songs from *Revolver* and was inspired by an LSD trip he experienced with actor Peter Fonda, the other Beatles, and members of the Byrds. The song features some of Harrison's dirtiest guitar work. "Good Day Sunshine" is not simply one of McCartney's upbeat songs; it features several musical influences, and the vocal round that serves as the song's coda is another Beach Boys–like touch. "And Your Bird Can Sing" featured Harrison and McCartney's detailed guitar work. "For No One" features McCartney playing most of the instruments on the recording, with Starr on percussion and Alan Civil on horn. This is an intimate love song that likely was inspired by his relationship with Jane Asher. "Dr. Robert" was inspired by a physician who was known for the special prescriptions he doled out to celebrities and rock stars. "Got to Get You into My Life" is McCartney's version of a Motown song. The Four Tops were one of Brian Epstein's favorite groups, and "Got to Get You into My Life" has more than a few touches that could easily have been delivered by the Four Tops and would be covered by a variety of artists in the years that followed. The final track, "Tomorrow Never Knows," was the first recorded for the album and remains one of the most extraordinary tracks in their canon.

Revolver featured a breadth of musical styles and influences, including rock, soul, musique concrete, raga rock, electronica, and world music, and along with 1968's self-titled album (*The White Album*), it demonstrated the variety of the Beatles' influences and inspirations and their own unrivaled originality. It arrived as the British capital was in the throes of "Swinging London" and is a soundtrack to that place and time. This was the last album Capitol released in the Beatles' catalog where the track order differed from its English (Parlophone) counterpart. "And Your Bird Can Sing," "Dr. Robert," and "I'm Only Sleeping" were included on the U.S.-only June 1966 release, *Yesterday and Today*, a grab bag of unrelated tracks from the U.K. versions of *Help!*, *Rubber Soul*, *Revolver*, and the single of "We Can Work It Out"/"Day Tripper." This album is best remembered for the first pressings that were housed in the infamous "Butcher" sleeve photographed by Robert Whittaker. The American version of *Revolver* was, for the first time in the Beatles/Capitol catalog, almost identical to its U.K. counterpart, with identical front and back cover graphics and eleven songs in the same order as on the Parlophone issue, minus the three tracks listed above. Whatever level of brilliance they achieved on *Revolver* exploded into something entirely unexpected with their next album.

THE BEATLES: *SGT. PEPPER'S LONELY HEARTS CLUB BAND* (JUNE 1967)

Sgt. Pepper's Lonely Hearts Club Band is the album around which the concept of psychedelic music has been constructed for over fifty years and is the album around which the concept of the *album* as a single work of art was first considered. In the rivalry between the Beach Boys and the Beatles, this album closed the race. What began with *Rubber Soul* led to *Pet Sounds*, which led to *Revolver* and then "Good Vibrations," which led to the final furlong where *SMiLE* and *Sgt. Pepper's Lonely Hearts Club Band* gave fans a reason to believe that popular music was about to explode in ways that could not have been imagined just five years earlier. As the Beatles released *Sgt. Pepper's*, Brian Wilson, who since winter 1967 had spiraled into a pitched battle of paranoia and self-doubt, believed that he lost the race with the Beatles, and in response, he abandoned *SMiLE* for over three decades. Once the Beatles released *Sgt. Pepper's*, it appeared that nothing could go wrong for them.

In June, the Beatles also participated in *Our World*, the first worldwide satellite-transmitted event that brought together eighteen countries who contributed content for the global broadcast in addition to thirteen countries who, though they did not contribute segments for the show, participated by broadcasting the event in their respective countries. It was on *Our World* that the Beatles premiered their next single, the anthemic "All You Need Is Love," which was released in early July. While they took time off that month, they returned to the studio to record songs that would end up in their next filmed project, *Magical Mystery Tour* (*MMT*). While in north Wales for their first studies in Transcendental Meditation, the Beatles learned their manager, Brian Epstein, had died on August 27.

They moved into fall with two weeks of location filming for *Magical Mystery Tour*, which, by all accounts, was disorganized and poorly executed. Paul was inspired to create this project after an April 1967 visit to California, where he saw Ken Kesey's Merry Pranksters and the larger San Francisco scene (it was this same trip where he visited Brian Wilson in the studio for a session where he was recording "Vega-Tables"). The film was broadcast on British television on December 26, and the savage criticism heaped on *MMT* marked the end of 1967's "Summer of Love" and the beginning of a new world for the self-governed Beatles. Just six months earlier, the Beatles' world was perfect, and *Sgt. Pepper's Lonely Hearts Club Band* was the voice upon which they ushered in the new era.

In the weeks that followed the conclusion of their final U.S. tour in August 1966, each of the Beatles went off to work on individual projects, which prompted some in the press to speculate the band had in fact broken up. In truth, John traveled to Germany and Spain to film his role as Pvt. Gripweed in Richard Lester's film *How I Won the War*. George traveled to India to study the sitar, Eastern philosophy, and yoga. Ringo stayed home with his family, and Paul scored the soundtrack for the film *The Family Way*. It should be noted that while Paul stayed in London during in the fall of 1966, he also familiarized himself with the burgeoning alternative psychedelic scene that had begun to peak in the fall of that year.

In November 1966, the Beatles returned to the studio to begin recording their next album. They began with "Strawberry Fields Forever," a song like no other in their catalog. The song, which John wrote while on location for *How I Won the War*, has its origins in Lennon's childhood. This would become one of the most loved tracks in their canon, but in the creation of the song, new recording and editing techniques had to be created for George Martin to bring the song to completion.

Released in February 1967, the double A-side single "Strawberry Fields Forever"/"Penny Lane" defined an entirely new sound for the Beatles. The hallucinogenic haze of "Strawberry Fields Forever" is a feat of songwriting, performance, and production. It is never clear what instruments you are listening to, and Lennon's dreamy and hallucinogenic journey into childhood carries the listener into his dream world. Both songs also explore a novella approach in the lyrics, presaging the style of narratives that would make up *Sgt. Pepper's Lonely Hearts Club Band*.

Sgt. Pepper's Lonely Hearts Club Band is perhaps the most written about, analyzed, and studied album in all of pop music. The record was a stunning achievement, and while they had never created a through-composed work before *Sgt. Pepper's*, they never again created anything so organic and whole as they did with this album. The record tallied impressive sales numbers and chart highs, but one of the lesser known details about this record is that *Sgt. Pepper's Lonely Hearts Club Band* was the first rock album to win the Grammy Award for Album of the Year. In addition to the Beatles, the album featured contributions from numerous session musicians (the most ever employed on their records) for "A Day in the Life," "She's Leaving Home," "When I'm Sixty-Four" and musicians from the London-based Eastern Music Circle for George's composition "Within You, Without You." The narrative of a fictional rock group, Sgt. Pepper's Lonely Hearts Club Band connected an eclectic collection of compositional and musical styles that required their producer, George Martin, along with engineer Geoff Emerick, to continue expanding traditional approaches to recording. Whatever technical expertise they reached with *Revolver* was expanded tenfold on *Sgt. Pepper's Lonely Hearts Club Band*. They recorded the album on the dependable Studer four-track machines in Abbey Road, but they were able to combine machines and capture every possible sound the Beatles wanted. "Lucy in the Sky with Diamonds" would forever be discussed as code speak for LSD, and the epic "A Day in the Life," which closes the album, is a masterpiece in terms of composition, recording, and performance.

The record received the most elaborate packaging ever accorded a rock album. It featured a gatefold sleeve designed by Peter Blake with Jann Haworth and art direction and photography by Michael Cooper. Also included in the album were a set of cardboard souvenir cutouts of the fictional Sgt. Pepper and military decorations similar to those found on the Beatles' costumes worn on the cover. Most importantly, the lyrics for every song were included on the back sleeve of the gatefold, so even if you did not buy the album, you could read the narratives for the thirteen novellas that comprise *Sgt. Pepper's Lonely Hearts Club Band*.

After creating such an extraordinary work, it might be expected the Beatles would take a well-deserved break from the studio. They recorded a couple of George's compositions, "Only a Northern Song" and "It's All Too Much," during the sessions for *Sgt. Pepper's*, but these were not finished to satisfaction and were held back for inclusion on the soundtrack to *Yellow Submarine*. In the month following the release of *Sgt. Pepper's*, they recorded "All You Need Is Love," "You Know My Name (Look Up the Number)," and songs for *Magical Mystery Tour*. The Beatles released five albums between *Sgt. Pepper's Lonely Hearts Club Band* and their final long player, *Let It Be*, which was released after they broke up. Each of the five are excellent records by any standard, but none has the thematic cohesion or richness in production values of their 1967 masterwork.

BLUE CHEER: *VINCEBUS ERUPTUM* (JANUARY 1968)

Blue Cheer is one of the most punk of 1960s psychedelic bands. They outstripped other garage rock bands of the period, such as the Seeds and Question Mark and the Mysterians, and created a sound that would not be duplicated in that period or in the decades that followed. Based in the San Francisco Bay Area, they chose a name, as many punk and new wave groups would do a decade later (e.g., Red Kross, Salvation Army, the Germs, and the Vibrators), that carried double meaning in the expanding consumer culture. In their case, Blue Cheer was the name of a laundry detergent as well as a code for a variety of LSD that was available in San Francisco.

If Jimi Hendrix, after his incendiary performance at the Monterey Pop Festival in June 1967, challenged social perceptions of race and rock music, then previous standards of sonic assault in rock could not have anticipated the January 1968 release of Blue Cheer's debut album, *Vincebus Eruptum* (Philips). While Hendrix's ferocious virtuosity introduced exotic visuals and intoxicating dynamics into psychedelic music, Blue Cheer challenged listeners to realign prior assumptions through their compressed and raw sonic power that laid the groundwork for the yet to be defined genre of heavy metal. They were loud and possessed no pretensions to virtuosity or subtlety. Their playing embodied a corpulent mass of ear-splitting volume in ways no group before them had dared to preserve on record. Dickie Peterson on guitar and vocals along with Leigh Stevens and Paul Whalley created an extraordinary attack on the senses with one of the loudest rock albums of 1968. They may have lacked Hendrix's exquisite image that was constructed on a visual collage of colors, but Blue Cheer bore more visual similarity to refugee bikers. The ethos of "peace and love" had no place in their work, and while the sheer cacophony of this album would soon be bettered on the Velvet Underground's sophomore LP, *White Light, White Heat*, Blue Cheer's *Vincebus Eruptum*, and in particular their extraordinary read on Eddie Cochran's "Summertime Blues," signaled the arrival of heavy metal and is the flashpoint where psychedelia begins to compress into the sound that would define many hard rock groups through the 1970s and 1980s.

BOB DYLAN: *BLONDE ON BLONDE* (JUNE 1966)

"That thin, wild mercury sound"—this is how Bob Dylan, in 1978, described the sound he looked to capture on *Blonde on Blonde*, the follow-up to his already classic album *Highway 61 Revisited*. How any record by Bob Dylan ends up in a collection on psychedelic music is justified by its being the second of three albums released within a six-month period during that magical spring/summer of 1966 that heralded the arrival of psychedelia. The tryptic of the Beach Boys' *Pet Sounds* (May), Dylan's *Blonde on Blonde* (June), and the Beatles' *Revolver* (August) opened a door in rock music that gave free rein for a model of creative expression that would explode upon the music world before the end of that year. It was the first double album released in rock music and was released two weeks ahead of another groundbreaking double album, *Freak Out*, Frank Zappa and the Mothers of Invention's debut album that was produced by Tom Wilson.

Dylan had experimented with LSD as early as 1964 and was ahead of the social curve when it came to be expanding his extraordinarily expressive psyche. *Blonde on Blonde* was the third of Dylan's electric albums released at a time when many purists decried Dylan's decision to move beyond his acoustic folk sound for the electric world of rock and roll. These three albums brought Dylan back to where he began, as an aspiring teenage rock musician, but these were in no way a regressive move for the artist. Across these albums, his influence on musicians of his own generation would be greater than would have been imaginable in 1961, the year he was signed to Columbia (CBS) Records.

In a career that is peppered with groundbreaking, forward-looking albums, *Blonde on Blonde* truly is a unique record in Dylan's canon. He had begun to work with Levon and the Hawks (who, by 1968, would become known by their more recognized name, the Band) as his backing group in concert, but he had not yet adopted them in full as his studio band. Working with his trusted session musicians in New York, Dylan found himself unable to capture the sound he heard in his head. Producer Bob Johnston suggested that he record in Nashville, an unexpected location for an artist of his stature. But it was in Nashville where he was ultimately able to capture that "thin, wild mercury sound" with a set of crack session players who helped Dylan to shape one of rock music's greatest albums.

Bob Dylan is perhaps the most prolific musical artist from the last half of the twentieth century, and his influence as a performer, composer, and artist continues into the first decades of the twenty-first century and will likely be sustained long after he sheds his mortal coil. His impact over the past half-century has resulted in the special citation he received from the jury for the Pulitzer Prize, the Presidential Medal of Freedom, and, in 2016, the Nobel Prize in Literature. For the young man from Hibbing, Minnesota, who absorbed so many varieties of music on late-night AM radio, his voice was shaped by the artists whose work he admired, from Hank Williams (his first musical idol) and Little Richard to the Staple Singers and Johnny Cash. Their extraordinary music was filtered through Dylan's enigmatic mind and enabled him to become one of the most prolific and diverse artists of his generation.

Johnny Cash had been the first person to recommend to Dylan that he take a shot at recording in Nashville, but the Columbia A&R men did not want their prized artist recording out from under their watchful eye in New York City. Dylan began sessions in New York City in late 1965 and into the winter of 1966, but nothing captured on tape matched what he heard in his head. With the support of his new producer, Bob Johnston, he decided to relocate to Nashville and work with a crew of expert musicians with whom he never had worked before.

Tom Wilson (who throughout the 1960s would produce Simon & Garfunkel, Frank Zappa and the Mothers of Invention, the Animals, and the Velvet Underground) shepherded Dylan into his electric albums, but after a falling out, he was replaced behind the board by Bob Johnston. While long-simmering tensions between Dylan and Wilson went back to the sessions for *Another Side of Bob Dylan* (1964), it was Wilson's criticism of Al Kooper's playing on "Like a Rolling Stone" that was the flashpoint for their break. Wilson produced "Like a Rolling Stone," which appeared on the album *Highway 61 Revisited*, but the remainder of the long player was produced by Johnston, who recommended to Dylan that he try to make the next record in Nashville. In his concerts during this period, fans listened through his acoustic set but booed their displeasure when he strapped on the electric guitar in the second half of the show. Dylan continued to redefine the boundaries of popular music, but he also had to contend with thousands of disapproving fans. In this cauldron of artistic rebirth, *Blonde on Blonde* was created, and, with it, rock music was forever changed.

When Dylan began album sessions at Columbia's studios in New York City, Hawks drummer Levon Helm temporarily left the group and was replaced in the studio by Bobby Gregg. In addition to the remainder of the Hawks, he rounded out his band with Al Kooper, Paul Griffin, and Bruce Langhorne, all of whom worked on Dylan's previous two albums. Johnston also added a Nashville-based musician with whom he was familiar, Joe Souter, who later in the decade, as Joe South, went on to have successful hits both as a songwriter and solo artist (he authored "Hush," which was used on Deep Purple's first album; "Down in the Boondocks"; "Rose Garden"; and "Games People Play"). "Visions of Johanna" was one of the first songs they tried to record in New York, but with no success. Bobby Gregg could not provide the rhythmic underpinning upon which the song could unfold, so each attempt at recording the song became an exercise in frustration. Outtakes from the initial New York sessions for what became *Blonde on Blonde* were released nearly a quarter century later on the multivolume *The Bootleg Series*.

Although Dylan's manager, Albert Grossman, opposed the move to Nashville, Dylan made the move, taking with him Robbie Robertson and Al Kooper. It is generally understood that he worked over two blocks of sessions in mid-February and early March 1966, though Al Kooper and guitarist Charlie McCoy maintain there only was one extended block of sessions. Regardless of whose memories are correct, what remains is the fact that Dylan worked with a group of musicians, who aside from Robbie Robertson and Al Kooper (and partly with Charlie McCoy), he had never worked with before. From a production standpoint, there was the possibility for failure and that the sessions might not result in anything better than what had been recorded in the less than successful New York sessions at the end of 1965.

Blonde on Blonde features a wealth of songs about women, love, and relationships. Dylan was recently married to Sara Lownds, after significant (and very public) relationships with Joan Baez and Suzi Rotolo (the woman who appears on the cover of *The Freewheelin' Bob Dylan*). Many of the songs are believed to have been inspired by his failed romance with Warhol actress, debutante, heiress, and society girl Edie Sedgwick. Dylan's friend, filmmaker Bob Neuwirth, was another rival for Sedgwick's affections, and Dylan's marriage to Sara reportedly was an emotional hit to her. Sedgwick may be the heroine of *Blonde on*

Blonde, but Dylan's obsessive focus on relationships is central in nearly every song on the album.

"Rainy Day Women #12 & 35" is the opening track on side one and was a No. 2 single in the United States. It is a howling wreck of a song with a demented Salvation Army–like band (a feature Syd Barrett would use to equal effect in "Jugband Blues" on Pink Floyd's sophomore album, *A Saucerful of Secrets*). The song is Dylan thumbing his nose at his folk audience. The wordplay of the lyric "everybody must get stoned" was about the biblical practice of stoning a convicted criminal, but the real pleasure for all involved was that they could record a song that would be played on American radio that extolled everyone to get stoned. "Pledging My Time"—originally titled "What Can You Do for My Wigwam?"—is laden with cynicism but informed by the classic blues of Robert Johnson. "Visions of Johanna" is considered by many to be one of Dylan's masterpieces. This was a track that he attempted in the initial New York sessions under the title "Freeze Out." T. S. Eliot's writing is believed to have been an influence on Dylan and this is borne out in the nocturnal lyricism of a song that some commentators believe is about Joan Baez. Side one closes with "One of Us Must Know (Sooner or Later)," the only recording to survive intact from the New York sessions. Released as a single well in advance of the album, it made no headway on the charts.

Side two opens with the thematically and structurally simple (for Dylan) "I Want You," a track that remains, after the album opener, one of Dylan's most remembered songs. It was the final song recorded for the album and one of Al Kooper's favorites and is the most accessible "pop" song on the album. The lyrics are unusually simplistic for Dylan, repeating the line "I Want You" in a way he did with no other song, while squaring this off with an extensive cast of characters; Wayne Moss's guitar runs are just one of the magical features of this classic work. "Stuck Inside of Mobile with the Memphis Blues Again" is a perfectly arranged song over Dylan's lyrical tale of loneliness and alienation.

Every arrangement on *Blonde on Blonde* was achieved through a process of multiple takes in which the virtuoso session players adapted and evolved their parts on each take until they locked into the sound Dylan heard in his head. Part improvisation and part instinct within the moment, this song, along with the album closer, "Sad Eyed Lady of the Lowlands," has one of the most organic sensibilities of any song on the album thanks to Kooper's sustained chords on the Hammond organ, which are punctuated with a demi-staccato blues countermelody. "Leopard-Skin Pill-Box Hat" is a direct commentary on his failed relationship with Edie Sedgwick, referenced by her penchant for wearing leopard print clothing. The blues progression on which this song is built is another moment of Dylan channeling his early influences, but this time, instead of Robert Johnson, it is Lightnin' Hopkins. The first record ends with "Just Like a Woman," a song whose theme would have passed in 1966 but may be seen as a work of unapologetic misogyny in the twenty-first century.

Side three opens with one of the shortest tracks on the album, "Most Likely You Go Your Way and I'll Go Mine," an atypically straightforward song about the breakup of two lovers that may refer to his unrealized relationship with Sedgwick. This is followed with the slow blues of "Temporary Like Achilles," a song that began as "Medicine Sunday." The part blues shuffle, part Memphis, and full pop sensibility of "Absolutely Sweet Marie" is an infectious song. "Fourth Time Around" is an interesting work on multiple fronts. It is one of the first songs Dylan took into the studios in Nashville. It was, for Dylan, an unusual number, as lilting triple-meter works were not a standard feature in his songbook.

Was "Fourth Time Around" the inspiration for the Beatles' "Norwegian Wood" or is the song Dylan's less than gracious answer to one of the most well-known songs by the Beatles? Bob Dylan's influence on the Beatles had been expressed in late 1964 with "I'm a Loser" and mid-1965 with the soundtrack to *Help!*, which featured Lennon's "You've Got to Hide Your Love Away," and later that year with *Rubber Soul* and "Norwegian Wood." Dylan may have believed the Beatles stole the song from him when he played an early version of the tune for them, but McCartney has defended Lennon by pointing out that he first composed the song in early 1965, before they met Dylan. Regardless, the song is a striking departure for the album and is one of the most accessible songs and least electric on the album. The third side closes with "Obviously Five Believers," another song of lost love and longing and an abrupt shift from the gentle waltz of "Fourth Time Around." Instead, this song borrows from "Good Morning Little Schoolgirl," a song written by Sonny Boy Williamson that was a standard among English blues groups. While known to blues aficionados in England, the work of Sonny Boy Williamson was less widely known among white musicians in the United States, except for those kids who, in the 1950s, were listening to blues on nighttime AM radio that was broadcast from far-off locations, just as Dylan first heard this music as a teenager.

The album ends with a song that takes the entirety of side 4, "Sad Eyed Lady of the Lowlands." This eleven-minute masterpiece is like no other in the canon, but it was not the first eleven-minute-plus song on a rock album. In April of that year, the Rolling Stones released the extraordinary "Goin' Home" to close out the first side of their Swinging Sixties musical novella, *Aftermath*. Like "Goin' Home," Dylan's song is eleven minutes and seventeen seconds in length, an otherwise unheard-of length for any song on a rock album. "Sad Eyed Lady of the Lowlands" is about Dylan's new wife, Sara Lownds, and he considered it the best song he had written up to that point. If "Just Like a Woman" is the misogynist Dylan, "Sad Eyed Lady of the Lowlands" is the opposite and is his most intimate and touching love song. Less than five years later, Pink Floyd would become known for works that inhabited an entire LP side, and the Floyd's Roger Waters was influenced by Dylan's expansive treatment of the song form. "Sad Eyed Lady of the Lowlands" has a solemn gospel feel and is the perfect conclusion to one of the most perfect albums released in the 1960s.

Barely two months after the release of *Blonde on Blonde*, the Beatles' *Revolver* was released in both England and North America, and Bob Dylan, always one step ahead of every curve, did not release an album of new material for a year and a half. After recovering from a motorcycle accident in July 1966, he returned to Nashville in the fall of 1967 to record the roots-inspired album *John Wesley Harding*.

THE BYRDS: *YOUNGER THAN YESTERDAY* (1967)

The Byrds are most widely remembered for the radio-friendly, jingle-jangle hit singles from their first three albums, *Mr. Tambourine Man* (1965), *Turn, Turn, Turn* (1965), and *Fifth Dimension* (1966), the latter of which included one of the first psychedelic hit singles, "Eight Miles High." But it is their February 1967 offering, an autumnal psychedelic masterpiece, *Younger than Yesterday*, that is the band's strongest and most cohesive purely psychedelic album. This was their second album as a quartet following the loss of lead singer Gene Clark, who departed in the early stage of recording the *Fifth Dimension* album (but not before coauthoring the aforementioned "Eight Miles High"). *Younger than Yesterday* signaled David Crosby's maturation as a songwriter of depth and originality, and under new producer Gary Usher, the band delivered a well-crafted album that incorporated a mélange of county rock, raga rock, and psychedelia. To complement David Crosby's rich songwriting and vocal skills, bassist Chris Hillman also emerged as a prominent songwriter on *Younger than Yesterday* and provided the album's opening track and hit single, "So You Want to Be a Rock and Roll Star," which featured South African trumpet virtuoso Hugh Masekela.

The strength of the album's opening track was sustained with the Hillman/McGuinn composition "Have You Seen Her Face," with its wonderfully discordant solo guitar lines that mesh with McGuinn's iconic jingle-jangle sound to create a wonderful psychedelic classic. McGuinn's interest in science fiction and his awareness of the recently developed quasar informs the proto–space rock of "C.T.A.-102," which includes an oscillator and pitch-altered voices on the song's coda. The country-flavored "Renaissance Fair" was inspired by a visit to Southern California's widely reknowned Renaissance Pleasure Faire. Hillman's "Time Between" could have fit perfectly on Jefferson Airplane's *Surrealistic Pillow* (1967) or *Crown of Creation* (1968), as McGuinn's guitar work and Hillman's vocals sound uncannily like the Airplane's Paul Kantner. What makes this track all the more extraordinary is that it marked one of Hillman's first attempts at songwriting.

Simmering creative tensions between McGuinn and David Crosby could be read into "Everybody's Been Burned," one of the finest tracks recorded by any configuration of the Byrds, even though Crosby composed the song before he cofounded the group. Usher's production highlights excellent guitar work that shows more than a touch of influence from the Beatles' *Revolver*, which was released five months prior to this album. The second half of the album features two songs each from Hillman and Crosby (the album's final track was coauthored by McGuinn) and one from Bob Dylan. "Thoughts and Words" is a heady slice of moody, West Coast pop, and Crosby's "Mind Gardens" creates an air not unlike one of Grace Slick's intoned and quasi-improvisational songs with Jefferson Airplane. "My Back Pages" features perfect vocal work by McGuinn and Crosby and McGuinn's signature guitar timbres in one of the band's best Dylan covers. The song also provided the band with a kernel of the album's title in the line "I'm younger than that now." Where this song may have marked Dylan's farewell to his early voice, it unknowingly marked the Byrds' transition into one of the most iconoclastic bands of the era.

Hillman's "The Girl with No Name" features future Byrd Clarence White and provides a hint of the country-hued sound they would refine on *Sweetheart of the Rodeo* and Hillman's later work with the Flying Burrito Brothers. The album concludes with the McGuinn/Crosby tune "Why," a sorely underrated track that shows the Beatles' influence in the choppy guitar work and serpentine vocal line. It appeared in a simpler version as the B side to "Eight Miles High" but was substantially revised in this iteration.

The 1996 reissue of *Younger than Yesterday* contained a rich collection of tracks from the period prior to the album's release. Crosby's "It

Happens Each Day" presages the style of songwriting he would soon master with Crosby, Stills & Nash. The McGuinn/Hillman "Don't Make Waves" was written for the Tony Curtis/Claudia Cardinale/Sharon Tate film of the same name. The song is slightly improved in this version over the edit that appeared in the film. The alternate version of "My Back Pages" with its more prominent organ part is believed to have been intended for the single release. A single released between this album and its successor, *The Notorious Byrd Brothers*, "Lady Friend" b/w "Old John Robertson" are the two gems that conclude the extended version of the album. The A side is one of Crosby's tour de force compositions, and the B side would appear in a remixed version on their next album.

THE BYRDS: *THE NOTORIOUS BYRD BROTHERS* (1968)

Between the Byrds' second and third albums, Gene Clark, their primary vocalist and songwriter, left the group. Rather than marking a decline for the band, it signaled a new and creatively rich period for the Byrds. At the peak of their creative trajectory in the summer and fall of 1967, and following the release of their fourth album, *Younger than Yesterday*, they splintered further with the departures of both David Crosby and Michael Clarke during the recording of *The Notorious Byrd Brothers*. Though recorded in the midst of an ensemble slimming from a quartet to a duo, *The Notorious Byrd Brothers* is one of the most progressive and rewarding records of the period and features some of the Byrds' most ethereal music. In their second Gary Usher–produced album, the Byrds threw themselves into psychedelia and confidently integrated pop, country, jazz, and electronic influences into their work. This is one of the earliest pop albums to feature the Moog synthesizer, and its colors enhanced the band's already rich aural palate. (A demonstration of a Moog synthesizer at the Monterey Pop Music Festival generated a great deal of interest from artists who performed at the festival, and in the last half of 1967, the instrument appeared on records by Diana Ross and the Supremes, the Doors, and the Monkees; however, the Byrds' use of the instrument on a number of songs was more than a timbral novelty.) After Crosby's firing, the band convinced Gene Clark to return to the band, and while he performed a handful of shows, his contributions to *The Notorious Byrd Brothers* are negligible, though the glorious vocal stack on "Goin' Back" gives reason for many to believe that Clark performed on this song.

The album opens with "Artificial Energy," a true-to-form drug song loaded with a funky brass accompaniment. It kicks the album into high gear and is followed by one of the band's most beautiful and striking cover songs, "Goin' Back," a haunting song by Carole King and Gerry Goffin. The song featured only McGuinn and Hillman because Crosby refused to play on the recording and Clarke had been fired from the group. Hillman's "Natural Harmony" blends the seemingly incongruous timbres of the Moog synthesizer and the pedal steel guitar in a near-perfect song. "Draft Morning" is a Crosby, Hillman, and McGuinn composition, and despite its, fractured gestation (Crosby was fired before the song was finished in the studio), its power and message are patently clear. A second King/Goffin tune, "Wasn't Born to Follow," is given a thorough country treatment thanks to the tasteful guitar picking of future Byrd Clarence White. The graceful five-legged waltz of McGuinn and Hillman's "Get to You" mixes equal parts psychedelia and country romance. "Change is Now" features more country sensibilities thanks to Clarence White, but the song veers off into a rambling Moog landscape with numerous overdubs.

Hillman and McGuinn offered a more strident read on "Old John Robertson" that works more effectively than the original arrangement on the flip side of "Lady Friend." The infrequent writing partnership of Crosby and McGuinn is featured on the requisite trip-out work, the 5/4 meter "Tribal Gathering," that relays the events of the January 1967 Human Be-In at San Francisco's Golden Gate Park. "Dolphin's Smile" features the Moog synthesizer in a classic jingle-jangle Byrds song. The album closer, "Space Odyssey," is inspired by Arthur C. Clarke's short story, two years before Kubrick's film based on the story ended up in cinemas. This sound effects–loaded song is a perfect closer to the Byrds' second psychedelic masterpiece.

The CD reissue of *The Notorious Byrd Brothers* features a pair of overlooked songs. McGuinn's "Moog Raga" should have been included on the album but likely was considered too esoteric for inclusion on a Byrds album. Crosby's "Triad" was rejected for the album because of its unconventional subject, in this case polyamory. It was covered beautifully by Grace Slick on the Jefferson Airplane's *Crown of Creation* album. Crosby's departure was precipitated in part by the band's rejection of this song in favor of the Goffin/King songs.

The Notorious Byrd Brothers is the final album to feature the McGuinn, Hillman, and Crosby configuration of the Byrds (while Crosby would be fired partway through making this album, Hillman would leave the group after their next album, *Sweetheart of the Rodeo*, to join Gram Parsons in the Flying Burrito Brothers). Clarke and Crosby's departures during the making of this album brought the curtain down on the band's first chapter. Many bands face an inevitable decline in quality and consistency when key members leave the group, but in the case of the Byrds, the band evolved into new and daring styles of music. Beyond *The Notorious Byrd Brothers*, the group released four additional albums (until 1970's *Untitled*) that mixed country rock with the new rock of the postpsychedelic counterculture. Each of the four is unique unto itself, and the richness of the songwriting and performing enable each of the albums to stand as a quartet of all but forgotten masterworks.

THE CRAZY WORLD OF ARTHUR BROWN: *THE CRAZY WORLD OF ARTHUR BROWN* (JUNE 1968)

The Crazy World of Arthur Brown is one of the handful of one-hit wonders in this volume, a majority of whom have been included in the essay on the *Nuggets* compilation. Regardless, the legacy of Arthur Brown's theatrical histrionics continued long after the band ceased to exist, and therefore his contributions to psychedelia are worthy of recognition. Arthur Brown was a student at Reading University when he began to perform with various blues bands and was briefly a member of the Foundations ("Build Me Up Buttercup"). He recorded under the Arthur Brown Set before reemerging as the Crazy World of Arthur Brown.

Brown's influence on the theatrical side of rock music would come to maturation in the 1970s with artists such as Alice Cooper, David Bowie, Peter Gabriel, and others. He was name checked by Frank Zappa in 1971, when, at a concert by Frank Zappa and the Mothers of Invention at Montreux Casino on December 4, 1971, a flare fired into the ceiling by an overenthusiastic fan created a fire that burned the building to the ground. As the conflagration began to get out of control, Zappa was recorded saying, "Fire! Arthur Brown in person." The fire was the source of the lyric for Deep Purple's 1972 hit "Smoke on the Water." The band was at the concert and was set to begin recording the album that would become *Machine Head*, which became Deep Purple's longest-lasting and most identifiable record.

The Crazy World of Arthur Brown was signed by Kit Lambert, the Who's manager, who produced (with Pete Townshend credited as associate producer) their self-titled first album on Track Records in the summer of 1968. That would be a banner year for Track Records. In addition to serving the Who, the label signed Jimi Hendrix and, beginning in 1967, released the three Jimi Hendrix Experience albums and the live album *Band of Gypsies*. In late 1968, the label also distributed the infamous John Lennon and Yoko Ono album *Unfinished Music No. 1: Two*

Virgins. Rejected by EMI, Apple Records' primary distributor, the album was picked up by Track Records. (In the United States, *Two Virgins* was distributed through Tetragrammaton, the U.S. label for Deep Purple Mk I). So, within a slightly anarchic company like Track, *The Crazy World of Arthur Brown* was a completely logical release.

The album's most famous song, "Fire," remains a staple of the late psychedelic period and is a clear inspiration for many of the theatrical rock acts that would soon flood the marketplace after 1970. The album reached the top 10 on the U.S. Billboard charts and the top 10 in the United Kingdom, Canada, and Australia. The album exists in multiple versions, though the stereo mix is the most widely known. Although released in the United Kingdom in both monophonic and stereo, the stereo mix had to be heavily edited for release in the United States. Atlantic Records felt that drummer Drachan Theaker could not keep a beat and ordered Lambert to "fix" the sonic deficiencies. He ended up overdubbing brass and strings to enhance the texture of the album. This version is the most widely known mix, though after 1991, alternative monophonic mixes were included as bonus tracks on the CD release.

The album is wonderfully suited to a hallucinogenic trip, and Brown's extraordinary vocals do not sound dissimilar to what Ian Gillan would deliver just two years later with Deep Purple Mk II. The heavy organ sound is somewhat similar to Jon Lord's sonic palate on Deep Purple's records, but it is also similar to the heavy organ swirl heard on countless freakbeat singles in 1966. His declamatory speech-singing style would be refined by the Doors, and the acid-tripping free-for-all sound would be expanded upon by Zappa and the Mothers of Invention. Brown's well-developed vocal stylings would become a hallmark in the early works of both David Bowie and Peter Gabriel, and the pyrotechnics and radical stage presentation would be seen in Alice Cooper's work starting in 1969. While *The Crazy World of Arthur Brown* is a dependable debut album, it was Arthur Brown's flair for production that has likely had the most influence in the field.

After *The Crazy World of Arthur Brown*, neither the band nor its namesake would have much success with later releases, although Arthur Brown would appear as a guest vocalist on a number of artists' records, notably with Kingdom Come and early progressive/psychedelic pioneers Hawkwind. While his career was not as incendiary in the post–Crazy World years, Brown's work remained as creative as ever. In the late 1970s, he lived in Africa and directed the Burundi National Orchestra, a rock group that played the songs of Hendrix alongside works by local artists. He studied guitar with Robert Fripp and had settled in Austin, Texas by the 1980s and released albums of synthesizer music.

CREAM: *DISRAELI GEARS* (NOVEMBER 1967)

Cream was the first pedigreed supergroup of the rock and roll era, three musicians who were the "cream" of the crop. They were also the first power trio of the era, in addition to being one of the finest psychedelic rock acts of all time. (An earlier band, the Big Three, was a Merseybeat trio that was part of the British Invasion, and though they were not a supergroup, a number of notable musicians cycled through that band.) Cream managed this while staying true to their creative vision and without any concern for the trends or styles that exploded in the years 1966–1968. Their legacy outlasted their brief existence, and the influence all three members have had on rock music remains a significant force to the present day.

Cream was composed of Eric Clapton (guitar), Jack Bruce (bass), and Ginger Baker (percussion), and together they created a most extraordinary sound from their shared blues lineage. Clapton was the original guitarist for the Yardbirds, but he left soon after the release of their breakthrough hit "For Your Love." He also did a stint with the legendary group John Mayall & the Bluesbreakers, where he played alongside future Fleetwood Mac bassist John McVie. After leaving Mayall's group, Clapton was replaced by Peter Green, who would go on to found Fleetwood Mac with two other members of the Bluesbreakers, McVie and Mick Fleetwood. Both Jack Bruce and Ginger Baker played with the Graham Bond Organisation, a brief but significant contributor to the English blues scene. Both men were known for their exceptional playing and had previously played in Alexis Korner's Blues Incorporated, a group who at one time or another had featured many of the best blues musicians in Britain, including future members of the Rolling Stones, the Artwoods (who would later feature future Deep Purple organist Jon Lord), the Graham Bond Organisation, and others. While their recorded output was minimal and they had little impact on the charts, the group helped to shape some of the leading musicians of the time, and both Baker and Bruce cut their teeth among Britain's finest blues musicians. After leaving the Graham Bond Organisation, Jack Bruce also played with Manfred Mann prior to joining Cream.

The terms *rock and roll* and *pedigree* would never have been used in the same breath if Cream had not created the model without any concern for labels. In their wake, the term *supergroup* would be used to identify any band composed of members who elected to leave a prior concern to join forces with like-minded musicians who also had chosen to leave their very successful bands to create something entirely new. A supergroup was not content to revisit previously existing models and styles but set out to shape an entirely new style of music. Over time, the definition of the model expanded to include groups whose members came together to make music along shared lines of interest over any desire to create a new hit style, and some were created with the intention of being short-lived excursions (e.g., the Honeydrippers, Humble Pie) designed to provide their members with a sense of creative freedom amid the pressures of being major-selling rock acts.

The inspiration for Cream came from Ginger Baker, who wanted to work with Clapton. Eric wanted to work with Jack Bruce, and while Baker was not keen on being in a band with Bruce, he agreed to it to realize his goal of working with Clapton. Although Baker and Jack Bruce had a volatile working relationship in their time with Graham Bond Organisation, that tension enabled Cream to create a quartet of extraordinary albums. Jack Bruce joined on after stints in John Mayall & the Bluesbreakers and, briefly, Manfred Mann. After seeing Buddy Guy at the Marquee on Wardour Street, Clapton had decided that a trio was the ideal composition for this new band. Where many white British blues bands made a sincere effort to emulate the authentic sound of the blues from the Mississippi Delta, Cream made a conscious effort to take the language of the blues into completely new territory, to a place where they did not sound like white English boys trying to sound authentic in their blackness. The exceptional improvisatory skills possessed by each of the three enabled their sound to explode both in concert and in the studio.

Cream's debut album, *Fresh Cream*, was released at the very end of 1966 and is a solid blues rock album. It may be heavier blues than that of other English blues artists, but at its core, it captured the energetic spirit of the era, when blues and beat music collided at the moment when psychedelia had just begun to take off. Released in England on Robert Stigwood's Reaction label, the ten-track album was slightly altered for the American release on Atlantic, and this version is the most widely known configuration. It opens with the Jack Bruce/Pete Brown song "I Feel Free," which gives what is otherwise a blues-based album a decidedly psychedelic bent. Released as a single in the United Kingdom, it was left off the album in their home country. The remainder of the album mostly features songs composed by the band, though songs by Robert Johnson, Muddy Waters, and Skip James frame the larger beat/blues album.

Ahmet Ertegun, the visionary head of their American label, Atlantic Records, brought the band to the United States to record their sophomore album in an American studio with American producers and engineers with the hope of capturing a feel with a more cohesive and identifiable sound. He had distinct views of what the band could become and envisioned the group with Clapton as the front man, although it was clear to everyone concerned that Jack wrote many of the songs and sang most of the vocals. Ertegun's attempt to reshape the structure of the band was just one of the outside influences that would wear on the band's already fragile structure. The legendary Tom Dowd engineered the album with Felix Pappalardi producing, and with this team, Cream delivered a record that matched the intensity and focus of their live shows. In November 1967, months after its completion, the psychedelic masterpiece *Disraeli Gears* was launched upon a market that absorbed everything that was new in popular music. The title, derived from a malapropism in describing the derailleur gears of a bicycle, was converted to borrow the name of nineteenth-century British prime minister Benjamin Disraeli.

"Strange Brew," the opening track on the album, remains one of the band's best and most recognizable songs. The lead vocal is delivered by Eric Clapton, who had to be convinced into singing it (he was allowed a broadly defined guitar solo in exchange). Jack Bruce was generally the front man on vocals, but this song featured Clapton's tentative falsetto alternating with Bruce's declamatory delivery and resulted in a perfect opening track. It is one of Clapton's few songs on the album and was cowritten with producer Pappalardi and his wife, Gail Collins. The next track, "Sunshine of Your Love," is one of their greatest songs. It was inspired from a bass line Jack Bruce played on an upright bass, and when it came together as a complete work, Ginger Baker's drums were the timbral and rhythmic core to Bruce and Clapton's interweaving textures, which include one of Clapton's most iconic solos. "World of Pain," composed by Felix Pappalardi and Gail Collins, is a good psychedelic pop song and a release after the tension of the two opening tracks. "Dance the Night Away" is another excellent Jack Bruce/Pete Brown composition that attempts to work as a tribute to the American sound of Buffalo Springfield and the Byrds, down to the jingle jangle of the twelve-string guitar lines and far outstrips anything recorded by the bands who may have influenced the work. Ginger Baker's solo composition "Blue Condition" closes the first side and features his sneering, nasal, yet charming vocals.

Side two opens with the amazing "Tales of Brave Ulysses," a tune composed by Clapton and Martin Sharp, the artist who designed the covers for this album and its follow-up, *Wheels of Fire*. For this track, Clapton was inspired by the dirty guitar sound created by Zal Yanovsky, of the Lovin' Spoonful, and the connection to the Spoonful's "Summer in the City" is very clear. "SWLABR" is Jack Bruce's sped-up blues stomper that features Pete Brown's wild lyrics and Clapton's virtuoso guitar work within Bruce's complex composition. "We're Going Wrong" was inspired by a fight Jack had with his wife and is the moodiest and most surreal track on the album. Baker's drumming is the glue that prevents this circular song from spiraling out of control, and Clapton's spare guitar touches are exquisite. It was constructed from two recordings in different keys, not unlike the Beatles' "Strawberry Fields Forever," and this technique contributes to the spiraling and disoriented quality of the song. The final three songs on the album are more directly connected to their blues roots. "Outside Woman Blues" is Clapton's arrangement of Arthur Reynold's song and a straightforward blues tune that is reminiscent of their earlier work. "Take It Back" is another Bruce/Brown composition and features Jack's vocals and harmonica playing. "Mother's Lament" is the band's arrangement of a traditional English show hall tune.

The deluxe edition of the album features the mono mix of the album, demo versions, BBC recordings, and "Lawdy Mama," a precursor of "Strange Brew." It features different lyrics and a slightly different arrangement and is interesting to hear against the classic finished product that contains the contributions of Felix Pappalardi and Gail Collins. Baker's "Blue Condition" is also included, but with Clapton's vocal instead of Ginger's harder delivery.

The cover for *Disraeli Gears* is one of the most recognizable album sleeves from a year in which numerous iconic albums were released with equally extraordinary artwork. It was designed by Martin Sharp, who shared a studio with Robert Whittaker, a photographer who created a number of iconic 1960s album covers, including the Beatles' infamous "Butcher cover." Sharp took Whittaker's photograph of the trio and washed it in electric colors, placing their image within a collage that explodes off the cover. Sharp created artwork for both the Middle Earth club and the UFO Club, and his work is recognizable among many images from that period.

CREAM: *WHEELS OF FIRE* (JULY 1968)

If any band from the 1960s would have been stamped with a date of expiration of the sort found on food products such as heavy, or whipping cream, it would have been the British supergroup Cream, who were destined for a short life span. The band was composed of three volatile personalities who were among the best blues and pop musicians in the world, and together they created work that was so groundbreaking and influential that it is a wonder that the band lasted as long as it did. Prior to the release of Cream's third album, *Wheels of Fire*, their manager, Robert Stigwood, announced that Cream would disband after one final tour (and ultimately a final album, *Goodbye*).

Wheels of Fire is vastly different from its predecessor but equally important in the band's catalog. *Disraeli Gears* was housed in Martin Sharp's technicolor collage, but *Wheels of Fire* featured the extreme opposite, a silver-toned cover loaded in explosive images, once again designed by Sharp. After the release of *Disraeli Gears*, Cream went on a seemingly endless cycle of tours. Their frequent appearances in the United States exposed the band to all levels of the 1968 edition of the American experience, and their playing impacted all musicians who heard them. Jefferson Airplane's Jorma Kaukonen and Jack Casady saw Cream during their extended residencies at Bill Graham's Fillmore, and they were inspired to expand their own sound to the wildest imaginable extremes. The social revolution happening in the streets over 1967 and 1968 accompanied Cream across the United States as they played any venue that manager Robert Stigwood deemed to be workable, and as a result, they were heard by thousands of American kids. Unlike *Disraeli Gears*, which was recorded in a matter of days, *Wheels of Fire* was recorded, both in New York and in London, over a course of months in between tours and other obligations.

The myth of "Clapton is God" was given free rein, as audiences could not get enough of the group. Their albums were often released months after they were recorded (balancing the demands of touring and the ongoing sales and chart action for records they already had in shops), and by the time the group was on the road, their sound had already begun to develop in a new direction. They became frustrated with the awareness that it did not matter what they played or how well they played it because the fans were hysterical for their sound, which did nothing to calm the creative and emotional turbulence around the band. They prided themselves on the extraordinary precision and virtuosity of their talents, but as it became harder to sustain this level of quality night after night, their patience with the band, with the music, with Stigwood, and with each other had become frayed to an utterly irreparable state. Amid the stresses of their endless tours and concert appearances, they managed to record an album every bit as diverse as the Beatles' self-titled double masterpiece, the *White Album*, which was released three months after *Wheels of Fire*.

The opening track, "White Room," is another Jack Bruce/Pete Brown masterpiece, and like "Strange Brew," which opened their previous album, it settles the listener in for an extraordinary ride. Clapton's contributions to the album included two blues covers, "Sitting on Top of the World" and, on side two, "Born under a Bad Sign," and both were given unbelievable treatments that enabled Clapton to extend his best work. "Passing the Time," composed by Ginger Baker with Mike Taylor, is a Syd Barrett–influenced slice of wistful childlike psychedelia that is interrupted with a speed-trip drone and is a work unlike any other in the band's catalog. Jack Bruce sings the lead on this song and sounds uncannily like Ginger Baker. The Bruce/Brown "As You Said" is another perfect slice of English psychedelia and is a track where Clapton is absent. The last two songs on side one feature two of the most unique arrangements they ever recorded.

Side two opens with "Pressed Rat and Warthog," another Baker/Taylor journey into a Syd Barrett–like fairy tale, with Felix Pappalardi playing the trumpet. "Politician" was one of the band's signature works in concert and allowed for extended improvisations during live performances. "Those Were the Days" is the third Baker/Taylor composition on the album and highlights the arrangement with marimba, hand bells, and tubular bells. Bruce and Clapton's deft handling of the vocal parts floats across treacherous metric changes. "Deserted Cities of the Heart" concludes the first album of this psychedelic timbral smorgasbord. Virtuoso playing runs across the whole work with a viola part delivered by Pappalardi over wild metric shifts and results in extraordinary playing from the band and their producer.

The second album of this set is a collection of live performances recorded at Bill Graham's Fillmore and Winterland Auditorium. They perform "Toad" and "Spoonful" from their debut album and the iconic "Crossroads" and "Traintime." The studio album demonstrates the extent of the band's virtuosity and ability to shape a variety of musical styles to their particular will. The diversity of aural experiences on the first disc makes this one of the richest albums in this volume. The single "Anyone for Tennis" is included on deluxe compact disc editions of the album. This Clapton/Martin Sharp tune is a most unexpectedly whimsical tune that would have been a natural inclusion on the album proper.

The album was released with an understanding that Cream had come to the end of its run as they prepared one final album that would be released after they split up. The appropriately titled *Goodbye* includes three live tracks recorded on their farewell tour performances at the Los Angeles Forum, where Deep Purple was one of the opening acts.

Recordings of both Deep Purple's and Cream's sets from this show have been available for some years and are a fascinating view into the emergence of hard rock, as it would soon explode with bands such as Led Zeppelin, Deep Purple Mk. II, and others. The live tracks are lengthened excursions of songs that appeared on their prior studio albums.

The three studio tracks give an indication of the directions that each of these artists followed in their next creative iterations. The Clapton/George Harrison tune "Badge" features a sound Clapton would develop further in his work with Derek and the Dominoes. Jack Bruce's "Doing That Scrapyard Thing" has a sound not unlike George Harrison's work on *All Things Must Pass*. The final song, Ginger Baker's "What a Bringdown," gives a taste of how his work would evolve in Blind Faith and Ginger Baker's Air Force. Fans and critics are split on this album, with some praising the live tracks but dismissing the studio tracks and others preferring the studio tracks over the remarkable live performances. The three studio tracks do give fans a glimpse of what Cream might have done if they had not decided to split up. This band may have been created with an expiration date, but none of the three had had any idea when that would be. In their brief existence, they left four excellent albums, each one unique and demonstrating the extraordinary musicianship contained in that unique trio.

Following Cream's demise in 1968, Clapton formed two more supergroups, Blind Faith and Derek and the Dominos, and the very definition of a *supergroup* would evolve over the next decades. Emerson, Lake & Palmer was perhaps the most successful and longest-lasting progressive rock supergroup. Crosby, Stills & Nash was born out of the beat and psychedelic movement (e.g., the Byrds, Buffalo Springfield, and the Hollies) and went on to shape the Laurel Canyon subgenre of the late 1960s and early 1970s. In the 1980s, some early heroes of rock and country formed supergroups that were a throwback to an earlier, more nostalgic time. Their music making was exceptional, and both the Highwaymen and the Traveling Wilburys brought full circle the concept of virtuoso artists who, early in their respective careers, sought new paths in popular and country music. In both cases, each group would highlight the styles that defined their legacies, with the result being a fresh take on some of rock's earliest influences and not a convenient trip down the lane of nostalgia.

DEEP PURPLE: *SHADES OF DEEP PURPLE* (JULY 1968)

Deep Purple, Black Sabbath, and Led Zeppelin comprise the pantheon of hard rock bands who helped to forge the genre at the end of the 1960s and carried it into the next decade as the full-blown genre that defined the first half of the 1970s. Most people remember Deep Purple for Richie Blackmore's iconic riff in the opening figure from their 1972 albatross of a masterpiece "Smoke on the Water," but their influence and importance extend far beyond that one song. They are the most enduring band and trademark in hard rock, as they have, excluding the years 1976–1984, in one configuration or other, been an active recording and touring concern from 1968 to the present day, despite the fact they have set their farewell tour to conclude in 2020. Before Deep Purple helped to shape the classic hard rock sound of the 1970s, they released three fascinating, if slightly uneven, albums with the lineup referred to as Deep Purple Mk. I: Rod Evans (vocals), Nick Simper (bass), Jon Lord (organ), Richie Blackmore (guitar), and Ian Paice (drums). The first of this trio of albums, *Shades of Deep Purple*, is a heavy psychedelic masterpiece.

Although Deep Purple has endured for fifty years, they are one of the most structurally fragile bands and have cycled through no fewer than eight configurations of the group. When inducted into the Rock and Roll Music Hall of Fame in 2016, members of the band's first three lineups were included, an acknowledgment of the commercial and creative impact that was served by the first configurations of Deep Purple. For many fans, the band is categorized into one of two frameworks, the Blackmore years and the non-Blackmore years, the latter having existed longer than the length of Blackmore's tenure in the band.

Shades of Deep Purple has unfairly been described as sounding like the "English Vanilla Fudge," though Purple were superior musicians to Vanilla Fudge and their first three albums display greater technical and interpretative skills than heard on the American quartet's impressive trio of albums. Jon Lord and Ritchie Blackmore saw Vanilla Fudge in their first British shows and expressed admiration for the group and their ability to expand the two-and-a-half-minute pop song into an eight- to ten-minute orgiastic assault on the senses. The comparisons to Vanilla Fudge are superficial, as Purple's influences were much broader and included not only classical music and jazz but Cream, Jimi Hendrix, and an array of early rock and roll styles.

Deep Purple was born from a concept called *Roundabout* that was developed by Chris Curtis, formerly of the Searchers, where he imagined a nucleus composed of a drummer, guitarist, and a keyboard player. It was later described by Lord as follows: "We (Blackmore and Lord) should be the center of the roundabout, and other musicians could jump on and off the roundabout as they chose . . . a lovely, psychedelic idea." Curtis initially approached the Herefordshire group Shakedown Sound and pitched his Roundabout concept, but they were less than enthused, though a few years later they would emerge in the center of the glam scene as Mott the Hoople.

It was Curtis's fortuitous timing and a few well-placed rejections that enabled him to bring Lord, Simper, and Blackmore onto the Roundabout concept. Jon Lord had played with the Artwoods, a rhythm and blues band led by Art Wood, the older brother of future Faces and Rolling Stones guitarist Ron Wood. They recorded a few sides on Decca and Parlophone but fell short in their quest toward stardom. They wanted to pursue a rock and classical fusion project but were nixed and ultimately dropped by Decca (one year later, Decca somewhat unexpectedly found itself with a rock classical fusion album in the Moody Blues' *Days of Future Passed*). The rock and classical fusion is one by-product of psychedelia that has not been fully recognized, but the work Lord premiered in 1969 with "Concerto for Group and Orchestra" and two years later with "Gemini Suite," plus the Moody Blues' classical-lite chart topper, *Days of Future Passed*, and Keith Emerson's work (first with the Nice and later with Emerson, Lake & Palmer) would become a significant influence on rock music throughout the following decade.

With Lord's rock and classical fusion ideas on hold, he, along with Nick Simper, joined a touring version of the studio psychedelia-lite novelty act the Flowerpot Men, whose single "Let's Go to San Francisco" was a modest hit in the United Kingdom. Curtis's Roundabout concept was precarious, but Lord and Simper were able to connect with Ritchie Blackmore, who had spent a good deal of time playing in Germany with a number of different groups. On the evening in November 1967 when Curtis introduced Lord and Blackmore, they composed "And the Address" and "Mandrake Root," both of which ended up on their debut album. They also worked out their arrangement of the Beatles' "Help," which also ended up on their debut LP.

Chris Curtis departed from the Roundabout but not before he connected the band with Tony Edwards, a successful clothier who was looking to invest in a musical group. Curtis met Edwards through his friend Vicki Wickham, the assistant producer for the legendary pop show *Ready, Steady, Go!* Edwards engineered a partnership with marketing consultants John Coletta and Ron Hire to form HEC Enterprises, who provided management and financial support to the embryonic Roundabout/Deep Purple. Without Curtis's connection to and commitment from Edwards, it is possible that Blackmore, and Lord, following Curtis's departure, might have chosen to return to their successful careers as sidemen in a variety of bands instead of taking the opportunity to shape the sound of 1970s hard rock.

HEC arranged for the band members to have a permanent location where they could live, rehearse, and write, like a professional and productive band. They moved the band to Deeves Hall, an old farmhouse outside South Mimms, Hertfordshire. They also invested in proper equipment that included a Hammond C3 organ for Jon Lord. Up to this time, Lord played either the piano or a Lowry electric organ, an instrument with a unique though relatively thin sound, but it was the Hammond organ that would provide the timbral core that became the signature for Deep Purple's sound. They started to work with drummer Bobby Clarke (some sources list him as Bobby Woodman) and auditioned over sixty singers, including Rod Stewart (who at the time was working with Jeff Beck), and the legendarily misadvised soon-to-be-star-that-never-was-realized Terry Reid, but could not settle on the right voice for the group. They crossed paths with drummer Ian Paice, formerly of the Maze, and in a pattern that would become the tenor of Deep Purple's Roundabout-like penchant for changing members, while they rehearsed and settled in with Ian Paice, management was left to fire Bobby Clarke. Paice recommended Maze's singer, Rod Evans, and with the band now in place, the Mk. I lineup set to work on a debut record and Scandinavian tour.

Blackmore and Lord had extensive connections through their years as journeymen musicians. Jon Lord, along with Jimmy Page, had played on the Kinks' "You Really Got Me," and Ritchie Blackmore, who played for Screaming Lord Sutch and a number of bands organized by producer Joe Meek, was used expressly by Meek to back his various artists. Through his tenure working with Meek, Ritchie Blackmore made the acquaintance of another independent producer, Derek Lawrence, who recorded him for a one-off single, "Little Brown Jug," as the Ritchie Blackmore Orchestra. Lawrence was connected to a number of industry people in the United States but had also landed a staff producer position at EMI. He heard the still unnamed group in their early rehearsals and saw their potential. He connected HEC with Arte Mogull, the head of the record division for Tetragrammaton Records, and also helped proctor a signing with Parlophone for U.K. releases. *Tetragrammaton*, an unusual name for a record label, is a Greek word defined as "consisting of four letters," which in Hebrew describes the four letters YHWH or JHVH to describe God, Yahweh, or Jehovah. The label was part of a multimedia organization owned by now-disgraced comedian Bill Cosby; his manager, Roy Silver; and two business partners. Although the label was host to a modest roster of artists, it invested heavily to promote its one rock act, Deep Purple.

Tetragrammaton might have been willing to invest in promotion for its new signing, but the label was not so generous in the more important areas that would enable the band to deliver a top product. This was a rock band, and an unknown one at that, and it was expected that they should not require a significant amount of studio time to deliver a single and album. *Shades of Deep Purple* was recorded and assembled over May 11–12, 1968, at ATV House, the home for Pye Studios. For an album recorded and assembled in two-and-a-half days, *Shades of Deep Purple* is an extraordinary debut album. Released in the United States in July 1968 and in the United Kingdom in September of that year, the album was a success in North America, buoyed by the hit single "Hush." The band toured the United States extensively through 1968 and 1969 but remained virtually unknown in their home country where their U.K. gigs were nowhere near as successful. Their stateside success was in part a result of Tetragrammaton's full-court press for "Hush" as a lead-up to the release of *Shades of Deep Purple*, both of which had been released in North America and registered chart success months ahead of the U.K. release.

In the United Kingdom, and ahead of their U.S. tour, HEC booked Deep Purple at significant venues, including the Roundhouse (where they opened for the Byrds), which had become a ground zero for the psychedelic movement in London. The band was seen as a poor man's Vanilla Fudge because of their reliance on cover songs, which were given the extended treatment by Lord and Blackmore. The Roundhouse show, their first major U.K. appearance. was not well received and was described by the Deviants' Mick Farren as "a slow and pompous din somewhere between bad Tchaikovsky and a B-52 taking off on a bombing run." One night they opened for the Sweet Shop (soon to become the glam rock sensation Sweet) and also appeared at the National Jazz, Pop, Ballads, and Blues Festival at Kempton Park (soon to become the Reading Jazz Festival), where they bombed in the shadow of Fleetwood Mac, the Nice, the Crazy World of Arthur Brown, Joe Cocker, Jeff Beck, and others. Although they faced the ignominy of their underwhelming British reception, they managed to get back into the studio, where, on Tetragrammaton's prodding, they recorded their second album, *The Book of Taliesyn*, which was completed before Parlophone released *Shades of Deep Purple*.

Each member of Deep Purple Mk. I came from a successful career as a working musician, but they were not prolific songwriters. Still, they managed to provide a few original tunes for *Shades of Deep Purple*. The album was a fair representation of their live show in 1968 and featured three-and-a-half cover songs among the album's eight tracks. Two of the covers, "I'm So Glad" and "Hey Joe," were more than ably covered by Jimi Hendrix, the Byrds, and Cream before Deep Purple committed them to tape. The album opens with the electrifying instrumental "And the Address," which was composed by Blackmore and Lord on the evening of their first meeting and featured the intricate guitar and organ interplay that would be the core of Deep Purple's classic sound. This is followed by "Hush," a cover of Joe South's tune that served as the hit single from the album. Another Jon Lord original, "One More Rainy Day," with Evans's less than inspired lyrics, is punctuated by the fierce, swinging instrumental interludes of Lord, Blackmore, and Paice that demonstrate the fantastic rhythmic and jazz-inflected grooves in their three-way solos that soon would become central to Deep Purple's sound over their next six albums. "Prelude" was an original group composition that tagged Skip James's "I'm So Glad" onto the second half of the song. Evans and Paice performed this song with the Maze, but Cream's masterful read of this song was featured on their debut album two years prior and was superior to Purple's very effective performance of the song. The other work composed that first night, "Mandrake Root," opened side two of the album, and while it begins rather unremarkably, the instrumental break is another Lord, Blackmore, and Paice three-way solo that presages Lord's *Concerto for Group and Orchestra*.

A cover of Lennon and McCartney's "Help" is a highlight of the album and one of the best covers of a Beatles song to come out of the decade. This arrangement went back to Chris Curtis's involvement in Roundabout and was further refined in the band's early days. Rod Evans' lead vocal takes the Beatles' upbeat downer hit and turns it into an extended blues drone with Lord's Hammond organ burbling beneath his crooning vocal. The album closes out with a throwaway tune, "Love Help Me," and a read on Jimi Hendrix's hit "Hey Joe" that is more menacing than what was delivered barely two years earlier with the Byrds. The influences of Hendrix and Vanilla Fudge is quite obvious on this song, but the inclusion of a thread from Manuel DeFalla's ballet "The Three-Cornered Hat" separates the Purple version from all others. The songs were linked across each side with a variety of sound effects nicked from BBC sound effects albums, giving the listener the feeling that the album was a single extended work.

Simon Robinson, in his liner notes to the twenty-fifth anniversary reissue of *Fireball* (1971), unfairly describes the Mk. I band as "a proficient but ultimately directionless underground outfit." *Shades of Deep Purple* had a cult following among Purple fans, but it would be the late 1990s before the album received a long overdue reassessment. All three Mk. I albums were unavailable (except in poorly bootlegged copies) for much of the 1970s, '80s, and '90s. This was partly because their American label, Tetragrammaton, possessed the masters for the band's first three albums, and EMI lost track of its copies of the tapes. When Tetragrammaton went out of business at the end of 1969, the masters were passed to Warner Bros., who picked up Purple's contract. In the wake of 1972's "Smoke on the Water," Warner Bros. released a two-LP compilation of tracks from the Mk. I albums with the title *Purple Passages*. This was the last legitimate release of the Mk. I recordings until EMI reissued the albums for the English market in the 1990s. This era of releases is drawn from LP transfers and later generation masters, but the recovery of the original master recordings in both stereo and mono led to the reissue of the Mk. I albums in both mixes during the 2000s, giving fans a sense of how the band originally sounded on record. They followed *Shades of Deep Purple* with two protopsychedelic progressive albums that are deserving of more than a cursory listen, *The Book of Taliesyn* (October 1968) and *Deep Purple* (June 1969). Both albums were released on Tetragrammaton in the United States and the United Kingdom on Harvest Records, the newly launched progressive label at EMI.

The heavy psychedelic sound of Deep Purple Mk. I ended in 1969 with the birth of Deep Purple Mk. II and Jon Lord's *Concerto for Group and Orchestra* (1969). The cacophonous barrage of "Speed King," which opens their fourth studio album, *Deep Purple in Rock* (1970), demonstrates how the formerly protopsychedelic artists, initially ignored in their homeland, forged a splendid model of hard rock that acquired international success and shaped the sound of the 1970s.

DONOVAN: *SUNSHINE SUPERMAN* (AUGUST 1966)

It could appear that giving three entries to Donovan in a volume about psychedelic music may be two, if not three, too many. Donovan may not be the first person who comes to mind in any discussion of psychedelia, but perhaps more than any other artist listed in this volume, he exemplified the ethereal and transcendent nature that so many artists attempted to capture as part of the era and the experience. Donovan was unlike any other artist of this period, and the records he made with Mickie Most between 1966 and 1969 are must-hear selections in the psychedelic canon. The three entries in this volume fully embody the psychedelic tenor of the era: *Barbajgal* (1969), *A Gift from a Flower to a Garden* (1967), and the subject of this entry, *Sunshine Superman* (August 1966). Not unlike Brian Wilson, the Beach Boys' mastermind, Donovan displayed utter and complete sincerity both in his life and his art, which made him a favorite among countless artists, and discounting Lennon and McCartney and Bob Dylan, no other artists in this volume have had their compositions covered in recordings by so many performers as Donovan. While his records from 1966 to 1969 are his psychedelic masterworks, he made significant inroads on the popular music scene in 1965 as a folk artist and was described in the press as a "Scottish Bob Dylan." That description was clearly incomplete, as his work after 1969 has been more diverse, though nowhere near as successful as his classic records.

Glasgow-born Donovan Leitch came of age among the beats and mods, but he evolved into a folk singer whose influences were classic American folk music and authentic rhythm and blues. Before his first record was released on the Pye label, he appeared on the groundbreaking television music show *Ready, Steady, Go!* on January 30, 1965, where he played the guitar and sang his songs live in the studio. Alongside show host Cathy McGowan, they were the epitome of the mod and beat sensibility of the British Invasion. With his first appearances in North America, Donovan was a part of the bridge of folk-rock artists (he appeared with Joan Baez at the 1965 Newport Folk Festival, the same festival where Dylan plugged in), alongside the Byrds, Jefferson Airplane, and the Grateful Dead, who would become the first wave of psychedelic groups from the United States.

One subject that runs through all of Donovan's albums from this period is the woman who was his muse—his "Lady of the Stars"—and, in 1970, became his wife, Linda Lawrence. Donovan and the Rolling Stones' Brian Jones had crossed paths in their earliest days on the rhythm and blues scene in London and made some of their earliest recordings at studios on Denmark Street, London's Tin Pan Alley and Linda Lawrence was an intimate point of intersection for Brian and Donovan. She had borne Brian's child (his third, each with a different woman) as an unmarried seventeen-year-old teenager. By all accounts, Brian cared deeply for Linda (at least as much as his damaged and troubled self could manage) and she for him. He left Linda in 1964, ahead of the Rolling Stones' tour of North America, and though they attempted a reconciliation in 1965, a complex three-way relationship developed between Brian, Linda, and Donovan.

Donovan met Linda in spring 1965 on the set of *Ready, Steady, Go!* and described her as "an astonishingly beautiful beat girl" and "achingly beautiful and very sad." She would not commit to Donovan, partly because she was still in love with Brian and also because she was afraid of a relationship with someone in popular music. Linda was the subject or inspiration for a number of Donovan's songs, including "The Entertaining of a Shy Girl," "Catch the Wind" (though he wrote this before meeting her, he insists that she was the still unknown subject of his longing), "Legend of a Girl Child Linda," "Sunshine Superman," "Celeste," and others.

Donovan began to record the *Sunshine Superman* album in December 1965 with a new producer, Mickie Most, and a new arranger, John Cameron. Most and Cameron were able to transform Donovan's sweetly plaintive songs into jazzy grooves, baroque pop, ethereal psychedelia, Arthurian-flavored minstrelsy, and hip blues. Unlike his previous work, this album had no songs of protest. These were flower power songs about dreams, myths, and his unrequited love for Linda. Cameron and Most treated Donovan's music as if each song was a miniature film score, so every track on the album was unique; sameness was not the order of the day. Recording for the album picked up in Los Angeles in early 1966, and the album was ready for release in August of that year.

A change of management from Ashley Kozak to Allen Klein occurred simultaneously with Donovan's transformation from a gentle folk-pop singer into a full psychedelic troubadour. Klein (who was also working to ingratiate himself into the Rolling Stones camp, that ultimately became one of his most successful coups) helped to place Donovan at Epic Records, where he would be Clive Davis's first signing at CBS and where *Sunshine Superman* would be the first major label release of a psychedelic album. From the colorful graphics and stylized lettering to the gentle songs contained within, this album helped to set the stage for the market to push psychedelia into mainstream American music. Side one opened with the radio-friendly title song, "sunshine" being code for LSD, with Jimmy Page providing guitar work, followed by one of the most beautiful songs on the album, "Legend of a Girl Child Linda." This love song to Linda Lawrence is loaded with Arthurian language and an exquisite arrangement for strings, winds, and harpsichord that helps to suspend Donovan's delicate guitar work. "Three King Fishers" is an Indian-flavored song in which the sitar provides a dreamy, mystical feel. "Ferris Wheel" is a delicate tune with a dominant bass and percussion accompaniment. The first side closes with "Bert's Blues," a lightly swinging tune about Scottish folk artist Bert Jansch.

Side two opens with another of Donovan's enduring hits, "Season of the Witch," with more of Page's inventive guitar work, and is followed by "The Trip" and "Guinevere." The first song is extolling the events of an acid trip, and the latter is another of his beautiful minstrel songs with numerous references to the Arthurian legends. "The Fat Angel" was composed for Cass Elliot, who never recorded the song, though Jefferson Airplane did service to the song on their first live LP, *Bless Its Pointed Little Head*. The final song, "Celeste," is one of Donovan's most achingly beautiful songs that, like "Legend of a Girl Child Linda," is suspended by an exquisite arrangement that features organ, harpsichord, electric violin, and sitar. His heartfelt expressions about the many challenges and changes that were happening in his life (all without Linda) resulted in one of the album's most perfectly realized songs.

DONOVAN: *A GIFT FROM A FLOWER TO A GARDEN* (DECEMBER 1967)

A Gift from a Flower to a Garden is not as well-known or well regarded as the studio albums by which it is bookended, *Mellow Yellow* (March 1967) and *Hurdy Gurdy Man* (September 1968), but it is Donovan's most psychedelically styled record in terms of content and presentation. Although Mickie Most is credited as producer, Donovan claims in his autobiography that he produced the entirety of the two-record set because he and Most disagreed on the construction of the album. Most received his credit and went on to produce Donovan's next two albums for CBS. This is not the first double album released in the rock era (Dylan's *Blonde on Blonde* and Frank Zappa and the Mothers of Invention's *Freak Out* preceded Donovan's set by a year), but it is one of the most elaborately packaged albums of the period. The Beatles' *Sgt. Pepper's Lonely Hearts Club Band* set a new standard for album art, but six months after *Sgt. Pepper's*, Epic Records released this beautifully packaged two-disc boxed set. Label head Clive Davis had to be convinced to invest in the special packaging, which features an infrared picture of Donovan on the cover and a standard photograph of Donovan with the Maharishi (two months before he would head off to Rishikesh to study with the Maharishi along with the Beatles, Mike Love, and Mia Farrow). Boxed set releases were not uncommon for classical music releases of opera and other collections, but they had not been widely used in rock music and had never required the six-color separation needed for the images on the cover. In an odd but cautious marketing move, Davis insisted that the label release the two-album set as two separate albums alongside the double set. Released as *Wear Your Love Like Heaven* and *For Little Ones*, Donovan's intended double album still managed to earn Gold record status in 1970.

The first album of the set opens with another of Donovan's enduring hits, "Wear Your Love Like Heaven," which sets the flower power tone for the first two sides of music. The ten songs on the first record are lovely, with one, "Under the Greenwood Tree," set to the words of Shakespeare. The second disc is an album of children's songs. When signing Donovan to Epic, Clive Davis was attracted to the range of Donovan's interests, which he said included music for children and a Broadway musical, and this album is Donovan's first foray into an album of children's songs. Every song on this disc is utterly charming, and it is clear Donovan's songwriting can easily reach into a faraway world of childlike wonder, not unlike the colorful songwriting of Pink Floyd's original front man, Syd Barrett. In late 1971, Donovan released another equally charming album of children's songs, *HMS Donovan*. Rejected by Epic, this two-record set was not released in the United States, but it was released in England on the Pye Records imprint, Dawn Records.

A Gift from a Flower to a Garden is one of the most overlooked albums from Donovan's canon and is easily lost among the records that provided some of his biggest hits. It is his most psychedelic album in terms of content, integrity, and packaging. While largely unavailable for over two decades, it began to show up on the compact disc reissue market in 1999. The original LP packaging for the album makes this one of Donovan's rarer finds for collectors and fans.

DONOVAN: *BARABAJAGAL* (AUGUST 1969)

Barabajagal is the heaviest of Donovan's Mickie Most–produced albums and his last commercially successful effort on either side of the Atlantic. The album features the Mickie Most–produced Jeff Beck Group with Donovan, and they are instantly identifiable on the album's title track and its follow-up, "Superlungs My Supergirl," a song that reintroduces the girl from "Mellow Yellow," but this time in a more adventurous and experimental frame of mind. This album was largely recorded in 1968, but it was held back because Epic released *Donovan's Greatest Hits*, a January 1969 release that collected his hit singles on a single album. The *Greatest Hits* album remained in print over the next two decades, and in the absence of the majority of Donovan's Epic Records catalog, that album was, for many, the only exposure or access fans would have to his music until the mid-1990s.

"Superlungs My Supergirl" was first recorded in the sessions for *Sunshine Superman*, but it was given an updated feel in the rerecording for *Barabajagal*. This is followed by another of Donovan's songs for

Linda Lawrence, "Where Is She," a work that returns to the simpler and sweeter sound of Donovan's earlier work. The piano and flute work are simple yet superb. "Happiness Runs" features a charming vocal round (sung by Graham Nash, Michael McCartney, and stalwart studio singer Lesley Duncan), and the last song on side one is the humorous "I Love My Shirt." "The Love Song" opens side two and carries a feel similar to his sound on the *Mellow Yellow* album with its cool jazzy grooves. "To Susan on the West Coast Waiting" is Donovan's return to the protest genre, though not as directly as he had in his earlier work. The song is a reflection of an era when youths no longer accepted the draft as an unquestionable or acceptable rite of maturity.

"Atlantis," like the Beatles' "Hey Jude" and the Velvet Underground's "Sister Ray," is a stunning example of the long-form narrative song. While shorter in length than those two masterpieces (though the long fade out of the chorus resembles "Hey Jude"), Donovan delivers the story of the mythical Atlantean culture in his most BBC-friendly Scottish tenor. After the serious tone of the last two tracks, Donovan provides some light, fun relief with "Trudi" and "Pamela Jo."

Barabajagal is Donovan' final offering from the Mickie Most–produced albums of the 1960s. Tensions between Donovan and his producer had reached an impasse, and to the displeasure of Epic Records, Donovan chose an entirely different sound with his next two albums. The first of his self-produced albums, *Open Road*, charted comparatively well, but the next album, *HMS Donovan*, a double-disc set of children's songs, was not well received on either side of the Atlantic (and was only available in the United States as an import). Donovan and Most reunited once more for 1973's glam-flavored *Cosmic Wheels*. This album was not a success; however, Donovan continued to make music throughout the 1970s and well into the new millennium.

THE DOORS: *THE DOORS* (JANUARY 1967)

The Doors were a psychedelic power trio in the guise of a four-piece ensemble who exploded onto the scene in early 1967 with the release of their self-titled debut album and the legendary single "Light My Fire." There was no shortage of musical groups in Los Angeles who represented the then current trends in popular music, but few acts were up to the unenviable task of defining a new Southern California sound. The folk-rock scene, composed primarily of groups or artists who migrated to Southern California, such as the Mamas and the Papas and the Byrds, was an honest competitor to the brilliant sounds created by Brian Wilson.

Progressive groups such as the Buffalo Springfield and less mainstream acts such as the Turtles and Frank Zappa also contributed to Southern California's eclectic music scene, but no act(s) can be credited with the creation of an entirely new Southern California psychedelic sound until the Doors (along with their Elektra label mate Love) crashed upon Los Angeles' music scene in 1966. For the Doors' Ray Manzarek (organ, keyboard bass), Jim Morrison (vocals), Robby Krieger (guitar), and John Densmore (drums), their seemingly overnight success was felt across the country as well as in England and Europe. Over the four years of their commercial record-making existence, they released six studio albums that to this day remain staples of the classic rock genre. They released two albums in the immediate wake of Jim Morrison's passing, *Other Voices* (1971) and *Full Circle* (1972). The posthumous *An American Prayer* (1978) features Morrison's recitation of his own poetry with improvised instrumental backing recorded by the Doors years after they disbanded.

    The Doors' power trio makeup was a result of their unique instrumental blend of otherwise traditional instruments: the guitar, keyboard, and drums. Added to this was a vocalist who wrote more than lyrics. Like Bob Dylan before him, Jim Morrison created unique poetic verses around which the instrumental trio created surreal soundscapes that could replicate an acid trip as easily as they could deliver the reassuring calm that concludes the private hell of that same trip. Chicago-born Ray Manzarek was the oldest member of the group and had completed his military service just prior to the buildup of the Vietnam War. Upon his stateside return, he enrolled in UCLA's film school, where he first met Jim Morrison. The baroque-flavored passages he coaxed from his Vox Continental organ harkened back to his childhood piano lessons, but they also reflected the influences he absorbed in film school. The Vox Continental was a favorite keyboard used by many bands of the period, but unlike a traditional band member who simply hammered out block or arpeggiated chords, Manzarek alternated blues licks with ornate contrapuntal lines and married them to the rhythmic sensibilities of a jazz keyboard player. His on- and off-stage appearance was unlike the other Doors and most every other musician on the West Coast scene. He was older than most of the other players on the strip, and his sartorial modern look was one he maintained throughout the Doors' existence.

    Guitarist Robbie Krieger was, like so many of his age, a first-generation Californian. Self-described as a "bad seed" in his teenage years, he was sent north to Menlo High School, a preparatory school for kids who expected (and hoped) to attend Stanford University or kids, like Krieger, whose parents sent them to the school with the hope of salvaging any opportunity of a postsecondary education. Living in such proximity to San Francisco, Krieger soaked in the emerging hippie scene, formed a jug band, and moved in the same music circles as Bob Weir and Jerry Garcia, who would later form the Warlocks, who then transformed into the Grateful Dead. He had developed formidable guitar skills by the time he attended university and could easily move between folk, flamenco, jazz, blues, and the rapidly expanding style of rock and roll. Long before it became à la mode, Krieger was studying non-Western musical styles and had learned how to play the sitar and sarod long before the Beatles or Rolling Stones incorporated these exotic instruments into their music. Krieger's ability to switch from modal scales to jazz harmonies to flamenco phrases and non-Western melodies enabled him to provide the Doors with a greater range of textures and structures than any other guitarist of that period could hope to accomplish.

John Densmore was another native Californian, and long before the Doors ever came into being, he and Krieger had attended University High School. The teenaged Densmore developed into a well-skilled jazz drummer, and it is likely that his time around the jazz set influenced his stylish manner of dress that, like Manzarek, was visually distinct from any other musician of that period. John and Robbie reconnected during their college years and met Ray Manzarek. All three were into smoking grass and taking the yet-to-be-outlawed drug LSD. They had been drawn into the emerging meditation scene that had taken hold in Los Angeles thanks to the Maharishi Mahesh Yogi, the same mystical Indian holy man who would seduce the Beatles and much of the Western popular music world just two years later.

Krieger's unique and diverse technical skills made him the perfect foil for Ray and John. As they were without a bassist, Ray played a Fender Rhodes keyboard bass. The rhythmic basslines from Ray allowed Densmore to call upon his impressive technical skills to fill a role beyond that of a standard drummer. Krieger was known for his bottleneck technique on the guitar, and the rhythmic and harmonic bed laid down by John and Ray allowed Robbie to create all manner of melodic textures upon which he could create an aural tapestry over a complex structure of rhythmic and timbral dynamics. The merger of three unequal equals led to a sound that no one else at that time had even dreamed could exist. To this was added the rich baritone of Jim Morrison, whose lyrics were unlike any being written by West Coast bands.

Jim Morrison, poet and singer, is the central figure around whom the Doors' legacy continues to be maintained. Jim grew up in a navy family and lived in towns on both coasts and in the South. The myth of Morrison as the dark, tortured artist developed in the wake of his death in 1971 and was enshrined in modern lore after the publication of his biography in 1980.

Morrison's siblings and parents recalled that Jim was an intelligent and thoughtful child as well as a prankster. With his father so often on duty, he assumed a certain level of authority as the man of the house, and according to his sister, Jim was a gentleman. His alternative biography, which can be traced back to his first bio sheet with Elektra Records, was likely authored to bring a sense of romance and rebellion to his professional identity but just as easily could have been authored as a way to avoid bringing potentially embarrassing attention on his family. His parents did not support his career choice as a singer in a pop band, especially since they paid for him to complete film school at UCLA. He and his father did not have the combative and unpleasant relationship that is reported in a number of biographies, and he apparently was afforded a great deal of freedom as a youth to come and go as he pleased. Jim's poetry completed the extraordinary musical tapestry begun by his bandmates. There is a depth in Morrison's writing that, aside from Bob Dylan, whom he greatly admired, would not have been heard in popular music in the mid-1960s.

Manzarek and Morrison met as film students at UCLA in 1963–1964 (both graduated in 1965, Ray with a graduate degree and Jim with a bachelor's degree), but it would be some months before they reconnected with the idea of being in a band. Ray ran into Morrison on the beach in Venice, where Manzarek lived with his future wife, Dorothy Fujikawa, and this was where the Doors was launched. Venice Beach in the mid-1960s was a rough-around-the-edges refuge for the hippie and beatnik set. It was popular for its cheap rents and ocean access, and this was where the Manzarek apartment served as a rehearsal space for the fledgling group. From the earliest days of the Doors, Morrison was known for his lack of punctuality and, on occasion, lack of attendance at band rehearsals and gigs.

Unlike earlier bands such as the Beatles, the Rolling Stones, the Yardbirds, and the Who, among others, the Doors did not pay the same level of dues as was required and expected of the previous wave of rock bands—playing long hours in a thankless circuit of gigs—but they still had to cut their teeth in a scene that was exploding with new bands and clubs. In early 1966, they had difficulty getting any club to hire them, but down the road from the Whisky a Go Go was a less than glamorous bar known as the London Fog. They stacked the place with friends and acquaintances on the night they were slated to audition at one of the least desirable clubs in town and were hired. They slowly became a fixture on West Hollywood's Sunset Strip, and while initially not popular, the intensity and drama of their shows began to draw larger audiences.

The band signed with Columbia Records, as that label was desperately trying to be current and relevant in the youth market. They were being considered along with a collection of other artists by a series of CBS house producers who were trying to decide what the next sound in popular music would be. The aging and conservative nature of Columbia's A&R men relegated the Doors to obscurity at Columbia. They had an option on the group but allowed it to lapse because they had not released anything they recorded. The Doors continued to evolve into a tight band thanks to their regular shows at the London Fog, but the lack of audience at the club prompted the club owner to drop them. While at the London Fog, one of the bookers for the Whisky a Go Go came by to hear them and signed them to be the house band who would open for their various star acts. In six short months, the Doors, who at the start of 1966 could not get into the Whisky, were now the house band. The need to play multiple sets per night in front of packed houses required the band to fill out their sets to cover for their modest repertory list. Out of necessity, the band called upon their improvisatory skills and expanded several of their songs to fill their sets.

In early summer 1966, Jac Holzman, the head of Elektra Record, came out from New York to hear this group about which he had heard so much. Arthur Lee, whose band, Love, was already signed to Elektra, had talked up the band to Holzman. He heard a few of their shows and was not overwhelmed, but after one show in which they played "Alabama Song (Whisky Bar)," a song by Kurt Weill and Bertolt Brecht, Holzman was convinced that this group had something and immediately wanted to sign them. He also had Paul Rothchild, a recently hired producer at Elektra, come to Los Angeles to hear them. Like Holzman, he was at first unimpressed but soon came around to Holzman's enthusiasm. Elektra signed the band to a three-album deal, and with that decision and investment, the band's legacy would be secured.

According to John Densmore, they recorded their debut album in six days. The songs they recorded were the core of their live repertory, so they knew every angle on each song. Despite the enthusiasm the group had in making the album, Morrison was high throughout most of the sessions and was the source of more than a few damages in the studio. Throughout the band's existence, the extraordinary skills and professionalism of Manzarek, Krieger, and Densmore propelled many shows where Morrison might be a no-show or was too incapacitated to perform.

In November 1966, the Doors traveled to New York City for their first shows out of Los Angeles, where they played one of the hippest clubs of the period, Ondine. Following that triumph, Jac Holzman convinced Bill Graham to hire them at the Fillmore in San Francisco. The antipathy between the Northern California and Southern California music scenes has long been deeply embedded into each city's emotional makeup. After initial boos when it was announced they were from Los Angeles, they managed to win over San Francisco's psychedelic trippers. There was no stopping the Doors until Jim Morrison's death in Paris four years after their explosive entrée into the rock canon.

Elektra released *The Doors* in January 1967 and promoted the band with a landscape-length billboard on Sunset Boulevard that featured the band portrait from the album cover and the Doors' name in the now familiar font that has been used on nearly every one of their releases. The album begins with "Break on Through (to the Other Side)," one of the most powerful album-opening tracks in all of rock and roll. The opening colors of Manzarek's Vox and his Fender Rhodes bass keyboard, Krieger's understated guitar work, and Densmore's jazz-inflected opening figures provided Morrison with an excellent opening that allowed him to explode into the song. This is followed by "Soul Kitchen," which features Krieger's blues playing at the forefront. After two gut-punching tracks, "The Crystal Ship" is our first introduction to Morrison's seductive crooning, a style for which he is seldom given credit. Manzarek plays both piano and organ, giving the song a very intimate feel. "Twentieth-Century Fox" is another hard track that leads into one of the album's two cover songs.

"Alabama Song (Whisky Bar)," composed by Berthold Brecht and Kurt Weill, is the song that flipped Holzman into seeing the group's potential when he first heard them at the Whiskey in spring 1966. The band's version of this classic song is part ska and part two-step blended into a psychedelic mélange. Even with the double tracking used to record Morrison, he had difficulty holding pitch, but this worked perfectly in this interpretation of the song. It is a version that bears little resemblance to Lotte Lenya's iconic performance, and in its Doors' version, it could never be replicated by another artist. Side one ends with "Light My Fire," one of the band's greatest and most successful songs. At seven minutes in length, it would be edited to a more digestible length of just under three minutes for the AM radio single, but its original version is a fantastic exploration into successive trance-laden solos, none of which crash into the others like a rude houseguest. The band had been playing this song for nearly a year and had developed it into one of the most perfectly crafted songs ever released.

Side two features a number of strong performances, but most of the songs are overlooked in favor of the album's closing track, "The End." For the first-time listener who is unaware of the album's conclusion, their cover of Willie Dixon's "Back Door Man" is a beautifully realized psychedelic blues classic. Morrison's howling vocal is accompanied by deft and minimal figures that take the listener to the limits of the song. "I Looked at You" is a cool, shuffling psychedelic tune. In lesser hands, this arrangement might have been tackled by the Strawberry Alarm Clock, but because it is the Doors, the song is anything but forgettable. "End of the Night" is a sinister precursor to the album's closing track and marries Jim's crooning with an eerie horror movie accompaniment. It is one of the earliest songs composed by the band and was used as the flip side of the single "Break on Through." Krieger's mournful crying figures on the guitar are absolutely perfect and beautifully punctuate the middle-eight of the song. "Take It as It Comes" is a seemingly harmless dance tune that could have been borrowed from (or covered by) any number of Motown artists. The final twelve minutes of the album are dedicated to the band's magnum opus, "The End." This song had been a part of the band's repertoire for some months and was developed and expanded during the band's run at the Whisky in mid-1966.

Much has been written about Morrison's interpretation of the Oedipus story, which was a late addition to "The End." The inclusion of the Oedipus fable supposedly led to the band being fired from the Whisky, as no one in rock music had ever deigned to sing about killing their father only to have sex with their mother. It would be some years before Lou Reed would write "Kill Your Sons," so "The End" pushed the envelope of parental civility and appropriateness to its limits. This song followed the Doors to every town, and authorities sought to shut the band down. The undeniable power of this song makes it a perfect choice for use in other media. Francis Ford Coppola used it in his 1979 masterpiece, *Apocalypse Now*, and it has been both parodied and covered by numerous artists. Nico (Christa Päffgen) covered the song almost as effectively as Morrison on her John Cale–produced 1975 album, *The End*.

The Doors were a band who moved from total obscurity, rehearsing in Ray Manzarek's flat on the beach in Venice, to playing for an empty club, moving to a hip club, and then recording and releasing their debut album, all in under two years. If they had been one-hit wonders with this album, their impact would not have been lessened, but this was the first in a series of six unique and wonderfully disturbing albums released by the Doors. Before the end of 1967, they released their second album, an even more psychedelia-soaked collection of charm and madness, *Strange Days*.

THE DOORS: *STRANGE DAYS* (SEPTEMBER 1967)

When *The Doors* was released in January 1967, the quartet had been a working unit for under two years. Their debut album was not only one of the great albums of 1967; it remains one of the most significant albums in all popular music. It might be expected that a sophomore release, a follow-up to the success of their debut album, would be a less-than release—less commercially successful, less groundbreaking, and less interesting overall. While chart showings and overall sales may have been less in comparison to their debut album, *Strange Days* is anything but a less-than album from the Doors. Elektra signed the group for three albums and left the band and producer Paul Rothchild to produce the music they wanted to produce. Jac Holzman had invested in the immense (by 1960s standards) billboard on the Sunset Strip that advertised the first album. The artistic yet austere portraits of the band are images that have been seared into the memory of time. The creative freedom granted to the Doors allowed them to offer one of the most underrated and challenging albums of the year.

The Summer of Love was at its apex in the summer of 1967, and the variety and wealth of albums released after the Doors' debut in January of that year represented an impressive body of music. Records from the Beatles, the Jimi Hendrix Experience, the Byrds, Pink Floyd, Jefferson Airplane, and the Velvet Underground, just to name a few, altered the landscape of popular music between the respective releases of the Doors' first two albums. A second record from a group that had just two years of experience under their belt would have been a challenge for any artist.

Strange Days is the more psychedelic album of their 1967 releases and pushes the boundaries of the band's musical experimentation. The move from a four-track studio to recording in an eight-track studio expanded their options to create an array of colors that is both soothing and frightening. Where their debut album presented a studio version of their live show, this album enabled the band to create more surreal and pointillistic sound beds. Many of the songs on *Strange Days* date from the same period as those on the first album, and two, "Moonlight Drive" and "My Eyes Have Seen You," date from some of the bands' earliest dates.

The album's title track (and opening song) features the band's first use on record of a Moog synthesizer. Although the album opener does not have the straight punch of "Break on Through," it sets a wonderful ambience that approximates an aural free fall. Session bassist Douglas Lubahn, who would serve in this role on a number of Doors' tracks, gives the songs on *Strange Days* a different timbral balance when compared to the parts Manzarek played on his Fender Rhodes bass keyboard, which always served as the band's live instrument and is more prominent on their first album. Manzarek's rhythmic swing on the bass keyboard set up a type of conversation with Densmore's fluid drumming, and while Manzarek still composed the bass lines, the swing of the instrumental bed would be slightly different when played on a proper bass.

"You're Lost Little Girl" is a wonderfully constructed ballad where the instrumental colors are introduced one by one and give the song the feeling of an impromptu jam session. "Love Me Two Times" was the album's lead single and has remained a perfect radio pop classic for the last fifty years. Manzarek plays the harpsichord on this song, and his stylized rhythmic figures against Krieger's bottleneck work provides a broad anchor for Morrison's vocal, one of his supreme vocal efforts. "Unhappy Girl" opens with Manzarek's baroque keyboard figures before launching into a song that appears to represent happiness more than unhappiness. "Horse Latitudes" is a spoken-word showpiece for Morrison's poetry and is accompanied with a wonderful musique concrète backing track. The intensity of this track segues into the wry sexiness of "Moonlight Drive," one of the earliest Morrison/Manzarek creations.

Side two opens with "People Are Strange," a song whose title and lyrical phrases have amply served the youth vernacular. "My Eyes Have Seen You" is a straightforward rock tune and a surprising relief from the mellow intensity of "People Are Strange." "I Can See Your Face in My Mind" is an overlooked track that highlights a marimba part within a standard blues song. The final track, "When the Music's Over," is an epic ten-plus-minutes showpiece, not unlike "The End." A roughly five-part song, it includes a number of iconic Morrison phrases, including the oft-paraphrased "We Want the World, and We Want It Now." This song's similarity to their earlier dramatic pièce de résistance, "The End," may be because it was composed before they had landed their recording contract and was developed into its expanded form during their early shows at the London Fog.

The Doors were part of the psychedelic wave that emerged from Los Angeles in 1966–1967, and though Northern California bands had a greater impact on the psychedelic music scene, the Doors were a major contributor to the entire movement and one of the few bands who could expand beyond the initial splash of psychedelia. While the Grateful Dead and Jefferson Airplane moved into different genres as the decade ended, the Doors contributed an array of styles on the remaining four studio albums they released before Morrison's passing in 1971. *Waiting for the Sun* (1968) shows a band trying to move beyond their traditional sound.

The album had an unusual array of studio guests whose contributions made the album a worthy successor to *Strange Days*. *The Soft Parade* (1969) was greeted with a good deal of confusion and criticism, in part because many of the songs included string, brass, and wind parts to enhance the work. They also began to credit their songs to the individual composers, eschewing the standard credit of "Composed by the Doors." While the stunning "Touch Me" is a product of this album, there were other particularly good tracks, even though their fan base was less than enthusiastic about the bands transition into something "soft."

The Doors returned to their blues roots for *Morrison Hotel*. The album lacks a strong opening single, but every track is an emotional roller coaster of inspired writing. Released in 1970, the album was a clear marker that the 1960s had died. It was the most *realismo* album of their career and featured a bare-bones production quality on exceptional songs. The following year's *L.A. Woman* is a moody masterwork that would have launched the band into another level of the stratosphere, if Jim had survived and returned from Paris. Instead, it served, albeit temporarily, as a fitting epitaph for the band.

ERIC BURDON & THE ANIMALS: *LOVE IS* (DECEMBER 1968)

Eric Burdon & the Animals is a simple yet confusing name in the history of rock music and probably rivals the multiples of configurations that represent Parliament-Funkadelic for this honor. Many bands change members throughout a group's existence, and some even change the style and direction of their music. But Eric Burdon & the Animals changed members, changed genre/style, and then regrouped the original members and played their original style of northern blues. They existed as an ensemble with a flexible membership that might feature only one or two original members, but they played their original sound before returning as a nostalgia act with their original front man, Eric Burdon.

The Animals were a hard-hitting five-piece blues band from Newcastle upon Tyne, in the northeast of England, who splashed onto the beat scene in 1964 and released a quartet of albums produced by guaranteed hitmaker Mickie Most. They were picked up for a pair of albums by Tom Wilson, newly arrived at MGM from Columbia, where he had worked with Bob Dylan and Simon & Garfunkel. The original group had dissolved by 1966, barely two years following their debut album. Burdon then released a pair of what ostensibly were solo albums, but by 1967, he had relocated to San Francisco and remade the Animals as a psychedelic outfit. Under this model of the group, they released four albums on MGM before Burdon shut down the enterprise in the wake of a disastrous Japanese tour. The psychedelic incarnation of Eric Burdon & the Animals was a heavier and more bluesy band, but unlike the original band, who had relied on making cover versions of various blues songs, the post-1967 group composed the majority of their music.

The band's first three albums as a San Francisco–based psychedelic outfit—*Winds of Change*, *The Twain Shall Meet*, and *Every One of Us* (the last being a U.S.-only release)—convey topical references and themes in "San Franciscan Nights," 'Yes, I Am Experienced," "Monterey," "Sky Pilot," and the single "A Girl Named Sandoz." Their fourth album, *Love Is*, is the final of the four post-1967 albums and is the most psychedelic album in their catalog. The expansive double album contains extended songs, most over six minutes, with only two that fall into the under-four-minute category. After three albums of mostly original songs, *Love Is* features a band going back to their earlier model of covering other people's songs and performing them in a style not far removed in spirit from Vanilla Fudge. Songs covered on this album include the Spector/Barry/Greenwich classic "River Deep, Mountain High"; the Bee Gees' "To Love Somebody"; Johnny Cash's "Ring of Fire"; and Traffic's "Colored Rain." This album also features the strongest lineup of the group with the inclusion of Zoot Money and Andy Summers (later to find fame on a global scale with the Police). The bass and organ parts are more prominent, and a number of expressive guitar solos cut across every track on the album and sadly are overlooked in most writings about the band.

Eric Burdon disbanded the group following an aborted Japanese tour and joined forces with War, an American funk band from Long Beach, California. He recorded two albums with the group, *Eric Burdon Declares War* and *The Black Man's Burdon*, both in 1970, with the former featuring the hit "Spill the Wine." Burdon was involved in various incarnations of the Animals on a number of reunion tours until the mid-1980s and then again after 2015. The 1967–1968 configuration of Eric Burdon & the Animals is a curio in the psychedelic canon. They left four albums of uneven quality but managed to capture the spirit of the period and have earned their spot in this volume.

THE GRATEFUL DEAD: *LIVE/DEAD* (NOVEMBER 1969)

No book on psychedelic music would be complete without an entry on the Grateful Dead. Aside from the Soft Machine, no other band included in this volume is so insufficiently represented on record as the Dead, who were best experienced as a live band and not as recording artists.

They released twenty-two albums over their three decades of activity, from 1965 to 1995. The core group of Jerry Garcia (lead guitar, vocals), Bob Weir (rhythm guitar, vocals), Phil Lesh (bass, vocals), and Bill Kreutzman (percussion) were in every iteration of the band from their beginnings as the Warlocks in 1965 until 1995, the year Jerry Garcia died. Percussionist Mickey Hart was a core member for nearly as long, joining the band in fall 1967, after the release of their debut album, and leaving briefly in 1971, though he rejoined a few years later and remained with the group until 1995. They cycled through multiple keyboardists throughout their tenure, with a number dying from excessive alcohol or drug use. They began with Ron "Pigpen" McKernan (1965–1972) and then Tom Constanten, who briefly supplemented McKernan from fall 1968 to winter 1970. Keith Godchaux also joined to cover for McKernan while he was on sick leave from the band. He stayed on to supplement McKernan and ultimately replaced him following McKernan's death in 1972. Brent Mydland had the longest tenure with the band, from 1979 to July 1990, a decade that saw their greatest commercial success in terms of concert attendance and record sales. Vince Welnick replaced Mydland following his death and remained with the band until 1995. The Dead were central to San Francisco's psychedelic scene and were, along with Jefferson Airplane, Big Brother and the Holding Company, and Quicksilver Messenger Service, one of the core psychedelic groups from the Northern California scene. Although they outlasted these groups, many of the Dead's members died at relatively young ages. Pigpen McKernan was twenty-seven, Godchaux was thirty-two (he died soon after leaving the band), Mydland was thirty-seven, and Garcia was fifty-three.

The Dead, for their position in the mid-1960s San Francisco scene, were nominally a psychedelic outfit. They were more of an eclectic group that incorporated rock, folk, country, jazz, blues, and psychedelic rock into a sound that set them apart from Jefferson Airplane and other San Francisco bands. They emerged from the jug band scene and, with McKernan, adopted a blues-influenced rock style. McKernan's choice of instruments, the Farfisa organ, Vox Continental organ, and Hammond organ, shaped both a garage and blues rock sound on their early records. As the band developed more deeply into psychedelia and improvisations, McKernan's style did not easily adapt to their expanded sound, which led to the band adding Tom Constanten on keyboards.

Live/Dead captures the Constanten/McKernan sound of the Dead and was recorded live at the Fillmore West and the Avalon Ballroom in 1969. It is the first live rock album recorded on sixteen tracks, and the album captures the band performing some of the most iconic songs from their first period, including the brilliant "Dark Star" and "St. Stephen." *Live/Dead* was their fourth album and first live LP. It is likely the Dead were the most recorded live act in all of rock music. Their fans, especially the redoubtable Deadheads (fans who traveled city to city to hear them wherever they appeared in concert), counted among them avid amateur ethnomusicologists who set out to record every Dead concert they could manage. The band encouraged their fans to record their shows, and fans exchanged homemade tapes from every concert. It was likely that multiple people recorded any given show, so multiple versions of individual concerts exist for most of their shows. This was in addition to the officially recorded concerts made under the supervision of their various sound engineers, including Owsley Bear Stanley and, after Stanley went to prison for manufacturing substantial quantities of LSD, Dan Healy. Dozens of their concerts have been officially released in multivolume sets as *Dick's Picks*, named after the band's tape archivist, Dick Latvala, and *Dave's Picks*, named after another band archivist, Dave Lemieux. These are in addition to the official multivolume releases, *Road Trips* and *Digital Download Series*.

The band never felt their studio albums represented their work in its truest form, so the carefully curated live albums were designed to give listeners a more authentic experience of the band. *Live/Dead* was the first live album recorded in sixteen tracks and raised the audio standard for live rock albums. The Grateful Dead's approach to live shows was unique because they did not rehearse their set in the way most bands prepared for a show. Instead, they selected songs on the spot in concert, which gave the shows a free, improvisatory feeling and afforded them a greater level of psychedelic credibility than did any of their individual songs or albums. *Live/Dead* captures the band at the end of the psychedelic movement in San Francisco, as they are about to embark upon the 1970s model of the band. In this period, they played all over the world, took a hiatus from touring, released a pair of excellent live albums, and began to embrace a more eclectic style throughout the next decade. For anyone who was unable to attend a Dead show before 1995, *Live/Dead* is a fair and smoke-free substitute for the actual experience.

Throughout the 1970s, the Dead released a classic series of albums: *Workingman's Dead* and *American Beauty* (1970), *Wake of the Flood* (1973), *Blues for Allah* (1975), *Terrapin Station* (1977), and *Shakedown Street* (1978). The latter showed the Dead trying to embrace a more mainstream soul/disco sound. In the 1980s, the Dead reached their greatest sales with *In the Dark* (1987) (with its attendant single "Touch of Grey" receiving a healthy level of exposure on MTV) and their final studio release, *Built to Last* (1989).

IRON BUTTERFLY: *IN-A-GADDA-DA-VIDA* (JUNE 1968)

Iron Butterfly was a prolific one-hit wonder, and *In-A-Gadda-Da-Vida* is the title track of their second album and also one of the most recognizable tracks of the period. The San Diego–based band was founded by organist Doug Ingle and was not substantially different from many other garage rock/psychedelic pop groups except that they created the epic "In-A-Gadda-Da-Vida," which filled the entire second side of their sophomore album. The six-track album was a massive hit and is believed to have received one of the first acknowledgments as a Platinum record, having achieved sales of one million copies. It was a mandatory long player in the collection of any self-respecting pot- or acidhead.

Organist and vocalist Doug Ingle played a Vox Continental organ, and this instrument was the core of their sound, particularly on the lengthy title track. Ingle's father was a church organist, and his exposure to protestant hymns of the sort his father would have played surely influenced Ingle's harmonic choices in many of his songs. Not unlike Procol Harum, who created the atmospheric "A Whiter Shade of Pale" on the back of a Bach-derived harmonic progression but had difficulty extending that style on successive albums, Iron Butterfly was also prolific; however, their sound was slow to evolve, and the group eventually came to an end after their fifth album, *Metamorphosis*.

All their albums were released on Atlantic Records' subsidiary Atco Records and received national distribution, which supported the massive sales of the record. Their music was built to accompany the flower power movement, and that very quality was its shortcoming, as it resulted in the band's brief existence. The group broke up in 1971, but they had a successful run as an opening act for Jefferson Airplane in 1968 and were scheduled to play at Woodstock; they never made it because they were stuck at LaGuardia Airport and could not get into the festival. Following the band's initial breakup in 1971, they were one of the early reunion groups of the psychedelic scene, and from the mid-1970s to the present day, there have been touring configurations of Iron Butterfly that feature any number of different musicians that play any city where fans want to hear "In-A-Gadda-Da-Vida." At the time of this writing, the only original member of the current touring group is drummer Ron Bushy, who is listed as a special guest with an otherwise proxy collection of musicians who work under the name Iron Butterfly.

Like the classic debut album by Vanilla Fudge, Iron Butterfly's albums have not received a proper remixing in line with current audio standards, so the CD issues of their albums have something of a stifled sound, a result of using later-generation master tapes. Another very good performance of "In-A-Gadda-Da-Vida" is on their fourth album, *Iron Butterfly Live*. This version is worth hearing because the electricity of the live version compensates for the tempered mix of the studio version.

JEFFERSON AIRPLANE: *SURREALISTIC PILLOW* (FEBRUARY 1967)

Jefferson Airplane was founded in San Francisco in 1965 by Marty Balin and Paul Kantner. Both men were part of the local folk music scene, but being turned on by all the changes going on in popular music, they wanted to create the next "other" that had yet to be imagined in popular music. From the mid-1960s to the mid-1980s, Jefferson Airplane spawned later collections of semicooperative groups: Hot Tuna, Jefferson Starship, and Starship. Membership within these groups could be very fluid, though Paul Kanter would remain the only constant member until 1985. Although the Mickey Thomas–led Starship scaled the charts in the mid and late 1980s, original members of both Jefferson Airplane and Jefferson Starship would regroup for specific projects. Over three decades, the group covered folk-rock, psychedelic rock, protest rock, blues rock, sci-fi rock, and progressive rock. More than any other group listed in this volume, this collective adopted a greater variety of musical styles than any other group before or since.

Jefferson Airplane signed to RCA Records and remained with Nipper's American label or their vanity imprint through RCA, Grunt Records, for the entirety of their recording career. When Jefferson Airplane set out to record their first album, RCA Records' artist lineup was in desperate need of modernization. From their earliest years to the middle decades of the twentieth century, RCA had been one of the greatest recording companies in the world, but with the arrival of rock and roll, they began their slide toward irrelevance that ultimately ended nearly two decades after they signed Jefferson Airplane. In 1965, RCA had one significant pop music act on their roster, Elvis Presley. Elvis made millions for the label, but they had no other artist in rock, a field for which they had no understanding. Jefferson Airplane provided the Radio Corporation of America with an opportunity to show they were still in the game.

To complete the first iteration of Jefferson Airplane, Kantner and Balin added singer Signe Toly Anderson, Jack Casady on bass, Jorma Kaukonen on guitar, and Skip Spence on drums. This lineup recorded their debut album, *Jefferson Airplane Takes Off*, a pleasant collection of folk-rock songs. It is an enjoyable album but not one that set the music world alight. Within a few months of its release, Skip Spence and Signe Anderson were replaced with a stylistically versatile jazz drummer, Spencer Dryden, and vocalist Grace Slick, whose vocals could slice through any other sonic timbres on command. The Kantner, Kaukonen, Casady, Balin, Slick, and Dryden combination, Jefferson Airplane Mk. II, is the classic lineup that released three of the greatest albums of the psychedelic period.

Both Jefferson Airplane and its later incarnation, Jefferson Starship, would endure despite multiple lineup changes, but Jefferson Airplane Mk. II was a perfect blend of conflict and experimentation. The music they released between 1967 and 1969 is some of the best music of the period by any artist(s). *Surrealistic Pillow*, the first Jefferson Airplane album to feature the new lineup, has endured for over a half century as one of the defining albums of the psychedelic era.

Grace Slick possessed a uniquely powerful voice and was one of the expansive personalities of the period, entering the scene around the same time Janis Joplin began to sing with Big Brother and the Holding Company. Slick had limited music experience but was known to the Airplane through the Great Society, a band in which she performed with her first husband, Jerry Slick, and brother-in-law, Darby Slick. She initially was not a fan of rock and roll, having grown up on musicals and classical music. In the early years of her marriage to Jerry Slick, Grace's proclivity to overimbibe was already apparent, but it was through an acquaintance, Ray Baxter, that she discovered LSD, peyote, and rock music.

The Great Society was a band that barely functioned, as they could seldom agree on a creative direction or business plan for the group. When two of its members went to India to study music, Grace accepted an invitation from Jack Casady to sing for Jefferson Airplane. Marty Balin had been the lead singer of the group, with Signe Anderson serving as the secondary vocalist, but Grace cut across Balin's dominance as the band's primary voice. Marty Balin's soulful, intimate tenor was the water to Slick's fiery contralto, and whether singing as a duo or in three-part harmony with Paul Kantner, the band had an unmistakable vocal presence. Grace's contributions were so unique for a female vocalist of this period that Kaukonen and Casady responded to her as they would another instrumentalist and expanded their own contributions by playing off Balin and Slick.

While all three Airplane records in this volume are psychedelic classics, the first and third records listed, *Surrealistic Pillow* and *Crown of Creation*, are, on the surface, entirely straightforward pop albums. There is no extensive instrumental meandering on these records, and all songs fit the then accepted standard length for pop songs (only one song on each album is over five minutes); however, these albums still capture San Francisco as the heart of the psychedelic counterculture in ways few other artists could achieve. The album title apparently was paraphrased from a remark Jerry Garcia made upon hearing a playback in the studio. Garcia's contributions to this album have been posed in two conflicting narratives. The band credited Garcia on the album's back sleeve as "Musical and Spiritual Advisor," yet Rick Jarrard, who produced the album, claims that Garcia was never present at any sessions and did not have a role in assisting on any song arrangements. Still, the recording logs for the album indicate Garcia's participation was more than cursory.

"She Has Funny Cars" is a Kaukonen/Balin composition and is a fantastically off-balanced song that is built on Casady and Kaukonen's unison lines with Balin's staccato vocal delivery. This is offset with Kantner and Slick's vocal on alternate lines, while Dryden's richly textured drumming creates a solid rhythmic bed in tandem with Casady's guttural and distorted bass lines, across which each of the other players is highlighted. "Somebody to Love," a work composed by Darby Slick, Grace's brother-in-law, and originally recorded with the Great Society, gets a full revision on this album with Grace's lead vocal that slices like a guillotine. "My Best Friend," composed by former Airplane drummer Skip Spence, is a charming and innocuous tune. If the Airplane ever wanted to do a soft-shoe cabaret song, "My Best Friend" fits the bill.

The final two tracks on side one possess an ethereal elegance that lifts the album into an intimate and emotional vein. "Today" is led by Marty's heartfelt vocal and is awash in reverb with, according to the recoding logs, Jerry Garcia on guitar. The delicately plucked guitar lines are understated, as so much of Garcia's playing was throughout his career. Dryden's subtle percussion textures become more prominent as the song progresses, while Kantner and Slick's background vocals emerge from the haze of dope smoke. This is followed by Balin's "Comin' Back to Me," an incredibly beautiful and tender love song that is punctuated with autoharp and recorder. This song features Marty's delicate guitar work, which holds the entire song in perfect balance. It is reported that Balin composed this song after partaking of some very potent weed, but how many Airplane songs were composed without the benefit of grass? Still, the intimate poetry of this song with Marty's sincere vocal makes this one of Jefferson Airplane's most beautiful songs.

Side two opens with Balin's hard and bluesy "3/5 of a Mile in 10 Seconds," which moved the Airplane toward a style of protest songs that they would deliver so richly on *Volunteers*. "D.C.B.A 25" harkens back to the earlier Airplane sound and serves Paul and Grace with the opportunity to refine their perfectly matched duet skills. The title is nothing more than a reference to the song's chord progression, and "25" is a reference to Albert Hoffman's legendary batch of LSD. "How Do You Feel" is the one song composed by Tom Mastin, an old acquaintance of Kantner and a friend of Rick Jarrard and someone outside of the immediate circle of Airplane members. Wonderful guitar work between Kaukonen and Kantner and Grace's recorder playing give the song a pop-folk sound not dissimilar to the Mamas and the Papas. "Embryonic Journey" is a sunshine-filled solo showpiece for Jorma Kaukonen, who wrote the work some years previous in a guitar workshop. It is a wonderful display for his fingerpicking technique on acoustic guitar and never would have made the album had Rick Jarrard not insisted upon it.

"White Rabbit," another of Grace's songs from her time with the Great Society, is the most recognized song from the album, with its references to Lewis Carroll's *Alice in Wonderland* and the effects of hallucinogenic substances. Maurice Ravel's *Bolero* is an obvious influence on this track, and Casady's serpentine bass line with Dryden's martial drumming provide a perfect bed for Grace's formidable vocal delivery; the line "Feed your head . . ." would become a perpetual rallying cry for acidheads in the years to come. The album closer, "Plastic Fantastic Lover," is an anticonsumerist party line against Middle America. The heavy weight of this song is achieved thanks to Jorma, Jack, and Spencer (Jerry Garcia is supposedly on this track as well). The tracking order for *Surrealistic Pillow* makes this album one of the most perfect offerings by Jefferson Airplane.

Post-2000 reissues of *Surrealistic Pillow* include both mono and stereo mixes of the album in addition to unreleased tracks from the recording sessions. Jorma Kaukonen's "In the Morning" is a standard blues number of the sort he and Casady would extemporize in Hot Tuna and features Jerry Garcia playing up against Kaukonen. Another Skip Spence tune, "J.P.P McStep B. Blues" is, like "My Best Friend," a charming and innocuous light shuffle of a song with a strong vocal delivery by Balin, Slick, and Kantner. "Go to Her" is a strong tune that was originally sung with Signe (an early version of the song is a bonus track on the *Takes Off* album) but was carried over in Grace's early days with the band. It would have been a good track on either of the first two Airplane albums, and it is a pity that it was cut from final listings. Jorma and

Jack's playing is positively flammable in the later version of the song. "Come Back Baby" is Jorma's rendering of a traditional folk song, and like "In the Morning," it is closer in feel to what Jorma and Jack would record with Hot Tuna.

JEFFERSON AIRPLANE: *AFTER BATHING AT BAXTERS* (NOVEMBER 1967)

With the incredible success of *Surrealistic Pillow* and the singles "Somebody to Love" and "White Rabbit," Jefferson Airplane was the San Francisco Bay Area's "it" band in the summer of 1967. Bill Graham had taken over as their manager, and under him, while they may have had more organization and a businesslike agenda, they were worked endlessly on the road and were one of the San Francisco–area bands chosen to appear at the Monterey Pop Festival in June of that year. Thanks to the increased press attention, Grace Slick was becoming the focus of the band, and as she explained it, "Any time you have four goats and one pig, you're gonna look at the pig."

RCA was making enormous amounts of money from their star act, and the label anxiously awaited their next record. But with no idea how to direct or manage a golden calf of the sort represented by Jefferson Airplane, RCA gave the band unprecedented studio time to record, and executives looked the other way when they caused damage to the studios or brought countless hangers-on in tow. If the label hoped for a repeat of *Surrealistic Pillow*, they were faced with music that sounded nothing like the eclectic and concise songs that had become hits wherever they were played. Unlike *Surrealistic Pillow*, which was recorded, mixed, and delivered in a matter of weeks, the follow-up album trickled out over the course of months. Despite this, the level of raw creativity upon which the band was riding throughout 1967 resulted in the release of one of the greatest albums of the era.

Marty Balin was the dominant songwriter and vocal presence on *Jefferson Airplane Takes Off*, and his smooth, emotive tenor was the timbral and thematic counterbalance to Grace Slick's electrifying range on *Surrealistic Pillow*. Although he delivered two gorgeous ballads and sang a number of songs on *Surrealistic Pillow*, with *After Bathing at Baxters*, he found himself pushed to the outer edges of the band he had cofounded. His lyrical, romantic songs became a source of criticism for Casady and Kaukonen, and his more even-tempered way of life fell outside the extremes being lived by other members of the band. The first two Airplane albums are Balin's work, but their third album, *After*

Bathing at Baxters, features more songs by Kantner than by any other member of the band, with Kaukonen, Casady, and Dryden delivering the band's most experimental work.

The group created a record that attempted to replicate, as closely as possible, the freedom and intensity of their live shows. Jorma and Jack had been exposed to incendiary playing of the British supergroup Cream and were determined to seek out ways they could integrate the level of virtuosity and power that Eric Clapton and Jack Bruce so naturally integrated into the mix of rock music's first power trio. Jorma and Jack continued to push the sonic envelope and incorporated the latest instruments and technical hardware to push Jefferson Airplane's sound into hitherto unimaginable territory. Ultimately, they splintered off from the Airplane and formed Hot Tuna, and while their contributions to the post-*Volunteers* Jefferson Airplane were good, they lacked the unbridled experimentation heard on the Balin-era albums.

Paul Kantner, in attempting to describe the dynamic of Jefferson Airplane, said, "Had we been a single organism, Jefferson Airplane would have been diagnosed schizophrenic." They were a band who wanted to function without rules or leaders, but when conflict arose, they had no tools to resolve matters without resorting to extreme measures. While their producer, Al Schmidt, allowed them the space to create and develop without external corporate pressures from his colleagues at RCA, he would have to organize a cohesive album from the seemingly unrelated finished tracks. To provide a narrative to this excellent collection of songs, they arranged the record into five "suites," under which they paired two or three songs per suite. "Streetmasse," "The War Is Over," "Hymn to an Older Generation," "How Suite It Is," and "Shizoforest Love Suite" provide the album with a pretentious sense of the dramatic, and the suite format worked wonderfully in gluing together an album that was created over the course of five tumultuous months.

Between *Surrealistic Pillow* and *After Bathing at Baxters*, San Francisco had faced enormous challenges dealing with thousands of kids from Middle America who wanted to, as exhorted by Timothy Leary, "tune in and drop out." San Franciscans, both inside and outside the Haight, saw their communities overrun and ultimately splintered by an endless stream of outsiders wanting to be at the heart of the scene. This was exacerbated by the perception by some that San Francisco was an amusement park for tourists, a place where the everyman could see "real hippies." Haight-Ashbury was forever changed, and the pressures to remain focused on one's values and intentions were becoming more difficult with each passing week through the summer of 1967. Into this cultural melee, Jefferson Airplane managed to create an album that captures the beauty and the mayhem of the period, and perhaps more than any other studio album by a San Francisco psychedelic band, *After Bathing at Baxters* is the sound of cultural and countercultural conflict and the almost complete rejection of Americans' suburban dream.

"The Ballad of You & Me & Pooneil" opens with Kaukonen's glorious feedback before exploding into one of Kantner's greatest songs. Paul's wordplay on "Pooneil" (a blending of Winnie the Pooh and Fred Neil, two of Kantner's favorite influences) would return in a darker and more sinister tone on their next album in "The House at Pooneil Corners," but on *Baxters*, it is a fantastic display of psychedelia exploding into its various progenitors that creates a minitour of "how we got to this place." Spencer Dryden was influenced by the anarchic sounds of Frank Zappa and the Mothers of Invention, and the next track is his homage to Zappa's influence. "A Small Package of Value Will Come to You, Shortly" is Dryden with friend Gary Blackman and future Airplane manager Bill Thompson creating a wave of nonsense constructed into a spectacular collage. This was the last track recorded for the album and was created on the heels of his work on "Spare Chaynge," the darkest and most emotionally wrought work on the album. Dryden went into the studio and recorded himself playing all manner of instruments at his disposal and then overdubbed multiple percussion tracks. He called in Thompson and Blackman, whom he recorded saying anything that came to mind. Gibberish or non sequiturs, it did not matter because Spencer created this humorous and brief collage that somehow became the one piece of levity on an otherwise serious and dark album. The first suite ends with Balin's "Young Girl Sunday Blues," his lone compositional contribution to the album. It is classic Balin, and regardless of Kaukonen's lack of interest in Balin's boy/girl love songs, he and Kantner delivered a very taut guitar-driven track. It is not Marty delivering a song that might have been left over from one of the two prior albums but a perfectly constructed song that manages to belie its conventional structure.

This is followed by two of Kantner's songs, "Martha" and "Wild Tyme." The former was inspired by Martha Wax, a teenager who was part of the Airplane's inner circle. She had arranged the meeting between Skip Spence and the band prior to *Jefferson Airplane Takes Off*. Her father was the mayor of Sausalito, a gorgeous seaside town south of San Francisco, and her free-spirited activities with the emerging masters of acid rock did not sit well with her family. "Wild Tyme" is a tight song with hypnotic guitar work and sounds as if it could have been sung by the Byrds around the period of the *The Notorious Byrd Brothers*. (Ironically, the Byrds recorded a pair of Airplane-like songs on *The Notorious Byrd Brothers*.) Paul's paean to the magical summer of 1967 would have made an excellent choice for a single, but RCA had difficulty in deciding "what" kind of song would be a hit for them.

Jorma's "The Last Wall of the Castle" sounds as if he's attempting to burn the vinyl with his incendiary solos. Side one closes with Grace's "Rejoyce," a dark, sinister song that is perhaps the most virtuosic song on the record. Grace's verse borrows from James Joyce, and she integrates tales on the moral challenges of the era. The song rides through a variety of meters and styles that highlight Slick's more esoteric musical upbringing. Dryden's jazz chops are allowed plenty of room to accent and flavor the final work. This is the most jazz-influenced work they would ever record, and one of the unique qualities of the song is the near absence of guitar work. There are brass and wind parts orchestrated into the song with rollicking piano sequences that hold it all together.

Kantner returns with "Watch Her Ride" to open side two. This is a traditional boy/girl love song, and the Airplane ratchets up the intensity and volume to the very end of the song. Kantner's very identifiable style of rhythm guitar is pitched into battle with Casady's bass to create a fantastic duel beneath Paul's strident vocals. Where Spencer's "A Small Package . . ." on side one is the light moment on the album, the track that follows "Watch Her Ride" is equally experimental but with very different results. "Spare Chaynge" is Spencer, Jorma, and Jack on their symbiotic high tide of creativity. The three most virtuosic musicians in the band created an avant-garde collage of emotional peaks and valleys that is pure acid music.

The final suite of the album features Slick's "Two Heads" and Kantner's "Won't You Try/Saturday Afternoon." Quite without reason, RCA thrust Grace's highly surreal and sinister work to market as the first single from the album. The label believed another Grace-led song would be a hit, just like her two songs on *Pillow*. They were wrong. Presenting this work as a single diminishes the beauty and mystery of Grace's verse. While AM radio could not figure out what to do with the song, it was a perfect work for the burgeoning FM listenership. Kantner's closing song commemorates the now legendary Be-In; the spontaneous gathering drew over twenty thousand in attendance at Golden Gate Park in January 1967.

The 2003 reissue of this album contained additional tracks. An alternate version of "The Ballad of You & Me & Pooneil" that clocks in over eleven minutes is a fascinating take on the song. It is more raucous and experimental than the official album version. The monophonic single version of "Martha" is simply beautiful, and the alternate version of "Two Heads," while interesting, does not match the officially released version. The final bonus track, "Things Are Better in the East," is actually two tracks. The first, a tender acoustic ballad of Marty's recorded in the immediate aftermath of *Baxter*, would remain unreleased until 1992's compilation, *Jefferson Airplane Loves You*. Tacked to the end is an early instrumental take of Marty Balin's "Young Girl Sunday Blues."

JEFFERSON AIRPLANE: *CROWN OF CREATION* (SEPTEMBER 1968)

After two years of rapid growth, Jefferson Airplane had evolved from a folk-rock band into the premiere psychedelic rock group in the United States. On the heels of the extremely creative *After Bathing at Baxters* (though less successful when compared to the sales of *Surrealistic Pillow*), plans began for a new album. In late 1967, Marty Balin recorded a couple of tracks, the excellent "Things Are Better in the East" and "Don't Let Me Down," but these were soon scrapped as contenders for the new album (though they have appeared on expanded editions and compilations). RCA wanted a new song and once more turned to Grace for the magic hit that had eluded them since "White Rabbit" barely nine months prior. The album released in September 1968, *Crown of Creation*, was substantially different from their previous two albums, and compared to *After Bathing at Baxters*, it was more accessible to many fans and featured songs where all members of the group were featured. If *Pillow* was a showcase for Marty's songwriting and *Baxters* featured Paul Kantner's songs, *Crown of Creation* is a far more democratic collection of songs in which everyone in the band had a near equal hand in its creation.

The successes the band experienced the previous year enabled them to invest in property, and their purchase of a turn-of-the-century mansion built by lumber baron R. A. Vance at 2400 Fulton Street allowed the band to have a central office and place of business. New manager Bill Thompson and his clerical assistant organized life for the ungovernable leaders of West Coast acid rock. For the first time in the life of Jefferson Airplane, there was order to their chaos.

Crown of Creation, their last psychedelic album, was recorded throughout 1968 and released in September of that year. The lightness of *Surrealistic Pillow* was gone. The serious and, at times, pretentious turn of rock music as art as heard on *After Bathing at Baxters* was gone.

In their place, *Crown of Creation* shows a band at the peak of their creative maturity, who, with their next album, the cathartic *Volunteers*, would begin to fragment into a sequence of disconnected operational realities.

"Lather" opens the album in a most innocent and heartfelt way. Composed by Grace Slick and largely inspired by Spencer Dryden, who, as the oldest member of the band, was about to turn thirty. "Lather" features Grace singing in her most childlike voice, and her fiery whiplash vocal colorings are nowhere in sight. The clever sound effects provide the song with an air of innocence that one might not expect to find on an album from Jefferson Airplane. The Kantner/Balin composition "In Time" is a subtly colorful song with Paul's lead vocal, Grace on background vocals, and Jorma's guitar solo. It is followed by David Crosby's "Triad," a song the Byrds had rejected for inclusion on *The Notorious Byrd Brothers* because of its subject matter, this being a ménage à trois, but it found a perfect interpretation with Grace's rich delivery. The maturity of her vocal on this song is in direct contrast to her childlike whimsy on "Lather." The band provides a perfectly balanced, mostly acoustic backing to Grace's intimate vocals.

Jorma Kaukonen's "Star Track" provides an opportunity for Kaukonen, Casady, Kantner, and Dryden to show their unique ensemble sensibilities. The looseness of tight playing, a style that few bands could ever achieve, was a natural hook for Jefferson Airplane, and on "Star Track," we have such a display in a strong but not overbearing rock number. "Share a Little Joke with the World" was used, in a different version, as the B side of "Greasy Heart," the first single from the album. In its rerecorded version on the album, it is one of Balin's most emotive songs, in which Jorma's ferociously melancholic guitar plays off Marty's vocal to give the impression that the singer is the only person who can hear his anxiety and pain. The power of that song is a perfect entrée into "Cushingura," another of Spencer Dryden's musique concrète experiments and a fitting conclusion to side one.

Side two opens with the Balin/Blackman penned "If You Feel," which is a masterful exercise in dark whimsy. Jorma, for whatever impatience he may have expressed for Balin's songwriting, manages to again deliver extraordinary guitar work that is in perfect conversation with Marty's vocal. The title track, "Crown of Creation," is Kantner's work through and through. Although not the best song in his catalog, it is among the most perfectly aligned songs of the period and intensifies the message of Jefferson Airplane that no other song of theirs could aspire to accomplish. If polite Americans felt threatened by the long-haired, loud, and at times sinister presence of Jefferson Airplane in their concert halls or on their television screens, this song is the band's statement that the world of the straights and parents was up for the taking. When asked a year earlier whether parents should be afraid of Jefferson Airplane's message, Kantner replied in the affirmative. "Crown of Creation" simply solidifies their stance of us versus them.

Jorma's "Ice Cream Phoenix" is a solid blues tune loaded with discussions of love and searching. "Greasy Heart," Grace's song that ended up as the album's lead single, is another of her piercing raga-like songs. Her vocal cuts across all other instrumental timbres and is filled with Slick's signature wordplay while the song bounces along from one random thought to another. The Balin/Kantner masterpiece is the album closer, "The House at Pooneil Corners," and references the lead track on their previous album, "The Ballad of You & Me & Pooneil." Where that song was innocent whimsy, "The House at Pooneil Corners" is a dark and foreboding dirge that builds in intensity to an ending of no exit.

When remastered in the early 2000s, *Crown of Creation* was released with bonus tracks, the majority of which are curios created by Dryden in collaboration with another artist. The single version of "Share a Little Joke" is the highlight of the bonus tracks. Although the first version does not have the taut interplay of the album version, Balin delivers one of the most unusual vocals on a Jefferson Airplane record.

JIMI HENDRIX: *ELECTRIC LADYLAND* (OCTOBER 1968)

In the brief twenty-seven years of his life, Jimi Hendrix revolutionized the role of the guitar in rock music. He also crossed barriers of race as an African American man who played rock and roll, the white man's by-product of rhythm and blues. His music blended rock, blues, and free improvisation with a raw power that had never been heard from any rock guitarist. He did not play just one type of music but absorbed a variety of musical styles and transformed them into a sound that was the precursor to hard rock. The extraordinary recorded legacy he left at the time of his death in 1970 stands among the greatest recorded catalogs in all of rock music. Three albums recorded with the Jimi Hendrix Experience, one live album with Band of Gypsys, and thirteen minutes of material released on the soundtrack to the film *Woodstock* make up the sum of the recorded output released in his lifetime. Since his death, there have been more than a dozen albums of previously unreleased material and many live recordings, both with the Jimi Hendrix Experience and with Band of Gypsys. He is a central figure in the psychedelic movement, and all three albums recorded with the Jimi Hendrix Experience qualify as essential albums in the psychedelic canon; however, his last album with the Jimi Hendrix Experience, *Electric Ladyland*, is a stunning artifact of the era and was the most experimental album of the three. Robert Wyatt of Soft Machine once described Hendrix's playing as being like Technicolor as it arrived in a black-and-white world. In that model, *Electric Ladyland* was the most acid-infused Technicolor sound to come out of the period.

Jimi Hendrix was born in Seattle, Washington, in 1942, and he served in the army from 1961 to 1962. Military service for a rock musician might have been a bit unusual, but faced with jail (for riding in stolen vehicles) or the military, he made the logical choice of the military. Once discharged, he began his career playing in bands backing numerous artists. He played for the Isley Brothers and Little Richard, in addition to Ike and Tina Turner and Joey Dee and the Starliters. He worked the infamous Chitlin' Circuit in the American South and clubs across the United States. In May 1966, a chance meeting with Linda Keith, the girlfriend of the Rolling Stones' Keith Richards, set his solo career into motion. Keith tried to interest Andrew Loog Oldham (the Stones' manager) and the now legendary industry maverick Seymour Stein in Hendrix, but they failed to see his potential. Linda Keith spoke about Hendrix to anyone who would listen because she believed so much in his talent. In summer 1966, Hendrix met Linda Keith, took acid, and heard Bob Dylan's most recent album, *Blonde on Blonde*. Although he worked his background gigs with Little Richard and others, meeting Linda Keith placed his career on a path that only ended with his passing in 1970.

Richie Havens took Hendrix to Greenwich Village's Cafe Wha?, where he began to play on a semiregular basis. Although this served to launch his solo career, he already had assimilated countless experiences to create the Hendrix sound. His first recording session in 1964 was playing on the single "My Diary," sung by his then girlfriend, Rosa Lee Brooks. The song "My Diary" was written by Arthur Lee (later of Los Angeles psychedelic pioneers Love), and the meeting of these two men initiated a respectful friendship and had an influence on the individual styles each would adopt for their public personae and their respective careers. Hendrix admired all manner of musicians, was familiar with Glen Campbell's playing on countless sessions, and could immediately identify the stylistically fluid sound Campbell created as part of the Wrecking Crew. Hendrix might have remained a curio in the Greenwich Village scene, except that Linda Keith convinced Chas Chandler, the departing bassist for the Animals, to hear Hendrix. Chandler saw artist management as a more effective way to make a living rather than having to depend on touring and the minor royalties from record sales. With Hendrix, he not only saw the future of rock and roll but also found his own ticket to success.

Chandler had no prior experience in artist management, so he partnered with former Animals manager Mike Jeffrey to help him manage this new and unsigned artist. Jeffrey is an overlooked character in the narrative of rock and roll history. Although short in stature, he maintained an air of mystery and intimidation. He had access to the monies that Chandler did not, and it was Jeffrey who enabled Hendrix to relocate to England. Chandler set out to promote and produce Hendrix as a new artist, but upon arrival in England, Hendrix lacked the appropriate work permits. Therefore, Hendrix's arrival in the United Kingdom in September 1966 was not made with a splash but with quiet and unofficial appearances performing with other artists. One of the first artists with whom Hendrix was connected was psychedelic artist Zoot Money and his guitarist, Andy Summers (who later played with Eric Burdon's psychedelic configuration of the Animals on the album *Love Is* and a decade later with the Police). By relocating to England and not experiencing the unchecked racism that was an accepted part of the American culture, combined with Chandler introducing him to many of the major artists in the London scene, Hendrix recognized that his days as a backing musician were behind him. Chandler helped to create the Jimi Hendrix Experience through the hiring of drummer Mitch Mitchell and guitarist Noel Redding. Redding had come to the audition hoping to join Eric Burdon's new configuration of the Animals but was convinced to play bass for Hendrix. Mitchell was selected over Aynsley Dunbar, who would go on to varying levels of fame in the 1970s as a member of the Jeff Beck Group, David Bowie's *Diamond Dogs* band, the Mothers of Invention, Journey, Jefferson Starship, and others.

With the Experience formed, Hendrix and his new bandmates traveled to France (where they could work) to back French rock and roll legend Johnny Halladay at the Paris Olympia. Kit Lambert and Chris Stamp, the Who's managers, took interest in Hendrix and wanted to sign him to a management contract, but Chandler rebuffed their offer and made it clear he was trying to land Hendrix a record deal. He had been rejected by Decca, and the majors could not see what Hendrix would come to represent in rock music.

Lambert and Stamp had been working toward creating a record label to serve the Who, a band they managed and that had bounced between a couple of labels in their first few years. They began at Brunswick and, with the hope of extricating themselves from Shel Talmy's production contract, had moved to Robert Stigwood's independent label, Reaction, before Lambert and Stamp set up Track Records. Like Stigwood did with his Reaction label, they made a deal with Polydor for distribution, which was a mutually beneficial arrangement for all parties. The role Polydor played in promoting new independent labels cannot be overestimated. The German record company set up shop in England, and rather than trying to build their own market share in popular music, they struck deals with enterprising businessmen (Stigwood, Lambert, Stamp, and others) and handled production and distribution for these new independent companies. This allowed Polydor to have a footprint at the front line of popular music and saved them the investment of having to develop an entire catalog on their own, and it also allowed these enterprising managers and businessmen to enter what had until then been a restricted and somewhat closed market.

With Hendrix signed to Track Records, Chandler could get down to business in capturing the Jimi Hendrix Experience on vinyl. Hendrix landed on the London scene and completely changed the face of rock music. The guitar greats Eric "Clapton is God" Clapton, Pete Townshend, Jeff Beck, Jimmy Page, the Beatles, the Rolling Stones, Donovan, and anyone who was riding the crest of popular music in 1966 could not avoid being influenced by the mysterious American who seemingly came from nowhere. Chandler sold his personal guitar collection to pay for an official debut at the trendy Scotch of St. James. Hendrix sat in with Cream at Regent Street Polytechnic, where Roger Waters heard him. This surely impacted Pink Floyd's evolution from being a blues cover band to one of the leading artists in creating the pathway from psychedelia to progressive rock.

With a record contract, Chandler produced Hendrix's first three singles: "Hey Joe"/"Stone Free" (December 1966); "Purple Haze"/"51st Anniversary" (March 1967); and "The Wind Cries Mary"/"Highway Chile" (May 1967). Hendrix's debut album, *Are You Experienced*, followed that same month. His records performed well in England, but the first singles released by Reprise in the United States did not do well in the charts. Paul McCartney recommended Jimi Hendrix to the organizers of the Monterey Pop Festival and insisted that they book him. In exchange for doing this, McCartney allowed his name to be listed among the organizers. The Sunday evening set on the final night of the festival launched several significant artists to U.S. audiences. The Who were not yet megastars in the United States, but their performance that evening launched their careers as artists of note. The hitherto unknown Janis Joplin performed with Big Brother and the Holding Company, which served as an epiphany of sorts for Columbia Records executive Clive Davis, who signed Joplin and launched her all too brief career. The Jimi Hendrix Experience was the third act to break through to the mainstream thanks to their appearance on the final night of the festival.

Brian Jones of the Rolling Stones introduced Jimi to the stage, and in the film *Monterey Pop*, the viewer can experience Hendrix's otherworldly performance, which climaxed with his burning his guitar at the end of his set. The reception to his performance at Monterey led Reprise to release *Are You Experienced* at the end of summer 1967. Over the next twelve months, Hendrix's career accelerated to unimaginable levels. His second album, the Chas Chandler–produced *Axis: Bold As Love*, was released in December 1967 and highlighted the expansion of Hendrix's sonic palate. Due in part to the staggered releases of *Are You Experienced* and the impact of his performance at Monterey Pop, *Axis: Bold As Love* was withheld for release so it would not affect the sales of *Are You Experienced*. Despite the incredible success Hendrix achieved in 1967, the following year would usher in the breakdown of the Jimi Hendrix Experience.

Bassist Noel Redding and Hendrix's combative relationship began to unravel in response to multiple points of frustration. Hendrix was a perfectionist in the studio and demanded retakes while also directing Redding on what to play. The excessive perfectionism also irritated Chas Chandler, who always kept an eye on production costs. Redding's frustration at being told what to play, the endless retakes of the same parts, and the limitations placed on him in contributing material to the group's albums became irreversible. A disagreement between Redding and Hendrix in Gothenburg, Sweden, led to Jimi's trashing of a hotel room and spending a night in jail. Hendrix's impatience with Redding invariably resulted in Hendrix decision to play many of the bass parts on the album.

Electric Ladyland, the third album from the Jimi Hendrix Experience was released in the fall of 1968 and was preceded by the single of Bob Dylan's "All Along the Watchtower," which became a hit in both the United Kingdom and the United States. The album reached No. 1 in the United States and was the first album that was not entirely recorded at Olympic Studios. Now recording in the United States, Hendrix's sound and image took on a more American identity.

This epic album begins with the just over a minute-long varispeed-altered track ". . . And the Gods Made Love," which leads into the title track "Have You Ever Been (to Electric Ladyland)," featuring one of Hendrix's best vocal performances. He always was self-conscious about his singing voice, but this song is a highlight in his vocal work. "Crosstown

Traffic" is one of the earlier recordings for the album. It was recorded at Olympic and brought over to the United States. Dave Mason from the Birmingham-based psychedelic band Traffic, sings backup on this song. The fifteen-plus-minute "Voodoo Chile" is a slow blues ride through Hendrix's aesthetic aims and features Jefferson Airplane's Jack Casady on bass and Traffic's Steve Winwood on piano. Redding's one contribution to the album is "Little Miss Strange," a danceable psychedelic tune.

Side three features three of the most original songs on the album: "Rainy Day, Dream Away"; "1983 . . . (a Merman I Should Turn to Be); and "Moon, Turn the Tides . . . Gently, Gently Away." Side four is the climax of the album with "Still Raining, Still Dreaming"; "House Burning Down"; "All Along the Watchtower"; and "Voodoo Child (Slight Return)." This sprawling album would be Hendrix's last studio album released during his lifetime.

Hendrix formed the Band of Gypsys with Buddy Cox on bass and Buddy Miles on drums. They produced one live album and were the band who accompanied him early on the final morning of Woodstock. By the time *Electric Ladyland* was in the record shops, Hendrix had broken off with both his producer and manager, Chas Chandler in addition to the Experience. The Band of Gypsys released one live album, which leaves *Electric Ladyland* as Hendrix's final word and psychedelia's most beautifully incomprehensible statement.

THE KINKS: *SOMETHING ELSE BY THE KINKS* (SEPTEMBER 1967)

The Kinks might not be described as a psychedelic band within the rock canon, and they surely did not frame themselves in anything remotely close to the spirit and creative milieu of the psychedelic era. For much of the 1970s and 1980s, their early work was, along with the Who and the Small Faces, lumped as being the work of a mod band, which highlights a misunderstanding of the group, their musical output, and their overall creative arc. Where the Who had Pete Townshend as their primary creative leader, the Kinks had Ray Davies, and, again, these comparisons continued to spiral into most writings on the band. The Who splashed onto the scene with such classic songs as "Anywhere, Anyhow, Anywhere" and "My Generation." The Kinks arrived on the scene with "You Really Got Me," one of the most copied riffs in all of rock and roll (successfully covered by Van Halen (1978) and Oingo Boingo (1981)), and "All Day and All of the Night," a similarly structured riff that was equally successful to its predecessor.

Like the Who, the Kinks were initially produced by American producer Shel Talmy, whose draconian business dealings allowed him to retain ownership of the master recordings for many of the artists he produced. And this is where any similarity to the Who ends. Where Townshend and company had inexperienced but risk-taking managers in Kit Lambert and Chris Stamp, who pried the band away from Talmy's aggressive ownership, the Kinks' management did not try to free the band from Talmy's production oversight, and they remained with him through 1966. The Kinks also survived a ban levied on them by the American Federation of Musicians (AFM) that prevented them from touring the United States from 1965 to 1969. The source of the ban was never precisely specified (one narrative maintains that Ray Davies punched an official from the musicians union on the set of a television show in response to said official's insults toward the all-British lineup scheduled for that episode), but it was slapped on them in response to what was viewed as "rowdy" behavior onstage. The band toured the world, but they were banned from performing in the United States during both the height of the British Invasion and the psychedelic movement.

In Britain, the band's records were released on the Pye label and suffered in part thanks to Pye's notoriously tight marketing budgets. In the United States, they were released on the Warner Bros.–owned Reprise label and while the AMF ban surely impacted their sales in the United States, Reprise continued to release their records. By the time of their third album, the label was releasing albums that generally followed the same track order as the albums that were released in the United Kingdom by Pye, long before London, Capitol, or Decca Records began releasing to the U.S. market the same albums that were being released in the United Kingdom by the Rolling Stones, the Beatles, and the Who.

The Kinks was a four-piece band throughout the 1960s and consisted of Ray Davies (guitar, vocals), his younger brother Dave Davies (guitar, vocals), Pete Quaife (bass), and Mick Avory (drums). The first album, *Kinks* (October 1964), was filled with American rhythm and blues numbers composed by Chuck Berry, Bo Diddley, and others. It did feature the brilliant single "You Really Got Me" as well as "Stop Your Sobbing" but was otherwise an unremarkable debut. Their debut single, a thin cover of Little Richard's "Long Tall Sally," gave no indication of the band's potential.

The second album, *Kinda Kinks* (March 1965), has the hallmark of many sophomore efforts and sounded rushed and poorly conceived. But this album featured mainly Ray Davies compositions in lieu of American rhythm and blues standards and featured performance techniques that were not yet widely adopted among pop bands, most notably a fingerpicking guitar style that was more commonly used in folk music than in rock. This was an early indication of Davies's creative range and compositional style. Although the album is decidedly uneven, it contains another pair of Davies's classics, "Tired of Waiting for You" and "Something Better Beginning." The Kinks released a U.K.-only EP in the wake of this album that featured the brilliant "Well Respected Man."

The band's last beat album, *The Kink Kontroversy* (November 1965), was an improvement upon its predecessor and featured another pair of Ray's iconic songs, "Till the End of the Day" and "Where Have All the Good Times Gone." In the wake of this album, the single "Dedicated Follower of Fashion" showed a distinct style of songwriting that Ray Davies would perfect over the band's next three albums.

Pye Records did not demonstrate their faith in the Kinks as album artists and promoted their singles with more consideration and care than they gave to their albums. For many fans, their singles are better remembered than their albums, but with their fourth album, this began to change. Ray Davies showed himself to be a musical visionary equal to Pete Townshend and would create a series of elaborate thematic, or concept, albums.

Face to Face was released in fall 1966, nearly a year after its predecessor, and showed the Kinks had evolved into a completely different ensemble. This might be considered their Swinging London album, from the Carnaby Street design cues on the album sleeve to the songs "Party Line," "Dandy," and "Sunny Afternoon." The Kinks had no interest in following the trends of the era, and their simple desires, mainly Ray and Dave Davies's attachment to their North London neighborhood of Muswell Hill, ran contrary to any typical rock star desire to conquer and inhabit the world. This album is their last with Shel Talmy listed as the sole producer.

Something Else by the Kinks, released in September 1967 (January 1968 in the United States), is their first contribution to the psychedelic music scene of 1967, despite the fact that the music on the album contains none of the expected tropes that were so prevalent that year. Released in the same year as *Sgt. Pepper's Lonely Hearts Club Band*, *The Piper at the Gates of Dawn*, *Between the Buttons*, *Disraeli Gears*, *The Who Sell Out*, *A Gift from a Flower to a Garden*, and *Are You Experienced*, this album is a perfect complement and companion to those classic works. Produced by both Shel Talmy and Ray Davies and recorded between the summers of 1966 and 1967, this album is considered by many fans and critics as the band's first masterpiece. It also marks the beginning of a dynamic that would always follow the band and its agenda. At the time of its release, both Ray and Dave were reported to have been planning solo albums, so despite the stylistic and thematic cohesion of this album, selected songs were released as Dave Davies solo singles: "Death of a Clown," "Love Me till the Sun Shines," and "Funny Face."

The album opens with "David Watts," a gut-punching opening track—and one covered eleven years later by the Jam on their most topically "English" album, *All Mod Cons*—that has few equals in the Kinks' canon. Although it appears to be about a horrid schoolboy, it was about a shady and dubious concert promoter known to the band. "Death of a Clown" was coauthored by Dave Davies and comes off as a minimasterpiece with Dave's lead vocal. "Two Sisters" is one of the two timeless tracks on the album, along with album closer "Waterloo Sunset." The narrative about two sisters was in truth a tale of the two Davies brothers. Ray, the married band leader, was more homebound and focused on creative pursuits, while Dave, three years younger, was still out on the town as he pleased, living more of the rock star lifestyle. Famed session keyboardist Nicky Hopkins provides a harpsichord accompaniment that is without equal in a pop song, save for Donovan's "Hampstead Incident."

"No Return" is a radical departure from the previous track with its bossa nova underpinning and could have been recorded by Antonio Carlos Jobin or any number of skilled bossa nova singers. The unexpected guitar plucking is a continuation from the timbral departure that Ray first used on *Face to Face*. "Harry Rag" is another music hall–like singalong tune, albeit one with a rather dark tone, perfect for a two-step or polka at the end of a drunken evening. "Tin Soldier Man" lacks the biting edge of "Harry Rag" but features a brass section. The first side of the album closes with "Situation Vacant" and is not, following in the wake of the album's first five songs, a terribly memorable song, but it is a perfect fit with its clever touches in phrasing, harmonic choices, and its overall arrangement.

If side one is a disjointed collection of brilliant and near brilliant songs, side two is where this album flowers into its full glory. Ray's sense of Englishness can be read through almost every song including the spectacular 'Waterloo Sunset." "Love Me till the Sun Shines" is a Dave Davies composition, sung by Dave, and was released as his solo single. Pete Quaife's thick, heavy bass line sounds like something John Entwistle would have played. "Lazy Old Sun," despite the nonpsychedelic intentions of the band, comes close as a psychedelic song and has a Beatles-like flair with backward guitars and drone-like percussion. It is one of the richest productions on the album and is a hidden gem. "Afternoon Tea" may be about the end of a love affair, but the very Englishness, using "afternoon tea" as a metaphor for daytime lovemaking, is far classier and simply a better song than a similarly themed song recorded in the mid-1970s by a forgettable American vocal group. Dave's country-like licks prevent the song from becoming too twee. The song carries a perfect balance of humor, irony, and affection in describing the end of a love affair.

"Funny Face" is another Dave Davies composition that was also released as a solo single. The story has a parallel to a sad and unfortunate real-life event in the life of the teenaged younger Davies. After "Lazy Old Sun," this is the next most psychedelic-sounding song. "End of the Season" is Ray Davies's homage/pastiche to Noel Coward. The early twentieth-century louche air to this song is simply beautiful. There are some Brian Wilson–channeled harmonic choices, and it is one of Ray Davies's most inventive songs on the album. The original album ends with the stunning "Waterloo Sunset" and what is perhaps the most beautiful verse composed about the formerly grimy and unromantic Waterloo Station. This is a perfect closing tune to a near perfect album. While "pastoral (or autumnal) psychedelia" can be an overused descriptor about the Kinks of the late 1960s, this song is a perfect example of this genre. The song was originally called "Liverpool Station," and the protagonists mentioned in the song went through a couple of name changes before Davies settled on "Terry" and "Julie." The composer has claimed some of the inspiration for this song came from observing the lives of his older sisters, but with Terry and Julie (was it Terrence Stamp and Julie Christie, two of the brightest and best of the British film scene in 1967?), it is possible to think of this as a perfect snapshot of a more personal and romantic side of Swinging London.

The album was available in both mono and stereo when first released, but the stereo version was adopted more readily in the United States than in England. As was the pattern of the day for many British groups, the artists spent time perfecting a mono mix; a stereo mix would have been a rush job or left to someone on the production team. For many fans, the mono mix is the preferable version of the two. The sound field in stereo is broad and cluttered, where, in mono, it is perfectly compacted, as if it were an audio novel. The deluxe edition of the album, released in 2011, offers both mixes, and listeners can compare the two versions. Also, the wealth of extra tracks includes singles from 1967 and early 1968 in both mono and stereo versions that appeared in other territories, alternate mixes of a few album tracks, and eight superb performances from the BBC radio show *Top Gear*.

THE KINKS: *THE KINKS ARE THE VILLAGE GREEN PRESERVATION SOCIETY* (NOVEMBER 1968)

Released one year after *Something Else by the Kinks*, Ray Davies and company delivered one of the most underrated and overlooked albums not only of the psychedelic period but of the 1960s. *The Kinks Are the Village Green Preservation Society* is perhaps the band's finest work and is both a masterpiece and statement of Englishness in pop music. While their previous two albums were released in near identical form both in the United States and the United Kingdom, *Village Green* was carried on a far more fractured route. In 1968, the band was still barred from performing in the United States, which did nothing to make their records a key component of Reprise's marketing prowess. With the goal of delivering a product tailored to each market, Ray Davies delivered a twelve-track album to Pye Records, the original *Village Green*, and for the U.S. market he delivered an eleven-track album to Reprise with the title *Four More Respected Gentlemen*. This collection featured a pair of tracks that were not on *Village Green*, thereby making an entirely different aural experience for fans. Davies decided to pull both the U.K. and U.S. configurations of the albums, but not before Pye Records jumped the gun and released advance copies to the press. Positive reviews began to accumulate for the original *Village Green*, but no album appeared in the shops because Ray had decided to completely reconfigure the album.

Davies did attempt to persuade Pye to release a double album (since the release of the Mothers of Invention's *Freak Out* and Dylan's *Blonde on Blonde*, the double album was becoming an accepted format for the extended artistic statement), something the label rejected no sooner than it was proposed. Had they allowed this, we would have had a masterpiece on the level of other double-LP sets released that same year: *Electric Ladyland*, *Wheels of Fire*, and the *White Album*. In the end, both Pye and Reprise released a fifteen-song *Village Green*, but the press had already given their collective thumbs-up to the original twelve-track album, making this official release a confusing collection among the press and fans. The result was one of the lowest-selling albums of the Kinks' career. It would be fifty years before the album qualified for Gold record status of one hundred thousand copies sold. The album also suffered at the register because the calm and gentle tenor of the record did not fit in with the sonic extremes of Hendrix, Cream, and the Beatles. Not unlike the Beach Boys' *Friends* album (also from 1968), *Village Green* was a relatively calm and peaceful album, and like *Friends*, it accrued negligible sales; only their hard-core fans would assign this record any importance in the larger catalog.

The Kinks Are the Village Green Preservation Society also marked a series of endings for the band. They would not have an album charting in the United Kingdom for many years to follow, and it was the last album on which original bassist Pete Quaife performed. This also marked the end of their relationship with session keyboardist Nicky Hopkins, who after delivering instantly identifiable keyboards to their previous albums (his contributions to albums for over half of the British rock scene in the 1960s made him one of the most easily identifiable session men in rock music) was not credited for his work on the album while Ray gave himself credit for playing keyboard. Though Davies played a handful of minor keyboard parts, this certainly did not warrant withholding or minimizing credit for Hopkins. He never worked with the Kinks again and claimed that he was never paid for his work on the record.

Along with contemporary album releases by Love, the Zombies, and the Beach Boys, *The Kinks Are the Village Green Preservation Society* is a classic work. While that is certainly true now, it was also true at the time of release, though no one took notice of this. Because of the album's fractured gestation, the wealth of songs composed during this period have allowed for an array of anniversary-themed reissues that feature multiple discs and virtually every track the Kinks recorded around this period.

The work of Dylan Thomas was an influence on Ray Davies's writing, and the romantic simplicity of an England that no longer existed (if ever it did) is a theme that runs through the album. The title track is a disarmingly simple song and would have been massively out of step in late 1968. "Do You Remember Walter," for its unusual title, is a simply beautiful song about the inevitability of relationships that fade into people's pasts and cannot be recaptured quite as naturally as one might wish. "Picture Book" has a jolly air with an underlayer of melancholy. "Johnny Thunder" is a portrait of a rebel biker that has moments of brilliance but never ascends to that height. "Last of the Steam-Powered Trains" sounds radically different from any other song on the album and was recorded in the period following Davies's decision to pull the original *Village Green* from its original release date. Steam trains had been replaced by electric and diesel trains both in England and North America, but the nostalgic desire for the power and rhythm of the steam train resulted in a style of writing that would become a standard form of white blues rock in the 1970s. "Big Sky" is a lovely song in which detachment from society and from oneself is a hoped-for state of being, and it thematically falls into a postpsychedelic genre of introspective rock music. "Sitting by the Riverside" closes side one of the original album, and what starts off as a simple, nostalgic tune falls into a slightly Beatlesque-inflected psychedelic wash. It is a minor song but one of the most imaginative on the album.

Side two opens with "Animal Farm," a simple tune with a deceivingly rich arrangement. It has no connection to Orwell's story and is solely about one's return to nature. By this point in the album, it is clear to the listener that Davies wants to experience an imagined and romanticized world of working-class British life. Although Ray was not actively seeking the lavish life of rock stardom, his desire for the vanishing world of his Muswell Hill neighborhood exposes his comfortable middle-class existence, one whose comforts of life were of a different world than any imagined England of old. "Village Green" was first recorded during the sessions for *Face to Face* and is the other side of the title song's statement. Nicky Hopkins' harpsichord lifts the song to another level, as he did on the previous album's "Two Sisters." David Whittaker's tasteful string arrangement gives the entire song a pseudo-baroque feel. On "Starstruck," Davies borrows from his not-too-distant beat past. It has a tight soul feel, and though it is an awkward fit on the album, Reprise chose to release it as a single in the U.S. market. "Phenomenal Cat" is, however much Davies tried to avoid following trends, a bona fide psychedelic song, with mellotron and all, and the subject of a feline, like Syd Barrett's "Lucifer Sam" on *The Piper at the Gates of Dawn*, shares similar qualities to Barrett's whimsical tenor from that album. "All of My Friends Were There" is a charming song in a turn-of-the-century music hall style, from the pump organ timbres to its jaunty change from a two-step verse to a triple-meter chorus. "Wicked Annabella" is a heavier tune than anything else found on the album, and Davies once again shares some of Syd Barrett's colors to create this spooky number. "Monica" is Davies's ode to a prostitute, but the cod-Caribbean accompaniment weakens the otherwise imaginary tale of a "hooker with a heart of gold." The fifteen-track album ends with "People Take Pictures of Each Other," a concluding song that combines the album's various themes of nostalgia, the awkward outsider, and the lost world of one's youth. The song is a wake-up call after the previous forty minutes of Ray Davies's various dreams of a long-ago world in which he never lived.

Although Ray and Dave Davies may have had no interest in participating in the LSD-soaked world of Swinging London, *The Kinks Are the Village Green Preservation Society* is one of the most complete psychedelic journeys into the mind of a leading artist from the period.

The Kinks' original lineup ended after this album, so the group's first era both as a beat band and as iconoclastic artists receives a gentle release into the recesses of our collective memories. After this album came *Arthur*; *Lola versus Powerman and the Moneygoround, Part One*; and *Muswell Hillbillies*, all brilliant albums from a 1960s group that shifted with ease into the new decade of rock operas, glam, progressive, and everything else that came tumbling out of the psychedelic 1960s.

The original twelve-track album that Ray Davies pulled from release (after it had been distributed to the press) is similar to the final fifteen-track release simply for the fact that ten of the twelve songs made it (with minor changes and alternate sequencing) to the final release, but the two songs that did not make it to the fifteen-track release, "Mr. Songbird" and "Days," give the album a substantially different feel. "Mr. Songbird" is a bouncy track not dissimilar to what Donovan might have written for the *Mellow Yellow* album. The mellotron textures are perfectly executed, and the theme of this song fits perfectly into the loose narrative about a desire for a lost England. "Days" is a minor masterpiece, a striking song of the quality of "Waterloo Sunset," and while it was dropped from the original track listing, it was released as a single and performed well in the charts. The prolific, talented, but now largely forgotten pop songstress, the late Kirsty MacColl, had a successful run with her cover of the song two decades after the release of the original single.

LOVE: *FOREVER CHANGES* (NOVEMBER 1967)

Love was a psychedelic band based in Los Angeles and led by Memphis native Arthur Lee. This band has largely been forgotten in the history of Los Angeles–based rock, sandwiched between the Byrds and Buffalo Springfield on one end and the Doors and the Mothers of Invention on the other. This is unfortunate because Love was a great band that could play garage rock, folk rock, hard blues, or psychedelic rock and should have been a more successful band. Lee was a difficult personality who had to have everything his way, but the challenges with substances, his bandmates, and the frustration at watching the scene begin to pass them by when they had been one of the first bands on the scene surely played into the disintegration of the core band following their third album, *Forever Changes*. In recent years, *Forever Changes* has received overdue recognition, and their other excellent albums, *Love* (1967) and *Da Capo* (1967), were the primer for the progressive psychedelia of *Forever Changes*. After this album, the original group disbanded, and Lee then worked with other musicians under the Love moniker for a surprising, though uneven at times, trio of albums: *Four Sail* (1969), *Out Here* (1969), and *False Start* (1970). This last album is memorable in part because its opening track, "The Everlasting First," features Jimi Hendrix on guitar.

The connection between Hendrix and Lee was complex, and, again, the legends tended to conflate the truth behind their valuable contributions to psychedelia. Lee and Hendrix certainly borrowed from each other in developing their individual public personae and styles. The idea of a black rock and roll artist was not easily understood by the public or record companies, and while neither Lee nor Hendrix copied the prevailing trends in black music, they adapted white rock music for black and white audiences. Both artists certainly influenced each other and had similar tastes in personal style, but Hendrix had the advantage of breaking into the scene in England, where audiences and fellow musicians from the Beatles, the Who, Cream, and others did not have the complications of race (at least not in the way American audiences were hamstrung) to prevent them from seeing a genius at work. Therefore, it is no surprise that Love maintained an English fan base long after the group disbanded. When Lee, following his release from prison, began to perform *Forever Changes* as an in-concert work, European and English audiences were wildly enthusiastic, whereas only the most dedicated and loyal fans took note of Lee's extraordinary comeback in the United States.

Arthur Lee and Jimi Hendrix also shared a prefame collaboration that was the first of two instances when they would work together. The teenaged Lee fronted various R & B groups in Los Angeles, and with future Love guitarist and childhood friend, Johnny Echols, he made recordings for Capitol Records in the early 1960s. He led a group called the LAGs (a West Coast takeoff from Booker T. & the M.G.'s) but also did uncredited work as a songwriter and singer. One overlooked songwriting credit is 1964's "My Diary," which was recorded by Rosa Lee Brooks on the Revis label. The song was inspired by Arthur's clandestine relationship with a neighborhood teen, who also inspired Love's "7 & 7 Is" and "A Message to Pretty." Brooks recorded Lee's song, and his desire to include a guitarist who could sound like Curtis Mayfield led label owner Billy Revis to recommend Hendrix, whom he had seen perform with another band. Hendrix was romantically involved with Brooks, which also helped connect him to this recording session. This may have been Hendrix's first appearance on record, but it would be the only time the two greats worked together in the studio until "The Everlasting First," which was one of Hendrix's last studio appearances.

Lee idolized Hendrix (whether he cared to admit it), and in interviews, Hendrix stated how much he loved Lee. These two African American men left an indelible footprint on the road from psychedelia to hard rock, and it was inevitable that they would be compared to each other. As a result, both men had to navigate rivalries, both real and imagined. Over successive decades, Hendrix's legacy became a part of the rock and roll historical narrative, but Lee's stumbled into near obscurity.

Lee's personal challenges with alcohol and drugs made him difficult to work with in most any capacity. Even when Lee had his postprison comeback, performing *Forever Changes* in concert, he was a difficult person and had to have an assigned handler within the band. Many of Lee's friends later claimed that even as a child, Lee could get whatever he wanted and never learned to take responsibility for his actions, simply because he believed he did not have to explain his actions. Despite being a difficult personality, his friends maintain that he was a quiet and introspective person, preferred small or intimate gatherings over large crowds, and could easily have his heart broken by one or another girlfriend.

As Hendrix's fame began to ascend to unfathomable heights in 1967, Love released their classic *Forever Changes*, but nearly two years would pass before they released their next album. In 1968–1969, Hendrix and Sly and the Family Stone released their now legendary records and changed the profile for African American men in rock music. Within a year of Love's return to the market, Parliament-Funkadelic crashed onto the scene, and Lee's music began to sound slightly out of step with the more progressive African American artists. Although his albums from 1969 and 1970 are not discussed here, they are good records and heavier versions of the original band. Sadly, everything he released after 1967 would be compared (often unfavorably) to *Forever Changes*. Arthur Lee's story has largely been constructed on legends and myths; it is only in recent years that his story began to receive the attention and detail befitting a musician of his talents and contributions.

Love was the first interracial psychedelic band signed to a national label, but they were soon followed by the Jimi Hendrix Experience and Sly and the Family Stone, both of whom would have greater commercial success than Love. *Forever Changes* was recorded in the summer of 1967 and has aged well in part because the music does not fall prey to the traditional aural hallmarks of psychedelia. It was a commercial disappointment at the time of its release but remained a favorite among Lee's most ardent fans. The extraordinary albums released in 1967 by the Beatles, Cream, Hendrix, and others can easily overshadow the looming seriousness that must have impacted the youths of that time. The military draft was absorbing more young men, with African Americans being drafted in disproportionate numbers. Fewer black men had college prospects after high school, and without college deferments, they were drafted in increasing numbers from 1967 onward. Both Lee and Echols were called up to report to their hometown draft boards, but they appeared strange enough and, if needed, pretended to be gay just so they would not be drafted. Under the darkening skies of the impending social and cultural deconstructions, Lee wrote *Forever Changes* with a sense of the foreboding, as if they could be his last words. Drugs had already begun to drive a wedge between various band members, but Lee managed to create one of the most focused and clearly articulated albums of the period.

By the time Love came to record *Forever Changes*, the band was already facing internal difficulties. Lee refused to tour, which made it difficult for them to build press interest in their work. Elektra's other psychedelic band, the Doors, was attracting far more attention and record sales (it was Lee who encouraged Elektra head Jac Holzman to hear them in 1966), which exacerbated the interpersonal challenges within the band. The arrangements for the songs were more complex than what they recorded on their first two albums, and it was coproducer Bruce Botnick who was able to move things along and bring the album to completion. He secured a few members of the legendary Los Angeles studio players the Wrecking Crew to play on a handful of the tracks. The working relationship between Lee and the band's other songwriter, Bryan MacLean, had also begun to break down, so by the time the album was released, there was little left of band (two other members had left prior to recording the album). *Forever Changes* had the poorest chart showing of their first three albums but was a top 25 album in the United Kingdom.

The last of the band's original members left the group soon after the release of *Forever Changes*, and Lee produced three more albums with a different lineup, the last of which, the aforementioned *False Start*, featured Jimi Hendrix playing lead guitar on the opening track. Lee would use the Love name on later albums, but his career never recovered from the unfortunate end to one of the most promising groups of the psychedelic era. He was sentenced to prison in 1996 for negligent discharge of a firearm and served a little less than half of his twelve-year sentence. Arthur Lee did live to see his musical legacy rehabilitated, and he performed concerts of the *Forever Changes* album. He was written off in the 1970s and was wrongly imprisoned in the 1990s, but upon his release, he discovered that people wanted to hear his music again. After his 2001 release, he appeared in concert with more frequency than he had at any earlier period in his career.

Arthur Lee is seen as a redemption story in rock music, especially when compared to the losses of Hendrix, Joplin, and Morrison. In spring 2006, it was reported that he was battling leukemia, and a series of benefit concerts were mounted to help provide the financial resources for his medical treatment. Still, his condition continued to deteriorate, and he died in August of that year.

THE LOVIN' SPOONFUL: "SUMMER IN THE CITY" (JULY 1966)

The Lovin' Spoonful were an American rock band that emerged from the Greenwich Village folk scene of the early 1960s. They were the lone jug band folk group of the period who would successfully transform into a rock and roll band. The Mamas and the Papas emerged from the same folk music scene, but their sound could best be described as folk rock or sunshine pop. One-half of the Mamas and the Papas, Denny Doherty and Cass Elliot, had sung with the Spoonful's John Sebastian and Zal "Zally" Yanovsky in the Mugwumps, and though the Lovin' Spoonful should have been a surefire success, they were misled by their shortsighted management team and lost their opportunity at commercial success in the emerging psychedelic scene. The Mamas and the Papas ultimately retained more of their folk roots than the Lovin' Spoonful, and John Phillips's vocal arrangements and Lou Adler's deft managerial style achieved far greater success and credibility among the counterculture.

The Lovin' Spoonful was led by John Sebastian, who would go on to greater fame as the author and performer of the mid-1970s television sitcom theme song to *Welcome Back, Kotter*, but in 1965, he and the Spoonful recorded catchy pop songs that fit comfortably into the maturing field of popular music. Songs such as "Do You Believe in Magic," "You Didn't Have to Be So Nice," and "Did You Ever Have to Make Up Your Mind" were catchy radio-friendly hit songs, but it was their sixth single, "Summer in the City," that earned them their first No. 1 single and a place in this volume. Sadly, this band never realized their full potential because of cowardly managerial advice in response to an aggressive drug bust against guitarist Zal Yanovsky and bass player Steve Boone. Drug busts made in the immediate wake of Yanovsky and Boone's arrest were supposedly initiated on information they were rumored to have provided to law enforcement, which ultimately damaged their credibility among the fans.

"Summer in the City" is one of the harder songs in the band's catalog, and the insistent, chopping guitar work of Zal Yanovsky would influence artists such as Eric Clapton, who acknowledged its influence in his own playing on "Tales of Brave Ulysses." The song's arrangement features two keyboard instruments, the Vox Continental organ and the Hohner piannet. The Vox Continental, conceived as a lighter and more portable alternative to the Hammond C3, possesses an iconic sound and provided the central timbre for several songs discussed in this book. The Hohner was a widely used instrument by bands such as the Zombies, the Beatles, and bands in the prepsychedelic era. It was an alternative to the Rhodes electric piano, which would find more widespread use in the 1970s. The dual keyboard timbres and Yanovsky's jabbing guitar chords were enhanced with touches of musique concrète (street sounds, jackhammers, and car horns), which brought a raw and gritty quality to the song and that would unfortunately not be replicated in their later work.

The Lovin' Spoonful and John Sebastian would continue to create accessible and enjoyable music, but "Summer in the City" would be the band's last No. 1 and Gold-certified single. Zal Yanovsky, whose guitar work provides the fascia that holds all of the wonderfully disparate timbres of the song in place, was threatened with deportation unless he was willing to assist undercover police in planting themselves into the scene with the goal of arresting more pot smokers and dealers. Despite the questionable legality of the police search and the dubious "offer" extended to them via their management team, which included attorney Melvin Belli and Charles Koppleman, Yanovsky was advised to take the deal, ostensibly to save his own skin and, by extension, also the band. Instead, their popularity began its slow descent, by which time Koppleman had moved on and was at work enhancing his own accounts while draining his next artists.

Predatory managers have existed in rock music for as long as the field has made money. Morris Levy and George Goldner are only two of the legendary managers with ties to organized crime. The Lovin' Spoonful's legacy would be shortchanged because of the legal gray area that was occupied by their label and managers. They were signed to Kama Sutra Records, a label founded by Artie Ripp, a pragmatic businessperson whose own strong-arm techniques served to benefit his ledger sheet at the expense of his artists/clients. Most famously, he would, a decade later, force Columbia Records and Billy Joel to pay royalties to his production company for years into the future in exchange for releasing Joel from his management and allowing him to sign with Columbia.

A label head possessed with this level of hard-edged acumen should have advised his label's best-selling band to consider other options instead of folding in response to the police. Belli (who had represented Lee Harvey Oswald's killer, Jack Ruby, just two years earlier) and Koppleman, who was relatively close in age to the band members, chose not to use their influence to push back against the charges. Ripp, Belli, and Koppleman understood that a band whose value was perceived to be on the decline could still be viewed as an excellent short-term asset if they could find someone to buy them. Over the next two decades, Koppleman made millions when he signed artists to private management contracts and used their creative assets as leverage to extract long dollars from various record labels. He was one of the first "super managers," before the era of David Geffen and Irving Azoff, and would expand his empire into the buying and selling of song copyrights and publishing companies.

Zanovsky eventually returned to Canada and opened the renowned restaurant *Chez Piggy* in Kingston, Ontario, a decade later. Charles Koppleman had pulled the plug on a band at the cusp of success in the psychedelic and counterculture movement. They had found their wider audience and achieved their first top-of-the-chart success, but they were left to a largely forgettable ending. In a story shared by many bands, the members of the Lovin' Spoonful made little money on their records. In a typical business play of the era, the band members were given substantial advances against future royalties, but they never saw additional monies in the years that followed, even though the records continued to sell or were licensed for commercial use or reissued on compilation albums.

THE MOODY BLUES: *DAYS OF FUTURE PASSED* (1967)

The Moody Blues emerged from Birmingham's Brumbeat scene, and though not a psychedelic band in its truest form, they were responsible for incorporating the mellotron, a relatively new and obscure keyboard-triggered electronic instrument, as a primary instrumental color into their sound. This instrument produced dramatic symphonic textures and new keyboard timbres into rock music at a brief period before the Moog synthesizer became a ubiquitous instrument for the emerging progressive rock bands of the late 1960s. The Moodies were not the first group to use this on record, but they were the first to feature its timbres as the core of their sound.

The Moody Blues Mk. I (Denny Laine, Mike Pinder, Ray Thomas, Clint Warwick, and Graeme Edge) were a good, though not memorable, English blues band and likely would have never achieved international fame if Mike Pinder had not begun to incorporate the mellotron into the band's aural palate in late 1966. It became a central instrument across the six classic Moody Blues albums (with Moody Blues Mk. II), from *Days of Future Passed* (1967) to *Seventh Sojourn* (1972). In the early 1960s, Moodies keyboardist Mike Pinder had worked for Streetly Electronics, the Birmingham-based company that designed and built the mellotron, and while Pinder did not own a mellotron at this time, he was aware of its potential for use in rock music.

The band was on track to become a one-hit wonder thanks to their second single, "Go Now," released in November 1964. Their debut album, *The Magnificent Moodies*, released on Decca in the summer of 1965, attained a moderate level of success, but like many albums from white blues bands of this period, the LP featured several cover songs with only a handful of original tunes. They were signed to NEMS under Brian Epstein's management, which led to their being chosen as an opening act on the Beatles' final U.K. tour in December 1965, where Pinder claims he introduced the Beatles to the instrument. Going into 1966, the Moodies follow-up singles continued to miss the charts, and their live bookings became fewer in number. Bassist Clint Warwick left the group in July 1966, and Denny Laine followed in October of that year. These departures led to their being dropped later that month by NEMS. Epstein had already lost interest in the group and had handed them to his assistant, Alistair Taylor.

In November 1966, John Lodge, on bass and vocals, and Justin Hayward (on a referral from the Animals' Eric Burdon), on guitar and vocals, joined the group. The band relocated to Belgium to rehearse and put the group back on its creative and financial feet. By December, they were opening for Tom Jones, but it was Pinder's acquisition of a secondhand Mellotron that enabled the band to develop their new sound. While Pinder worked at Streetly Electronics, the price of a new mellotron, at £3,000, put the instrument out of his financial reach. It was on the recommendation of his contacts at Streetly that he was able to purchase a used mellotron from the Dunlop Tyre Factory social club. He began to incorporate it into the band's sound during the Belgian rehearsal sessions and in their live shows, which still featured their earlier blues-based repertory. The first record on which Pinder incorporated the mellotron, "Love and Beauty," was recorded in July 1967, and later that fall, he added the mellotron to Justin Hayward's new composition, "Nights in White Satin." With this, the band's iconic sound was secured.

The Moody Blues were on the verge of obscurity throughout 1965–1966, but with a wealth of new songs by Pinder and Hayward that featured the mellotron; their collaborative partnerships with producer Tony Clarke and engineer Derek Varnals; and, of equal if not greater importance, the support of the visionary executive producer Hugh Mendl, the band would achieve extraordinary successes from 1967 to the mid-1970s.

Their work from 1968 until their self-imposed hiatus following the tour in support of *Seventh Sojourn* (1972) could best be described as cosmic rock rather than psychedelic rock. The band pokes light fun at their earlier work with Ray Thomas's "Veteran Cosmic Rocker" on 1981's *Long Distance Voyager*. In the video to their smash 1986 single "Your Wildest Dreams," the band members are in a party scene where they ape their psychedelic/cosmic rock past by putting the vinyl record of *In Search of the Lost Chord* on a turntable. Although *Days of Future Passed* restored Decca's faith in the band, the record was not an immediate smash upon its first release. The album made the top 30, and the singles "Nights in White Satin" and "Tuesday Afternoon" crept into the top 25. It remained a steady seller on the charts, but on the album's reissue in 1972, it acquired the tag of "masterpiece." On its second issue, the album reached the top 5 on Billboard, and the single "Nights in White Satin" was top 10 in the United Kingdom and top 5 in the United States.

How the group evolved from an unremarkable blues band into pioneers of the psychedelic and progressive rock movement has been presented in two conflicting narratives. What is true is that the Moody Blues, a nearly obscure group two years past their last successes, were a gamble for Decca. The most widely promoted story, supported by the band and critics, had the group contracted by Decca to record a rock version of Antonin Dvorak's *Symphony No. 9* to promote Decca's new stereo technology, which they marketed as Deramic Stereo Sound, or DSS. Once in the studio, the legend maintains that the band convinced Tony Clarke (their assigned producer) and Peter Knight (conductor of the London Festival Orchestra) to let them record their idea for an album.

While that story has the appropriate David and Goliath conflict that pitched Decca *against* the Moody Blues, Derek Varnals, the engineer who recorded the band's classic albums from 1967 to 1972, has stated that the Dvorak story was fabricated after the fact and that he first heard it in the early 1970s. He recalls that Decca wanted to expand their DSS series (the label featured several light and pop orchestral titles prior to *Days of Future Passed*) with an album that combined a rock band with a symphony orchestra. He also states that the hit singles "Nights in White Satin" and "Tuesday Afternoon," along with "Dawn is a Feeling" and "Peak Hour," were composed before the concept for an album was developed. However accurate Varnals's memories may be on this point, his assertion that the band recorded the song for BBC Radio's *Saturday Club* in the months prior to the album's release may not be entirely correct. Still, we can correctly suppose that Decca received a final product that none of the label managers (apart from Hugh Mendl, who supported the project from its earliest days) could have anticipated.

While much has been written on the mixture of rock and orchestral textures in *Days of Future Passed*, the album consists of songs performed by the Moodies that are connected through orchestral interludes created by Peter Knight, who worked from the materials the band recorded for the album. It is only at the end of "Nights in White Satin" that the orchestra is heard *with* the band. The album opens with Peter Knight's sweetly majestic "The Day Begins." Knight did splendid work at incorporating the Moodies tunes into his orchestral arrangements, which provided the album with a through-composed structure. Knight created an overture in which themes from many of the band's songs are introduced. The orchestral fade-out features Mike Pinder's recitation of "Morning Glory" to create a seamless transition to the dreamy "Dawn: Dawn Is a Feeling," a Pinder composition in which the mellotron continues with the rich timbres of the symphony orchestra. Pinder's piano playing on this album provided a core texture and rhythmic groove within the band's sound palette. On later Moody Blues albums, he would move away from the piano and rely more on the mellotron, organ, and other instruments.

A romantic orchestral interlude provides a connection to "The Morning: Another Morning," Ray Thomas's jaunty tune that opens with his double-tracked flute. Ray's wonderfully plummy vocal delivery and rich tenor were another of the band's strengths, and this song hits upon playful and whimsical themes. This is bookended with an appropriately sprightly tune that keeps up a frantic pace in anticipation of the final song on side one. The next orchestral interlude leads us to "Lunch Break: Peak Hour," one of John Lodge's pure rock songs in which Pinder's stabbing gestures on mellotron and organ provide a lead-in to Justin Hayward's guitar solo and sustain the song through its end-of-side-one climax.

Side two opens with "The Afternoon," a two-part song that begins with one of Hayward's most famous songs, "Tuesday Afternoon." Lodge's bass and Pinder's mellotron colors provide a rich and magisterial air to this ballad. Hayward's acoustic guitar provides a delicate balance that allows the longing in his vocals to draw the listener more deeply into the song. Before going into the second half of the "Afternoon" section, another grandiose orchestral interlude sets up for Lodge's "(Evening) Time to Get Away." Again, the band's excellent ensemble work creates a delicate atmosphere for the song, which features John's falsetto vocals, a soon to become familiar timbre in the Moody Blues' sound. The "Evening" section includes Pinder's "The Sunset" and Ray Thomas's "Twilight Time." Pinder's growing interest in Eastern mysticism and exotic sounds is apparent in this song. Another brief orchestral interlude connects "The Sunset" to Thomas's "Twilight Time," one of the more purely psychedelic works on the album.

The concluding section, "The Night," opens with the band's most famous song, "Nights in White Satin." This song incorporates all the now-recognized Moody Blues tropes: a spacious arrangement, the dark colors of the mellotron, the falsetto backing vocals, a flute countermelody in the middle-eight, and Justin Hayward's heartfelt lead vocal. The single edit of this song lacks the orchestral part in the final verse, but in either version, this song is one of the band's most perfectly crafted songs. A final orchestral transition leads to the album's closing track, Graeme Edge's "Late Lament." In later Moody Blues albums, either Edge or Pinder provides overly dramatic, though utterly sincere, poetry segments on the openings and closings of their records. But it is on *Days of Future Passed* that we are first introduced to the Moody Blues as psychedelic troubadours whose albums would take willing listeners into cosmic journeys across time and space.

THE MOODY BLUES: *IN SEARCH OF THE LOST CHORD* (1968)

Cosmic rock and progressive rock are two of the many genres in popular music that evolved from psychedelia, and on *In Search of the Lost Chord*, the Moody Blues make lyrical and musical references to themes at the core of the psychedelic movement while their sound begins to evolve into the cosmic rock genre for which they are most remembered. While *Days of Future Passed* rescued the band from obscurity as the one-hit wonder of 1965, it redefined an otherwise competent blues-based band from the Midlands into psychedelic/progressive musical travelers and enshrined their position in popular music history. Peter Knight and the London Festival Orchestra provided the artistic gravitas and tone on *Days of Future Passed*, but for *In Search of the Lost Chord*, the Moodies performed every instrument on their one truly psychedelic offering and created an album equal, if not greater, in scope to its predecessor.

The album opens with "Departure," a Graeme Edge spoken word prelude accompanied with a cod-Indian/mellotron soundscape that leads into a classic John Lodge tune, "Ride My See-Saw." Ray Thomas follows this serviceable rock song with his whimsical "Dr. Livingstone, I Presume." With its prominent mellotron and organ accompaniment and the Moodies' falsetto backing vocals, it expands upon the sounds they created on *Days of Future Passed*. Lodge's "House of Four Doors" is a complex, mystical, and at times lilting song in which Lodge demonstrates his newly acquired skills on the cello. Ray Thomas follows again with "Legend of a Mind," one of the first works recorded for the album. His paean to San Francisco's hippie and acid scene, in which he name-checks acid guru Timothy Leary, is underscored with his double-tracked flute and Pinder's rich mellotron accompanient. Justin Hayward and Mike Pinder engaged in a level of experimentation, surely influenced by both the Beatles and the Rolling Stones, and acquired enough technique to use Indian instruments, in this case the sitar and the tanpura, to add a rich Eastern flavor to Thomas's song. This leads into part two (in truth more of a coda than a second part) of Lodge's "House of Four Doors," which concludes side one of the album.

Side two of the record is stacked with great songs from both Hayward and Pinder. It begins with one of Justin's masterpieces, "Voices in the Sky," which set a template for the intimate tenor of Hayward-penned songs that would dominate future Moodies albums. Pinder's sincere interest in Eastern philosophy is apparent in the lyrics for "The Best Way to Travel." With any other band, it likely would have acquired the drug connotations of the sort that dogged the Byrds' "Eight Miles High." This is another of the band's psychedelic classics and is filled with studio effects, distortion, and an expansive mix from producer Tony Clarke, the range of which is not heard again on their records.

Justin's "Visions of Paradise" is one of the most satisfying songs on the album. It features Hayward's sitar playing, a prominent flute part performed by Thomas, and expertly double-tracked vocals. The mellotron seemingly rises from nowhere to carry the b-section of the song into a final verse. This is followed by another Hayward tune, "The Actor," which is fitted with rich lyrics and an understated arrangement that features a prominent flute countermelody. The b-section of the song features one of the band's best vocal ensemble arrangements and is one of the highlights of the album. On "The Word," drummer Graeme Edge delivers one of his shortest contributions on a Moodies album and leaves it to Pinder's delivery to lead into the Pinder/Thomas collaboration "Om," a logical continuation of the themes introduced in "The Best Way to Travel." A showcase for the Indian instrumentation they utilized across the album, it has a more prominent and virtuosic role in the arrangement for Hayward, Pinder, and Edge. Ray Thomas's flute holds together all the instrumental colors between verses.

Two songs recorded during these sessions, though not included on the original album, Hayward's "What Am I Doing Here?" and "King and Queen," possess a magisterial troubadour-like air that would inform many of his future hit songs. Although they were left off the original album (they were first released on 1977's *Caught Live + 5* album and given a first release on compact disc a decade later on *Prelude*), both songs are included on the various expanded reissues of the record. Deluxe and expanded editions of the album feature not only the outtakes recorded during sessions for this album but also alternate mixes that were streamlined for the album. There is a longer version of the album opener, "Departure," with wild, stabbing mellotron textures; a mix of "The Word" with the mellotron placed higher into the mix; and a beautiful extended version of "Om" that concludes with a stunning vocal coda. One of the most surprising exclusions from the album is Mike Pinder's "A Simple Game." There were two recordings, one each with Mike and Justin on lead vocal, though Mike's version was used as the B side of the album's lead single, "Ride My See-Saw." This song was given a more powerful interpretation by the Four Tops in their version released in 1971 as a U.K. single. The production by Moodies producer Tony Clarke captures the strengths of Mike's composition with the Tops' powerful delivery. The single was eventually released in the United States but did not have comparable chart success.

THE MOTHERS OF INVENTION: *WE'RE ONLY IN IT FOR THE MONEY* (MARCH 1968)

The Mothers of Invention will never be categorized as psychedelic artists, but their arrival on the commercial market in 1966 overlapped with the emergence of psychedelic music. Frank Zappa, the titular leader of the Mothers of Invention, is perhaps the most prolific artist of the rock era. His extensive catalog of recordings includes over sixty albums released in his lifetime, and after his passing, the Zappa Family Trust released another fifty albums, making his discography the largest in rock music.

The first three albums released by the Mothers of Invention, *Freak Out* (1966), *Absolutely Free* (1967), and *We're Only in It for the Money* (1968), are extraordinary for their unconventional content and the fact that such consistently unconventional work was released by a major record label (following the releases on Verve, Zappa released his records on a variety of smaller labels that included his own self-managed label in addition to Warner Bros. Records). The band's debut record, *Freak Out*, was only the second double album released in rock music, and for many years, it was the only debut album accorded the freedom of a double set. It was released a few weeks after Dylan's *Blonde on Blonde* and was a wild and sprawling mass of music that is unlike anything else released by a rock group in the psychedelic era. Unlike the many bands from this period who recorded free improvisations in the name of compositional/artistic experimentation, Zappa treated his band the way a conductor handles an orchestra, and he expected his band to play exactly what he composed.

We're Only in It for the Money was released in March 1968 (it was Zappa's fourth album, as he had released his first solo album, *Lumpy Gravy*, between *Absolute Free* and *We're Only in It for the Money*), and it is the strongest of Zappa's early works and features one of the best cover parodies in all of rock music. The intended cover was a parody of *Sgt. Pepper's Lonely Hearts Club Band*, but MGM feared legal action over the cover and chose to instead put a photograph of the band on the cover and the parodied image on the inside of the record's gatefold sleeve. This album is a parodied rip-off of numerous psychedelic tropes, but after this album, Zappa directed the Mothers of Invention into a variety of different directions. The next record, *Cruising with Reuben & the Jets*, was a return to his early penchant for doo-wop, and *Uncle Meat, Burnt Weeny Sandwich* and his second solo album, *Hot Rats*, tread further into experimental and jazz styles.

In the climate of the second decade of the twenty-first century, Zappa's shock value, especially in album and song titles, lost its impact and appeared to many as being juvenile and sexist. *Burnt Weeny Sandwich*, "Twinkle Tits," "Don't You Ever Wash That Thing," "Carolina Hardcore Ecstasy," "Titties & Beer," and "The Illinois Enema Bandit" are just a few of his titles that never found a commercial market.

San Francisco is considered by many as the home of West Coast psychedelia, but Los Angeles, with groups such as the Doors and Love, represented a much different genre of music. Zappa and the Mothers of Invention were pure anarchy. For many decades, Los Angeles was, despite the presence of Hollywood and the film industry, a conventional and conservative part of the state. Agriculture, petroleum, and the aerospace industry was California's financial base, and these communities tended to lean on the conservative end of the political spectrum. In 1967, the state elected Ronald Reagan as governor, and the future U.S. president promised to end the anti-war and antiestablishment protests and movements. He sent the National Guard into Berkeley and criticized university administrators for tolerating protestors. He did not believe in appeasement when dealing with those he perceived to be "the enemy";

his governorship was simply a practice run for his controversial two-term presidency.

The Los Angeles Police Department was known for its strong-arm and harassment tactics in addition to racial profiling. By the mid-1960s, the police were distinctly antifreak, antilonghair, and antihippie, so people who fell under the category of "freaks" were frequent targets of police brutality. Zappa's song "Plastic People" (the opening track on the Mothers' sophomore LP, *Absolutely Free*) is about police violence on the Sunset Strip. Zappa's iconoclastic musical voice was shaped by many factors, including his brief (and entirely unwarranted) incarceration and his disdain for conventional social structures, public education, and organized religion.

Satire was one of Zappa's greatest skills, and however much he disliked societal convention and straight society, he held an equal level of disdain for liberal hypocrisies and their lifestyle. Many of his works are not necessarily an attack on the right wing of the political spectrum but are likely an attack on the artificiality of the so-called counterculture; the sound of the Mothers of Invention is a reflection of the Los Angeles scene at that point in the decade. On *We're Only in It for the Money*, it is clear that Zappa had developed a firmer command of the ensemble, and on this album Zappa turned the proverbial mirror back onto the audience, who demanded such for the purpose of entertainment. With one or two exceptions, the mainstream rock press panned the Mothers' first two albums, and their third album won no more supporters among critics.

Although the Mothers of Invention were a Los Angeles–based group, Zappa relocated the group to New York City, where they were the resident band at the Garrick Theater on Bleecker Street. They played two shows nightly, six nights a week, and out of this came *We're Only in It for the Money*. This album is the sound of a Los Angeles freak band in New York. Not long before, the city had been the musical heartbeat of the country, but in 1968, it was in a transitional period in the run-up to glam and punk. Los Angeles had become the musical capital of the country; however, one of the city's most unique groups had relocated to New York City, and their third album reflected Zappa's disdain for the hippie movement that, by 1968, had overrun San Francisco.

We're Only in It for the Money contained all new songs, where their first two albums had featured songs from Zappa's formative pre-Mothers years. He had been one of the early freaks in Los Angeles, but now he saw the entire movement as having been washed out, commodified, and killed and replaced by dropouts, publicity-hungry kids, and social opportunists. This album is a combination of songs with extended interludes/

bridges, so half of the album's tracks are ninety seconds or less. The record opens with "Are You Hung Up?" (Julian Cope did a brilliant cover of this song in April 1991 on a John Peel BBC show as part of a work he titled "Soul Medley." In this, Cope opened with a cover of Funkadelic's "Free Your Mind and Your Ass Will Follow" before falling into his "Everything Playing at Once," which leads into an acid trip–worthy read of Zappa's song before concluding with "Hung Up and Hanging Out to Dry" from *Peggy Suicide*.)

The broad range of songs on the album features doo-wop, rhythm and blues, musique concrète, surf music, collage tape compositions, and parodied quotes from a variety of sources, not the least of which is from Scott McKenzie's "San Francisco (Be Sure to Wear Flowers in Your Hair)" in "Who Needs the Peace Corps." "Flower Punk" is a clear parody of "Hey Joe," a mainstay for many early psychedelic groups. "Concentration Moon" considers the interning of hippies in the World War II–era concentration camps where the American government held Japanese Americans during the war. That shameful period of American wartime policy had conveniently been swept into silence, so Zappa's acknowledgment of the camps' very existence could be read as subversive or anti-American. "Mom & Dad" addresses the generation gap that had riven many families in Middle America. "Telephone Conversation" is a party line that leads into another bridge, "Bow Tie Daddy," an old-time novelty riff. This bridge along with the two that follow, "Harry, You're a Beast" and "What's the Ugliest Part of Your Body," are rip-offs about the vapid, superficial cons that are so much a part of (in Zappa's view) Middle American life. The waltz "Absolutely Free" is a take on the hippie ethos of freedom and social unity, poking deep holes into the hippie mode of life. The depths of Zappa's satire drive to their fervent conclusion on side one with "Flower Punk" and the blink-or-you'll-miss-it run-out groove of "Hot Poop."

Side two opens with the musique concrète exercise "Nasal Retentive Calliope Music." The record speeds from here to the end of side two with scathing attacks on American life. "Let's Make the Water Turn Black" sounds as if Zappa had landed on the set of the television show *My Three Sons*. The remainder of the side deals with politician fathers, mothers who are prostitutes, and soul-stomping tunes amid various studio experiments and a reprise of "What's the Ugliest Part of Your Body." The album concludes with the longest track on the record, "The Chrome Plated Megaphone of Destiny." This Dadaist collage is not one that most Zappa fans would gravitate toward, but it gives the composer room to flex his insolence at the listener.

The Mothers' albums on Verve were unavailable for much of the 1970s and early 1980s and among the rarest albums in his catalog. When managed and distributed by MGM Records, Verve Records was often victim to some of the more unsavory practices of the era. MGM Records was known for its creative "accounting" practices that included overruns from the pressing plant, which served the needs of organized crime in the record industry. Zappa believed the biggest development in modern music was its transformation into big business.

NUGGETS: ORIGINAL ARTYFACTS FROM THE FIRST PSYCHEDELIC ERA, 1965–1968 (OCTOBER 1972)

This entry is the only posthumous release from the psychedelic era to be included in this volume. The original two-album release on Elektra Records was compiled by Lenny Kaye, the soon-to-be guitarist for the Patti Smith Group, in 1972. Kaye has had an extraordinarily diverse and lengthy career, though his time as a clerk at New York's Village Oldies record store helped to connect him with Elektra Records president Jac Holzman, who commissioned Kaye to compile this first-of-its-kind album (Village Oldies was renamed Bleecker Bob's Golden Oldies before it closed in 2013 and was replaced by a frozen yogurt shop). It was released four years after the end of the psychedelic movement and four years before the launch of punk rock, two of the most dissimilar yet complementary musical movements since the arrival of rock and roll. The album found an almost immediate audience with kids who may have been too young to have recalled the original garage and psychedelic music scenes and were on the cusp of launching the punk movement. This influential album spawned similarly themed albums (*Pebbles* and *Back from the Grave*), and upon reissue on compact disc, it included additional volumes that featured songs that were left off, or never considered for, the original album. A *Nuggets II* featured early psychedelia, and the 1998 boxed set with over 125 songs is a worthy collection in which to immerse oneself. This entry is focused on the original 1972 issue. In the liner notes, Kaye discusses the selection process he utilized in narrowing the original album to a two-LP set. Licensing and copyrights played a hand in removing certain songs from his preferred track list, but many of these would show up later on the 1998 four-CD reissue.

Garage rock is an often-forgotten stylistic doorway that informed many of the early psychedelic bands in North America. In Britain, movements such as freakbeat served a similar function, but regardless of the terminology, the music contained on the original *Nuggets* features songs from a number of bands who were significant contributors to the original psychedelic movement, the punk movement of the late 1970s, and the neo-psychedelia of the 1980s. While not as direct a relative, the ambient grooves that first appear in the 1970s from Köln, Berlin, Düsseldorf, and London also found their way through the pre-twilight dark with these unique and, at times, inconsistent samples of distorted heaven. Some of these songs were the lone hit for these bands, but in later years, some of them would be recognized as bona fide hits on oldies radio. But in 1972, the lo-fi aesthetic of these songs was a perfect tonic for a genre of music that was expanding and en route to becoming a bloated caricature of itself.

Side one opens with the Electric Prunes hit "I Had Too Much to Dream (Last Night)" that was originally released on Reprise Records in January 1967. Produced by Dave Hassinger, this single was from the original Seattle-based band. By 1967, after dealing with a group who lacked the initiative to expand their sound, Hassinger brought together five new members as the Electric Prunes and recorded *Mass in F Minor*, a quasi-psychedelic/medieval chant album. This album was significant because a track from this record appears in the cinematic counterculture masterpiece *Easy Rider*. The Standells' "Dirty Water" from November 1965 would become a standard on oldies stations in future decades. This Los Angeles–based band was signed to Capitol Records' subsidiary label, Tower Records (the same U.S. label that released Pink Floyd's first three albums). They had been on the scene since 1963 and had cycled through a variety of styles before having this minor hit as a psychedelic outfit.

"Night Time," by the Strangeloves, was coauthored by famed songsmith and producer Richard Gottehrer. The "band" was an artificial construct for the production team of Gottehrer, Jerry Goldsmith, and Robert Feldman. The Knickerbocker's "Lies" from March 1967 acquired a longer shelf life than perhaps it was due from this minor New Jersey outfit. The Vagrants' read on the Otis Redding composition (and Aretha Franklin hit single) "Respect" is a now forgotten take on an otherwise classic song. It didn't hurt that the single was released on the Atco Records label, a subsidiary of Atlantic Records, home of Aretha Franklin. "A Public Execution" by Mouse is one of the more obscure tracks on the collection. Mouse, a nom de plume for Ronny Weiss, also performed as Mouse and the Traps and were active in Texas' prolific psychedelic scene, though Weiss later went on to be part of a soft-country duo on RCA, Rio Grande.

Side one closes with the Blues' Project's "No Time Like the Right Time." This Al Kooper–penned single from February 1967 has a sound not dissimilar to the work of any number of English beat groups from 1966. The group landed on New York's blues scene in 1965, and Kooper, who had appeared on a number of Dylan's recent hits (most notably, "Like a Rolling Stone" and *Blonde on Blonde*) went on to form Blood, Sweat, and Tears with guitarist Steve Katz. Of even greater importance than this record, Kooper was responsible for getting Clive Davis to release the Zombies' *Odessey and Oracle* after CBS had passed on it for a U.S. release. Two of the first three albums of the Blues Project were live albums on the Verve label. Following Kooper and Katz's departures, the band soldiered on with a couple of replacements before the original group came together early in 1973 to release a live album of a concert in Central Park.

Side two opens with "Oh Yeah" by the Shadows of Knight, a Chicago-based blues band that recorded on the Dunwich label. Leaning more to the garage, rather than the psychedelic, sensibility, their sound owed more than a bit to the British blues bands of the era. The Seeds' "Pushin' Too Hard" remains a classic slice of garage psychedelia. Led by Sky Saxon, the band might have remained as a popular curio of the Southern California scene except for their manager, Tim Hudson, who was able to promote their flower power image. Their simple driving tunes were catchy, if not terribly original, but the sneering vocals of Sky Saxon and his Vox keyboard drones give their albums an irresistible, if at times dated, sound. Saxon was already thirty by the time the Seeds had their first hit. Over a decade after the Seeds disbanded in 1969, Saxon was living in Hawaii with two common-law wives and, by his own admission, praying to dogs. Saxon went on to lead a spin-off project, the Sky Saxon Blues Band, and in the 1990s, he oversaw a thirteen-CD release of psychedelic tribal music recorded in the 1970s by Ya Ho Wa 13. In the decade before his 2009 death, he became an active creative force with a variety of musical projects, and his influence on millennial pro-topunk bands such as the White Stripes and Smashing Pumpkins has been widely acknowledged.

The Barbarians had appeared both on *Shindig* and the *T.A.M.I. Show*, and their song "Moulty" is about one of the members of the Barbarians. This Laurie Records single is an odd countryfied three-chord stomp. The Remains' "Don't Look Back," composed by Billy Vera (later of the Beaters), is a good stomping beat tune from a band who would open for the Beatles on selected dates of their 1966 U.S. tour. The Magicians were a regular fixture at the Night Owl Café in New York and have largely been forgotten except for the heavy swinging tune "An Invitation to Cry." "Liar, Liar" by the Castaways, released on Amos Heilicher's Soma

Records (the same label that released "Surfin' Bird" by the Trashmen), is a classic slice of garage punk, and their brief existence bears this out. The band hailed from Minneapolis and made the rounds playing frat parties in the Twin Cities. They reached the No. 12 spot on the charts with this song. As quietly as they arrived on the scene, they just as quietly disappeared into the recesses of oldies radio. Their hit song would be granted an extended life through its inclusion on the soundtracks to *Good Morning Vietnam* (1987) and *Lock, Stock, and Two Smoking Barrels* (1998).

The side ends with the incomparable 13th Floor Elevators' performance of Roky Erickson's timeless classic "You're Gonna Miss Me." The 13th Floor Elevators were constructed from remnants of two Austin, Texas–based bands, the Lingsman and the Spades. They performed several times at Bill Graham's Avalon Ballroom and were often mistaken for being a California group. The band were supporters of marijuana and psychedelic use, and Erickson's alarming change of personality, possibly exacerbated by psychedelic use, led to his being diagnosed as a paranoid schizophrenic. Over a four-year period spent in mental hospitals, he was subjected to electroconvulsive therapy and Thorazine treatments. Erickson was the subject of a 1990 tribute album, *Where the Pyramid Meets the Eye: A Tribute to Roky Erickson*, and Arch Druid and neo-psychedelic artist Julian Cope released the lo-fi masterpiece *Droolian*, an official bootleg Cope released on the Zippo label to help raise funds for Erickson's legal fees. Sadly, Roky Erickson's personal story casts a tragic shadow over his prolific and colorful work.

Side three opens with Count Five and the title track from their Double Shot Records album *Psychotic Reaction*. The members of this band were still quite young and preferred to gig around their hometown of San Jose, California, never breaking beyond this minor, though active, market despite having a top 10 hit with "Psychotic Reaction." The Leaves provided an early reading of Billy Roberts' classic tune "Hey Joe." Michael and the Messengers are a unique inclusion on the collection because they were noted for not having any original tunes but were instead an excellent cover band, in this case, their note-for-note cover of the Reflections' hit "(Just Like) Romeo and Juliet." The Cryan' Shames were one of a handful of Chicago-area pop bands who covered others' hit songs, in this case, the Searchers' "Sugar and Spice." The Amboy Dukes should have been a one-hit garage punk wonder with their cover of Them's "Baby Please Don't Go," but guitarist Ted Nugent would not leave good enough alone and kept the band producing generally unremarkable albums as Ted Nugent and the Amboy Dukes before officially going forward as a solo artist in 1975. Side three ends with one of the most contrived groups featured on this collection, the Bronx-based the Blues Magoos, whose debut album on Mercury, *Psychedelic Lollipop*, features "Tobacco Road."

The final side of the original album opens with the well-remembered but little-known Chocolate Watchband. The San Jose, California, band released three albums on Capitol Records' subsidiary label, Tower. Their debut album, *No Way Out*, featured "Let's Talk about Girls," a solid early Stones-style blues rock stomper. The band had a perfect name, little documentation on the band's origins or makeup, and three albums on a major label, but it is not necessarily deserving of its own entry in this volume because they were not an influence on other bands as much as they were a mélange of various styles that preceded them. They appeared in the period-era film *Riot on Sunset Strip*, but apart from occasional moments of reemerging popularity, they are more a curio than a major influence of the period. The Mojo Men were an early San Francisco group, contemporary with the Beau Brummels, and appeared on Autumn Records. They were originally known as Sly and the Mojo Men and featured the soon to be Sly Stone. When Autumn Records was purchased by Warner Bros. Records, Lenny Waronker and Van Dyke Parks produced "Sit Down, I Think I Love You," a Stephen Stills tune with a Sly-less Mojo Men that hit the top 40 in early 1967.

The Third Rail's "Run, Run, Run" was a studio construction of Artie Resnick (the Rascals' "Good Lovin'" was his prior creation) and his wife, Joey Levine. The opening of "Run, Run, Run" sounds not dissimilar to New York's premier vocal group Frankie Valli and the Four Seasons. Gary Usher, who was responsible for producing a trio of the Byrds' best psychedelic albums (in addition to his work with the Beach Boys and his own studio construction, the Super Stocks), hitched on to the burgeoning baroque psychedelic pop train with Sagittarius. The track "My World Fell Down" was highly polished and had the input of many of California's top arrangers/producers, Terry Melcher, Bruce Johnson, and Curt Boetcher. Released in May 1967, the single found favor with Murray the K's new progressive rock show. While Usher was in the midst of his own excellent work at Columbia, the influence of his former collaborator, Brian Wilson, can be heard all over this album. Future progressive rock demigod Todd Rundgren led the Nazz, a Philadelphia-based band on the excellent "Open My Eyes" from their self-titled debut album. With hints of where Rundgren would travel into the next decade, "Open My Eyes" is a perfect mélange of English beat music with a level of guitar work equal to what Jorma Kaukonen was providing to Jefferson Airplane and tight pop sensibilities. If the Zombies had come from Philadelphia, Rod Argent and Colin Blunstone might have sounded not too dissimilar to the Nazz. If Question Mark and the Mysterians were the Mexican American contribution from the Midwest with their protopsychedelic "96 Tears," the Premiers were Los Angeles' premiere Chicano-rock act who helped to lay the foundation for garage rock. Signed to Warner Bros. Records and recorded live, the Premieres were a tight club band. Since they landed a year or so ahead of other Los Angeles acts, such as the Turtles and doo-wop insurgent Frank Zappa, this band would have been lost in the narrative of early psychedelia if Lenny Kaye had not included them on the original *Nuggets* collection. They wore matching lounge suits and played Fender instruments; in short, they were sharp members of a bygone era, a link between Richie Valens, Question Mark and the Mysterians, and a takeoff of "vato" rock that Cheech Marin would perfect with Tommy Chong in the early 1970s.

The collection closes with another Philadelphia-based group, the Magic Mushrooms, whose single "It's-a-Happening" was released on A&M Records. Legend has it that neither of the two label bosses at A&M knew what magic mushrooms were, but once they were clued in, they pulled the single, but not before it bubbled just inside the top 100 at the end of 1966.

PARLIAMENT: *OSMIUM* (SEPTEMBER 1970)

Although psychedelic music has its origins in African American music through its relationship to rhythm and blues, few black music groups are afforded credit for their contributions to psychedelia. The Temptations are just one group that fostered a genre now referred to as *psychedelic soul*. Beginning with *Cloud Nine* (1969) to 1973's *Masterpiece*, the Temptations provided a unique take on soul music, and while their producer, Norman Whitfield, was initially not interested in this aspect of their sound, he still produced/coproduced their albums during this period. African American–fronted groups may have incorporated a psychedelic sound after the heyday of 1967, but they were not following a bandwagon; they used the style to develop a harder and more elusive form of funk music. The Parliaments/Funkadelic/P-Funk megaband is, along with Sly and the Family Stone, one of the finest examples of psychedelia in its marriage/rebirth with funk music. Funk and hard funk in the 1980s owe a debt to bands like Parliament and its' companion group, Funkadelic. Both groups were founded by George Clinton, who in the 1950s led a doo-wop group from Plainfield, New Jersey, under the name the Parliaments.

Clinton arrived on Motown's radar in 1963 when he walked into Motown's New York offices, located in the legendary Brill Building. Raynoma Gordy (later Raynoma Gordy Singleton) was one of Barry Gordy's ex-wives and, more importantly, the woman who cofounded the Motown label. She headed the label's New York office in 1963 and took note of Clinton when he came to sell his songs to the label. Contrary to his later outlandish, theatrical appearance, Raynoma recalled him being "clean-cut, soft-spoken, with a beautiful smile." He was producing a variety of groups, and Motown hired him as a writer, though the label never took up his group. He relocated the group to Detroit, and, as Parliament, they recorded some sides for the small Detroit soul label Revilot. When Revilot filed for bankruptcy, Clinton lost the rights to the Parliament's name and began using Funkadelic.

George Clinton used the names Parliament, Parliament-Funkadelic, and Funkadelic for several his group configurations, many of which shared the same players. Critics attempt to differentiate the two groups, but never to any agreement or understanding, by claiming one is more funk, the other more R & B, and another being psychedelic soul. What is true is that George Clinton had more creative ideas than could be contained in a single group, and his contributions to psychedelia, soul, and funk music are seldom recognized.

When Clinton launched Funkadelic with their self-titled album on Detroit's Westbound Records in February 1970, he had regained control of the name Parliament (removing the final *s*) and recorded *Osmium* on Invictus Records in September 1970. The Invictus Records story is one of the most complex and ignored stories in Detroit's music history. The label was started by the legendary songwriting/production team of Holland-Dozier-Holland following their acrimonious departure from Motown in 1968. While Motown began to move the entirety of its operations to Hollywood, Invictus and its companion label, Hot Wax, were two of the most exciting new labels in the country and were a positive voice in Detroit at a time when the city was losing both its population and its business core in the wake of the 1967 rebellion. If there is any need to compare Funkadelic to Parliament, one might agree that Funkadelic is a straight-ahead funk group, albeit a very experimental and progressive group, and Parliament is the truly experimental psychedelic/soul/funk outfit. *Osmium* contains songs that represent a diverse range of styles, from a funk beat sound (the opening track, "I Call My Baby Pussycat") to a neoclassical sound ("O Lord, Why Lord/Prayer"); a swinging mixed-meter R & B tune ("Put Love in Your Life"); psychedelic soul ("Moonshine Heather"), and a panoply of other styles. In

1970 alone, he released three albums, two under the Funkadelic name and *Osmium* under Parliament. The diversity and range of styles he created across the three albums are equal in artistic depth and influence to the three studio albums from the Jimi Hendrix Experience and Janis Joplin's albums, from *Cheap Thrills* to *Pearl*. Sadly, his work is often highlighted in isolation and seldom credited for the evolutionary continuum sustained over the length of his extraordinary career.

Though psychedelia had largely died out by 1970, artists such as George Clinton were dissecting pieces from psychedelia's sonic textures and using them to develop entirely new worlds of music. He returned in July 1971with Funkadelic's third album on Westbound Records, *Maggot Brain*, which picks up where *Osmium* left off and takes funk into a harder and more liberated style of music. *Osmium* features many of the original Parliaments ensemble, and important collaborators Bernie Worrell and Tiki Fulwood also appear on this album. Clinton's combination of the two group names, Parliament-Funkadelic, would be abbreviated as P-Funk (even when he later resumed using the Parliament moniker on its own in the mid-1970s), which is widely understood as a particular and completely independent form of funk music that could only flow from the mind of George Clinton.

PINK FLOYD: *THE EARLY SINGLES* (1967–1968)

The Early Singles was a bonus disc first packaged in the 1992 *Shine On* boxed set and featured the A and B sides of Pink Floyd's five U.K. singles from 1967 to 1968. Only one of the songs included was an album track at the time of its initial release, though some of the songs appeared on the rare Columbia (EMI) compilation *The Best of Pink Floyd* (1970) that Harvest Records later reissued as part of a compilation series released in France, Germany, and other Western European territories as *Masters of Rock, Vol. 1* (1974). A few other tracks appeared on the early compilation *Relics* (1971), but it was 2016 before all five early singles were made widely available on *The Early Years 1967–1972: Cre/ation*.

"Arnold Layne" b/w "Candy and a Currant Bun," released in March 1967 on EMI/Columbia, is the only Floyd record produced by Joe Boyd, who, as one of the founders of the UFO Club, saw great promise in the group. As an A&R man for Elektra Records' U.K. office, he hoped to get the band signed to Elektra but also had Polydor interested in the band following the production of their first single at Sound Techniques Studio. Pink Floyd's booking agent, Bryan Morrison, was able to secure what appeared to be a better deal at EMI, and this is how Pink Floyd became a part of "The Greatest Recording Organisation in the World." The "better" deal at EMI may have been more appealing on the surface, but it was the typically parsimonious contract that EMI offered to many new groups. They were locked into a ten-year contract with a £5,000 advance and an 8 percent royalty against which their studio time was charged. They later renegotiate this to a 5 percent royalty in exchange for unlimited studio time, which became a necessity as their increasingly elaborate records took longer to bring to fruition. They were signed not on a demo but with the first completed single in hand. Under EMI's policy, the band would have to work with one of company's in-house producers instead of Boyd, who so effectively captured the band's sound on "Arnold Layne." A song that dealt with transvestitism, or at the very least a fetishist with a penchant for young girls' undergarments, was seen as being too impolite for BBC radio, and the record was banned both on the BBC and on pirate stations Radio London and Radio Caroline. The group made a promotional video for the single and were filmed for *Top of the Pops*. Despite the radio ban, the song reached No. 20 on the charts. The B side, originally titled "Let's Roll Another One" but renamed for the recording, is a perfect mélange of pop, feedback, and disjointed lyrics all tossed amid a cavalcade of sonic colors. Pink Floyd never lacked original ideas, but this single, in all its perfection, would never be replicated in any of their other works.

Syd Barrett's compositions also dominated the band's sophomore single, "See Emily Play" b/w "Scarecrow," released in June 1967 and recorded during sessions for their debut album *The Piper at the Gates of Dawn*. The sparkling A side is a perfect slice of acid-tinged psychedelia in recognition of the Games for May concert at Queen Elizabeth Hall in May 1967 and is one of Barrett's most magical moments captured on record. Where the first single bore alternate meanings for those in the know, "See Emily Play" is both a perfect record and one whose meaning is purely on the surface; it hides no underground references while capturing the sparkling innocence of psychedelia circa 1967. Barrett loved the English countryside, and his imagination was anchored in a world of idyllic wonder. Ironically, Procol Harum's Gary Brooker reviewed the record in *Melody Maker* and was less than kind in his evaluation of the band, criticizing their "horrible organ sound." The B side of the single is a track culled from *The Piper at the Gates of Dawn*. "Scarecrow" contains some of Barrett's most wonderfully discordant lyrics over a triple-meter Ferris wheel accompaniment.

"Apples and Oranges" b/w "Paintbox" was the band's third single and the last single on Columbia before moving to EMIs new progressive/

contemporary imprint, Harvest Records. It is also the last released single with Syd Barrett. The song is wonderfully messy, a bit of a psychedelic freak-out, and though Roger Waters has claimed that Norman Smith's production ruined the song, its merits stand on their own. This song was supposed to be mimed on their debut American TV appearance on *American Bandstand*. Their performance is a highlight of Barrett lore, for while Syd (with his "obligatory Hendrix perm" as Waters sang on "Nobody's Home" from 1979's *The Wall*) stood at the front, barely expending any energy into miming or playing the guitar, his bandmates awkwardly but gamely carried on and made a brave face. It is doubtful that American TV audiences had witnessed anything of this sort, and the tragedy of Syd's story would become a larger-than-life myth among fans of Pink Floyd. "Paintbox" is keyboardist Richard Wright's debut composition on a Pink Floyd single. His lead vocal, with his plummy, wistful accent, possesses a certain calm, whereas Barrett's vocals on the A side veered from manic to sinister to playful. This song is an emotional departure for the band, and though it has a fairly conventional song structure, the mélange of instrumental colors that includes Barrett's lovely, mournful guitar work provides the listener with a dreamy psychedelic wave upon which one could drift away.

The band's fourth single and first without Barrett, "It Would Be So Nice" b/w "Julia Dream" must have given fans reason to wonder whether the group had in them no more than a few singles and an album. It was released in April 1968, a few months prior to their sophomore LP, *A Saucerful of Secrets*. It begins promisingly enough with a full throttle psychedelic pop opening, but it devolves into a whimsical novelty song with uninspired lyrics. In between these trivial verses, there is a promising middle-eight and a return to the opening, but it ultimately returns to another forgettable verse. Although Richard Wright composed or cocomposed some of the most beautiful moments in the Pink Floyd canon (the final movement of "Wish You Were Here," large sections of "Echoes," and, of course "The Great Gig in the Sky" are proof enough of his skills), none of the unique harmonic touches or his simple yet beautiful melodies can be found here. The band distanced themselves from the song, laying blame with the label for hustling them to produce hit singles, and though it was released in the *Shine On* boxed set, it was not easily available until 2016. The flip side, "Julia Dream," gives us an indication of the future Pink Floyd. A solo composition from Roger Waters, this song presages the pastoral psychedelia of "Fat Old Sun" and "Grantchester Meadows" and has beautifully layered guitar and flute lines that weave amid Waters' verses. If not a beautiful song, it is a taste of the ethereal grandeur that would soon become Floyd's pastoral sound. This song was made more readily available when it was included on the 1971 compilation album, *Relics*.

The last of the early singles is the Waters/Gilmour composition "Point Me at the Sky" b/w "Careful with That Axe, Eugene." Released six months after *A Saucerful of Secrets*, this is the last single from the band until 1979's "Another Brick in the Wall, Part II." The A side has too many ingredients, and while Gilmour delivers a good lead vocal on a tepid introduction, the song breaks into a full-out chorus in which the vocals deflate the power of the instrumental track.

The B side is a powerful song that became a regular feature in live Floyd shows through the early 1970s. This group composition also appeared in various settings with an array of different titles. There was "Keep Smiling People" followed by "Murderistic Woman" for an early BBC performance. Then, as part of a live set known as "The Journey," it was known by "Beset by Creatures of the Deep," and on the soundtrack to Antonioni's post–*Blow-Up* counterculture film *Zabriskie Point*, it was retitled as "Come in No. 51, Your Time Is Up." Each setting of the song would be substantially different from the original (or traditional) version of "Careful with that Axe, Eugene." This song is worth hearing in its various iterations, especially on *Ummagumma* and in the film *Pink Floyd, Live at Pompeii*, where each of the performances is harrowing and intense. Some versions are shorter, most are longer, and while the structure remains constant, it contains a number of classic Pink Floyd tropes, most notably Roger Waters' blood-curdling scream and Richard Wright's exquisite cathedral-like harmonies that float over the nervous and suspenseful action that occurs within the song. Despite its brooding sensibility, its various live performances at the BBC (for which a number are now officially available) provide a palpable tension that they would not achieve again until the late 1970s albums *Animals* and *The Wall*.

PINK FLOYD: "VEGETABLE MAN"/"SCREAM THY LAST SCREAM" (1967/1968/2016)

"Vegetable Man" and "Scream Thy Last Scream" would remain unreleased in the Pink Floyd canon until 2016, though both songs could be found on countless bootlegs. For many years, both songs were believed to be Barrett's last single for the group before he was removed from the band, but, in truth, it was supposed to follow "See Emily Play." Rejected by EMI, "Apples and Oranges" was released as the follow-up to that song. The lore behind this single is greater than any other early Pink

Floyd record, but along with "Jugband Blues" on *A Saucerful of Secrets*, it offers a disturbing glimpse into the creative mind of one of rock music's great songwriters who perhaps was too sensitive to survive the demands that audiences require of our popular music stars. Both songs are harrowing psychedelic masterpieces and are a preface for his two solo albums, *The Madcap Laughs* (1970) and *Barrett* (1970). Although he would be "fired" from the group in early 1968, these two songs show Barrett at the precipice of his reality, and through which he delivers two of the greatest psychedelic songs of all time. Sadly, unless one collected the various bootleg recordings on which these songs were released, you would have to wait until 2016 before you could experience Barrett's mind in a state of perpetual deconstruction.

After the delicious and innocent whimsy of *The Piper at the Gates of Dawn*, these two songs throw the listener into the incipient madness of one who was there at the birth of English psychedelia and who composed some of the most enduring music of 1967. Members of Pink Floyd recount in various sources that "Have You Got It Yet," a song Barrett brought to the band, was an intentional effort to make inaccessible music. The title of the song was used to describe the band's inability to play the work because, on every take, Barrett would play something different, which warranted the response, "Have you got it yet?"

"Vegetable Man" features Barrett reading off the mundane details of his wardrobe and activities for that day (not unlike Brian Wilson's "Busy Doin' Nothin'" on *Friends*; with no interest in writing about anything of note, the author simply recounts the minutiae of his vacant days) over a sloppy accompaniment that pounds away with no change in dynamics or colors. Barrett's increasingly breathless vocals trail off into nothing. The middle-eight of the song is the only part that resembles anything close to his mastery of sing-song verse. "Scream Thy Last Scream" is a slightly more traditional song, but its cacophony and barely present rhythmic structure prevent it from becoming anything too conventional. Both songs sound underrehearsed, but this was likely Barrett's intention.

It's a pity that Pink Floyd held on to these songs for so long, but their difficult relationship with Syd in late-1967, and whatever conflicted feelings they had about their former bandmate, must have played into their decision to hold them from release for nearly five decades. Syd was a reluctant pop star. He did not have the ambition or drive for success that brought together the remaining band members to create Pink Floyd. Syd was out to create work that had no commercial potential, and his increasingly erratic behavior with the band gave pause to consider exactly how long they could work with him.

While both songs are posthumous releases in Syd's output, they are a perfect entrée to Barrett's two solo albums. When Syd was let go from the band, the group's representation, Blackhill Enterprises, kept Syd on their rolls but dropped Pink Floyd. Syd authored most of their songs and was considered by management to be the brains behind the group. It took Pink Floyd some time to find their post-Syd identity, and few expected the band would reemerge as a successful unit without Barrett. Malcolm Jones, the label head at Harvest Records, wanted to get Syd back into the studio, and throughout 1968–1969, Peter Jenner (one-half of the Blackhill management team), followed by Jones, attempted to get Barrett to create in the studio. The Jenner sessions yielded little. Some of these tracks would end up on the compilation album *Opel* (1988), and although Jones was able to get Barrett to be a little more productive, David Gilmour and Roger Waters were drafted to help Syd finish the album. The final product is different from anything he produced with Pink Floyd, and upon its initial release in January 1970, it managed a decent chart showing, which prompted EMI to request a follow-up album.

Barrett was recorded in the winter of 1970, but with David Gilmour and Richard Wright behind the production desk. These songs are slightly more realized and organized than his work on *The Madcap Laughs*, but the album generated less interest than its predecessor. The general lack of interest both from Barrett and his label allowed these albums to fall out of print and become cult favorites. In the wake of *Dark Side of the Moon*, EMI reissued the two records as a double-album set in 1974 with the hope of generating fresh interest in Barrett's music. Subsequent reissues, first with *Opel* in 1986 and various reissues of the original two albums, made every scrap of minutiae Syd recorded in the studio available to fans.

PINK FLOYD: *THE PIPER AT THE GATES OF DAWN* (AUGUST 1967)

Pink Floyd's debut album, *The Piper at the Gates of Dawn*, is Syd Barrett's album with Pink Floyd. The title, lifted from the title of the seventh chapter from *The Wind in the Willows*, Kenneth Grahame's novel for children, is a reflection of Barrett's own personality. Released after the band's successful sophomore single, "See Emily Play," this album, in response to EMI's financial dictates for unproven or new bands, guaranteed that the production budget would be minimal, and their job, while being allowed to make an album, was to capture the same market that purchased their first two singles.

The Beatles were EMI's cash cow, and the company was not looking for another artist to redefine the field; it wanted musicians whose works would translate to sales at the lowest cost of production. In return, EMI received one of the greatest albums of 1967, and the company has been able to continue selling an album that has not embarrassed itself by appearing dated and out of step. The sound of the early Pink Floyd influenced countless neo-psychedelic groups in the 1980s and 1990s, and though it may not have been the mature masterpiece that was *Sgt. Pepper's Lonely Hearts Club Band*, it is one of the first sounds of a new musical voice from a band who would transcend all records for sales and chart longevity and influence artists for decades to come.

Of the eleven tracks on Pink Floyd's debut album, eight were composed by Barrett; two were group compositions or, more accurately, improvisations; and one work was composed by Roger Waters. This album was a studio capture of their live show in early 1967 and is the most consistent artifact of how this group likely sounded to audiences who had never heard anything quite like it. Syd's vocals and guitar playing drive this album, but it is keyboardist Richard Wright, and not Roger Waters, who is the second most prominent musician in the mix. Wright's Farfisa organ provides the timbral underpinning of the album. This record is Barrett's magical moment, when his world of tales, creatures, and childlike wonder come to life in one of the most enchanting albums ever produced.

By the time of the album's release, Barrett had already begun to unravel from the pressures of the band and their increasing success, but most of all, if one chooses to believe the multiple first-hand reports of bandmates, friends, and acquaintances, from his copious drug intake. It would be irresponsible to refer to him as an acid dropout or burnout, as the truth is much more nuanced. Whether by choice or necessity, he retreated from the music business and his daily life as a musician in general to a life of quiet existence. His return to Cambridge to live with his mother and, after her death, his sister requires that we respect his family's wishes to not make Syd Barrett's life something tangible for his fans.

In keeping with the spirit of the space age that was a central feature of the Cold War rivalry between the United States and Russia during the 1960s, the opening track, "Astronomy Domine," enters with Morse code and the recitation of astronomical names (as if delivered by a bored waiter) before it breaks into a sonic flood in which each of the instrumentalists is playing at full dynamic levels. This song remained in the band's live set into the early 1970s. The live/studio double-album set, *Ummagumma*, opens with a powerfully liberating performance of the song.

"Lucifer Sam" is about Syd's Siamese cat and his Cambridge girlfriend, Jenny. The guitar, organ and bass interplay are some of the best ensemble playing on the album. It is a song that is clearly of the period but has remained fresh and exciting a half century later. "Matilda Mother" is one of Barrett's most beautiful turns on the album. The vocal opens not with Barrett but Rick Wright, whose unmistakably plummy dialect is perfect in all his work with Pink Floyd; Barrett joins him on the choruses. The instrumental interlude prevents the song from becoming a maudlin lullaby. The final verse, this time with Barrett on lead vocals, builds in intensity, and the dreamlike fade-out is carried by a chorus of wordless vocals. "Flaming" features some of Syd's most wickedly charming lyrics and is arranged with layers of percussive effects, piano, guitar, and vocals. The nightmare soundtrack in the middle-eight is a microcosm of how their improvisatory sets must have sounded in their early days.

"Pow R. Toc H." is a group composition, an instrumental that had its nearly six-minute length reduced from a much longer improvisation in their live set. Their producer, Norman "Hurricane" Smith, had to take their expansive live sets and edit them into short digestible tracks that could be captured in the studio, and he accomplished the task on this album. Roger Waters, who would become the driving force of the band and, after 1975's *Wish You Were Here*, Pink Floyd's chief songwriter, is given one song on the album, "Take Up Thy Stethoscope and Walk." Waters later dismissed this early effort, which clearly has its origins in one of their long improvisational sets. Wright's organ solo in the first half of the song is fantastic and allows Syd and Roger to set up their feedback-washed interplay. Waters and Barrett share the lead vocals, not that the song's lyrics have any particular meaning.

Side two of the album opens with the group-credited instrumental "Interstellar Overdrive." This song, like the album opener, remained in the band's live set until the early 1970s. The structural makeup of the song gives a hint of the direction they would take on "A Saucerful of Secrets" and "Echoes." The layered multipart composition enables you to forget this is a thirteen-plus-minute track, and one that was surely cut to album size by Norman Smith. Whether the track listing was intentionally designed by either Norman Smith or the band or was simply the result of the draw, side two takes the band into far different territory than is heard on side one. "Interstellar Overdrive" is a perfectly constructed aural representation of an acid trip, and the final four songs that follow this are at turns nightmarish and charmingly unsettling but utterly harmless. "The Gnome" is Barrett's folksy nursery song, not terribly unlike what Donovan was recording on the *For Little Ones* album (the second disc in the set *A Gift from a Flower to a Garden*). This is chamber music when compared to the songs on side one. The vocals are delivered as if Barrett is singing a nighttime lullaby to an imaginary niece or nephew. The title and lyrics of "Chapter 24" have their origins in the I-Ching, the ancient Chinese "Book of Changes," a book of divination and cosmology that has been used in numerous studies of religion and philosophy and have been a source of inspiration for musicians from John Cage to Syd Barrett. This sing-song droning tune is of the type Julian Cope would create in generous amounts on the last records of the 1980s neo-psychedelic band the Teardrop Explodes. "Scarecrow" is another of Barrett's nighttime nursery songs, this time accompanied by a clip-clop track that sounds like the mechanical unwinding of an elaborate toy, and features Wright's wonderfully sinewy organ lines. The vocals are once more shared by Wright and Barrett.

The final track on the album is the classic "Bike." This song has a completely innocent feel, but you can hear the road Barrett would later travel with "Vegetable Man" and other songs on his solo albums. Syd's wonderfully elaborate verse is delivered as if it is an utterly normal conversation. The unwinding of the toy shop closes this track with a panoply of disjointed sound effects.

The Piper at the Gates of Dawn was released in England and the United States (albeit with an altered track list) in both stereo and mono. The stereo version became the standard version known around the globe, but with the reissue of the mono version for the album's fortieth anniversary in 2007, fans should give both mixes equal listening time, as they represent very different albums. Phil Spector and Brian Wilson mastered the art of the mono recording, making it a superior artefact to any stereo mix of their records. Although the producers and engineers at EMI mastered fantastic mono mixes for the Beatles, Pink Floyd was a different sonic world. Norman Smith's monophonic mix is interesting, but it lacks the depth and spaciousness of the stereo mix.

PINK FLOYD: *A SAUCERFUL OF SECRETS* (JUNE 1968)

Within days of the release of *Piper at the Gates of Dawn*, Pink Floyd returned to the studio to begin work on what would become their second album, *A Saucerful of Secrets*. The first sessions featured Barrett's "Vegetable Man," "Jugband Blues," "Scream Thy Last Scream," and "In the Beechwoods," plus the commissioned but unrealized soundtrack titled "John Latham." Wright's "Paintbox" and "Remember a Day," the group composition "A Saucerful of Secrets," and Waters' "Set the Controls for the Heart of the Sun" are representative of Pink Floyd's sound more than anything by Barrett at this stage of his time with the band. Syd was still considered to be the primary songwriter for Pink Floyd, and they recorded his "Scream Thy Last Scream" as a possible follow-up to "See Emily Play." "Scream Thy Last Scream" and "Vegetable Man" acquired cult status through their inclusion on various bootleg albums until their official release in 2016.

Within days of returning from their first U.S. tour, the band joined a seven-group show on the Jimi Hendrix U.K. tour. In between tour dates, they recorded shows for BBC Radio and continued work on *A Saucerful of Secrets*. David Gilmour began to rehearse with the band in the second week of January 1968, and the new five-man Pink Floyd resumed their work on the road; but this ultimately fell apart. With Syd's removal from the group, the new four-piece Pink Floyd composed a film soundtrack for Peter Sykes' *The Committee*, which did not see an official release until 2016.

The band's next single, "It Would Be So Nice" b/w "Julia Dream" (April 1968), was the first record released in the wake of Barrett's departure and arrived in the shops a few months before the *Saucerful of Secrets* album. The Wright-composed A side is a slice of sunshine psychedelic pop and is unlike anything else in the Floyd canon. Lightweight and poppy, with verses that are reminiscent of a Ray Davies English music hall work, the song was not a hit and did not accurately represent the band's real sound. The B side would have wider familiarity thanks to live performances and its inclusion on 1971's *Relics* compilation. The Waters-penned song is a moody and evocative work, though, for Waters, it is an optimistic piece that points toward the pastoral psychedelia they would continue to develop over the next few years. The psychedelic-pastoral heyday of 1968–1969 was brief, and while many bands would begin to fade away or disband, Pink Floyd had the unenviable task of recapturing the fleeting magic and success they had achieved barely a year earlier. For their efforts, they were rewarded with an entirely new identity, faithful audiences, and the freedom to release some of the most experimental pop records ever distributed by a major record label.

To accompany the slightly schizophrenic quality of their singles from this time, the band's transitional period is apparent on *A Saucerful of Secrets*. Three songs include Barrett ("Set the Controls for the Heart of the Sun," "Remember a Day," and "Jugband Blues"), and four feature David Gilmour ("Let There Be More Light," "Corporal Clegg," "A Saucerful of Secrets," and "See-Saw"). With Barrett becoming increasingly unreliable, Wright and Waters became the central writers/singers in the group, and Wright began to replicate Barrett's very English style of writing. This is the first Floyd album cover designed by old Cambridge friends Storm Thorgerson and Aubrey Powell, who worked under the professional name Hipgnosis. The cover is awash in colors and images and is the second of three albums in their entire output to feature a picture of the band on the cover, though in this case they are barely present through a small fish-eye view buried in the visual collage. The most noticeable difference in their sound is thanks to Rick Wright, who began to include the Hammond organ, mellotron, and vibraphone.

The "new" Gilmour-era songs are a mix of the fantastic and the ordinary. "Let There Be More Light" is a Waters composition and is a workman-like study in how to write a psychedelic song. "Corporal Clegg" is Waters' first unapologetic foray into the military and war themes that would come to a climax on *The Wall* (1979) and *The Final Cut* (1982). The opening track on side two, "A Saucerful of Secrets," is the first classic Pink Floyd song with the Waters-Gilmour-Wright-Mason lineup. Clocking in at nearly twelve minutes, this four-part thematically cohesive composition set the tenor for so many of Pink Floyd's greatest works and remained in their concert sets for years to come.

The Barrett-era songs are a mix of old and new. Rick Wright's "Remember a Day" features Syd's melancholy slide guitar. The haunting "Set the Controls for the Heart of the Sun" continues on from "Julia Dream" with its slow build and sotto voce vocals. Barrett's guitar is barely discernable as it floats across the track, as Wright's keyboards and Mason's drumming are foremost in the mix. This song became one of their live stalwarts and is an early highlight of the band's dramatic skills. "See-Saw" is, in Thorgerson's words, "delicate psychedelic pop" and is another of Rick Wright's charming lullaby-scented works. It was roundly dismissed by the group, who referred to it as "The Most Boring Song I've Ever Heard, Bar Two." As with "It Would Be So Nice," the band has distanced themselves from this song, seeing it as an embarrassment, but it carries a certain Syd-like charm in its magical cumulus-soaked timbres. The album's concluding track, "Jugband Blues," is Syd's final track on a Pink Floyd record and one of the most poignant songs ever recorded by Syd or Pink Floyd. Is this Syd's very lucid response to his bandmates and the methods they used to dispose of him? Is it simply the mind of a sensitive artist who wants us to know he no longer can play a role the public prescribed for him? Whatever the meaning, the song is the most emotionally shattering work on the album. In the nonlinear compositional style for which Syd had become known, the song features a Salvation Army brass band riffing on whatever they wanted with no relation to the song. The final two lines—"What exactly is a dream? What exactly is a joke?"—are a deafening coda to Barrett's time with Pink Floyd.

Having exhausted the club and cinema circuit, Pink Floyd began to acquire a new following thanks to the rapid expansion of new universities across England that provided the band with new venues of open and willing audiences. Although *A Saucerful of Secrets* did not further the band's fame or marketability, it marks an important stage in their development with the inclusion of long-form compositions. In concert at London's Royal Festival Hall in April 1969, the band unveiled the Azimuth Coordinator, which allowed for the creation of a 360-degree canvas of sound that encompassed the venue. In an era when elaborately designed live concert audio was in its infancy, Pink Floyd introduced hardware that produced a primitive surround sound experience, distancing them even further from the mainstream audiences who came to hear the average pop band. Their increasing popularity led to an invitation from the BBC to provide music for their coverage of the Apollo 11 moon landing, a recognition that the band had a unique ability to create sonic pictures.

PINK FLOYD: "ECHOES" (OCTOBER 1971)

Although Pink Floyd continued to sustain their popularity as a live act in Europe, Asia, and North America through the late 1960s and into the early 1970s, their record sales in North America never matched their draw as a live act. Capitol Records, an EMI subsidiary, was often challenged when marketing its contemporary artists. Beyond the Beatles and the Beach Boys, the label had little idea how to promote bands like Pink Floyd. Between *A Saucerful of Secrets* and 1971's *Meddle*, the album that featured "Echoes" on the entirety of side two, Pink Floyd released two soundtrack albums to films by Barbet Schroeder; contributed to a soundtrack for Michelangelo Antonioni's counterculture film *Zabriskie Point* (they composed the entirety of a soundtrack score, but Antonioni decided to use recordings from a number of artists, using only a few of the Floyd's tracks); and released the live album *Ummagumma* and the proto-progressive masterpiece, *Atom Heart Mother*, their first No. 1 LP in Britain, which also featured one of the most iconic album designs in all of rock music.

Although the psychedelic era had finished three years prior to "Echoes," this track is the culmination of a style they first created with Syd Barrett in their shows at the Roundhouse and UFO clubs, continued with Gilmour on "A Saucerful of Secrets," expanded into orchestral rock with "Atom Heart Mother," and concluded with "Echoes." After *Meddle*, the album that featured "Echoes," they recorded the second of their Barbet Schroeder soundtracks and the landmark *Dark Side of the Moon*, after which Roger Waters became the driving creative voice of the band. They continued to develop long-form works on *Wish You Were Here* and *Animals*, but "Echoes" is the concluding masterpiece of their creative youth.

When the band entered the studio in January 1971 to begin work on the album, they were lacking for ideas and decided to simply record anything they wanted to commit to tape. They collected enough material that they first named it *Nothings*, then *Son of Nothings*, and then *Return of the Son of Nothings*, and they numbered their best works from one to twenty-four to indicate the number of "nothing" pieces they had catalogued. Although the work sounds entirely organic and improvised, it was constructed over the course of six months. In its final form, their individual ideas coalesced into a coherent, brilliant, and expansive structure to create one of their greatest works and one that would have a healthy life in concert for many years. One notable feature of "Echoes" is the vocal duet of Wright and Gilmour, as they capture a pure Englishness in their music that could never be copied by any other band.

Just prior to the release of *Meddle*, the band traveled to the ancient city of Pompeii to be filmed by the Anglo-French filmmaker Adrian Mabew for a Pink Floyd concert movie that would be played in the empty amphitheater. Mabew wanted to upend the traditional concert film that typically included cutaway shots of screaming or stoned fans and instead focus only on Pink Floyd. The movie was intended for television, but it ended up playing in theaters. Mabew added sequences filmed in a French studio to bring the film to a length required for a feature film. Although "Echoes," "A Saucerful of Secrets," and "One of These Days" were the only three songs filmed in the amphitheater, with the combined studio segments, the film feels like a complete work. The director also captured the band walking among the volcanoes for artsy shots that he interjected into footage of the band's performance. The first work performed in the film is the first half of "Echoes," and the second half is used as the concluding work in the movie.

PROCOL HARUM: "A WHITER SHADE OF PALE" (1967)

Procol Harum, a Gary Brooker–led band, originated in 1964 as the Paramounts with Robin Trower on guitar. Following a brief breakup, the group reformed (minus Trower) in early 1967 as Procol Harum (loosely translated from Latin as "Beyond These Things"), and in May of that year, they released their first single on Deram Records, "A Whiter Shade of Pale." As with many English pop groups of the era, Procol Harum began as a blues-based rock band, but "A Whiter Shade of Pale" stands as their iconic contribution to psychedelic music. In later songs "Homburg" and "A Salty Dog," they attempted to recapture the slow, drone-laden atmosphere of "A Whiter Shade of Pale" but could not match the success of the Bach-inflected debut single.

Some commentators have posited that "A Whiter Shade of Pale," a distinctive calling card of English psychedelia circa 1967, is constructed on a harmonic progression used by Johann Sebastian Bach in the "Air" movement of his Suite No. 3 in D, BWV 1068. Others have noted its similarity to a progression used in Bach's cantata "Wachet auf, ruft uns die Stimme," BWV 140, known by its English-language title, "Sleepers Awake." While the Hammond organ figures played by Matthew Fisher may sound Bach-like, the chord progression in BWV 140 is studied by many organists who learn to improvise over this standard figured bass chord progression. "A Whiter Shade of Pale" does not directly quote from any one work composed by Bach, but its baroque-inflected figures were likely influenced by Fisher's musical training at the Guildhall School of Music as much as they are a direct quotation from J. S. Bach. The song was composed by Gary Brooker and Keith Reid before Fisher joined the band, but his distinctive organ solos were acknowledged as deserving of coauthorship credit in 2006.

The single was produced by Denny Cordell, who had previously produced the Moody Blues' first album, *The Magnificent Moodies* (July 1965). Although "A Whiter Shade of Pale" was released on Deram, it was licensed by Straight Ahead Productions, who then transferred rights to the newly resuscitated EMI imprint Regal Zonophone, who released Procol Harum's eponymous debut album. The song was not included on the U.K. edition of the album, but Robin Trower had returned to the group after the success of "A Whiter Shade of Pale" and does appear on the album. Successive albums moved away from a psychedelic sound toward a progressive, symphonic rock sound.

"A Whiter Shade of Pale" remains Procol Harum's signature tune, and its worldwide fame among younger audiences was secured when the song appeared in the original movie soundtrack for *The Big Chill* (1983).

QUESTION MARK AND THE MYSTERIANS: "96 TEARS" (1966)

The tri-city region of Michigan (Midland, Saginaw, and Bay City) sits north of Flint, Michigan, that for many years was the second-largest city in the state and has, for over three-quarters of a century, been home to a substantial Latino immigrant population. Mexican Americans, primarily from Texas, and migrants from Mexico's northern states, have made their way to mid-Michigan for decades to work in the automotive and agricultural industries. *Campesinos* travel every summer to work the orchards and farms throughout the state, but we seldom hear about Latinos' cultural contributions in the region.

It is notable that a quintet of Michigan transplants from Texas who formed a band in 1962 released their first single, "96 Tears," as ? (Question Mark) and the Mysterians on the local Pa-Go-Go Record label in August 1966. The single landed airplay in the Flint and Detroit markets before it spread across the country. The record was picked up by Philadelphia-based Cameo-Parkway Records, who later that year released the band's debut album, with the hit single serving double duty as the album's title. The band was equal parts garage band and psychedelic pioneers, and their first album, like debut albums by the Velvet Underground, the Seeds, and (a decade later) the Ramones, is a landmark work for its unconventional originality. Their lo-fi, organ-drenched, two-chord/two-note vignettes set a standard for punk bands to come, and though they managed to chart a total of five singles in 1966–1967, "96 Tears" was their biggest record and tagged them as a one-hit wonder.

The band was picked up by Cameo-Parkway thanks to Neil Bogart, who had recently joined the label as the head of A&R. He produced the band's debut album, which helped, albeit temporarily, to revive the label's flagging fortunes. The following year, Cameo-Parkway was sold to ABKCO Records, and as a result, licensing issues related to the master recordings for ? and the Mysterians (and all other Cameo-Parkway artists) kept these records off the shelves in the years that followed. Through the 1970s and into the 1990s, the records heard by former Cameo-Parkway artists such as Chubby Checker and ? and the Mysterians were rerecordings of their classic hits. By the 2000s, ABKCO began to release the original recordings and made available most of the Mysterians recordings from 1966 to 1967. When Cameo-Parkway was absorbed by ABKCO, Neil Bogart went on to Buddha Records and later founded Casablanca Records, where he struck gold with Donna Summer, KISS, Cher, and the Village People.

Rudy Martinez (Question Mark) reformed the band in the early 1970s with new members, but in 1984, the original band members performed for a one-off reunion concert and came together again in 1997 when they rerecorded their debut album. Martinez lost his home, band memorabilia, and his Yorkshire terriers in a house fire, but he continues to perform with a new generation of Mysterians. Unlike Madonna, Bay City's more famous resident, ? and the Mysterians have been recognized by the city, and the single "96 Tears" was declared the rock and roll song of the city.

THE ROLLING STONES: "WE LOVE YOU"/ "DANDELION" (AUGUST 1967)

If you believed the spin of their original manager, Andrew Loog Oldham, the Rolling Stones were the anti-Beatles. They were also the first of the London-based groups from the British Invasion who, while retaining their American blues roots across their records through 1965, would rapidly evolve into one of the most eclectic bands of the early psychedelic era. Their work from *Aftermath* (1966) through *Their Satanic Majesties Request* (1967) features some of the best Swinging London, Carnaby Street, and prepsychedelic pop and includes the delicate minstrel stylings of "Lady Jane" (June 1966); the raucous feedback and reverb-washed "Have You Seen Your Mother, Baby, Standing in the Shadows?" (September 1966); the charming if slightly schizophrenic *Between the Buttons*; and the flower power ballad "Ruby Tuesday" (January 1967). This all led to their turn with musique concrète–hued psychedelia on their mid-1967 single "We Love You"/"Dandelion." In early 1968, the band moved swiftly back to their blues-soaked roots, but their brief foray into psychedelia is an important marker both for the band and for the evolution of the genre.

Founding member Brian Jones was responsible for the introduction of exotic instruments and unusual timbres on the group's most exciting records. He provided the authentic blues harp on many of their early sides, introduced a jazz grooves on the marimba for "Under My Thumb," the dulcimer on Jagger/Richards' faux-minstrel love song "Lady Jane," the sitar on the deliciously ominous "Paint It Black," the recorder for the prepsychedelia and flower power "Ruby Tuesday," and the mellotron on their August 1967 single "We Love You," the band's first truly psychedelic record.

Although Jones was rapidly retreating from his front man position within the band, by mid-1967, he along with Jagger and Richards were dealt a significant blow by the Establishment with drug busts and unrelenting harassment from the press. While bassist Bill Wyman would say, "Instinctively, we all felt that this would be a year of change," no one outside of the group had any idea that real pressures had reached a breaking point in the first half of that year. The very eclectic cabaret prepsychedelia on *Between the Buttons* was not an instant hit for the band and was their lowest-selling album at this point in their career. The relationship with manager and producer Andrew Loog Oldham would break down before the year was through, and interpersonal relationships among band members wore at the group and bruised their creative drive. Mick, Keith, and assorted girlfriends and hangers-on were arrested in a high-profile drug bust at Redlands, Keith's home, and Anita Pallenberg left Brian Jones to take up with Keith. Breaking the formerly tight relationship between the band's two guitarists was unfortunate and unavoidable, but in addition to court appearances, declining record sales, and the outrageous sentences they received for their drug "crimes," it is no wonder the band was creatively bereft.

Brian was busted that summer and later hospitalized for exhaustion; Mick was sentenced to three months and Keith for twelve. While out on appeal, the band produced their last two songs with Oldham, which became the single with which they might have to sign off, however temporarily, if they were unable to appeal their sentences. In August 1967, they released their last record produced by Andrew Loog Oldham, "We Love You"/"Dandelion" and their first single since January's "Let's Spend the Night Together"/"Ruby Tuesday." This record was ostensibly in support of the fans who stood with them through their various rich pop star troubles. "We Love You" sought to capitalize on the peace-and-love ethos so effectively displayed on the Beatles' "All You Need Is Love," but with undertones that were much darker than anything conjured by the Beatles before the "White Album."

The record opens with the sound of a jailer's footsteps and the clang of a jail door closing. The doppler/phase-shift effect of the vocals is accompanied by a cacophonous accompaniment driven by Nicky Hopkins' insistent piano ostinato and baying mellotron riffs by Brian Jones; Lennon and McCartney provide uncredited backup vocals on this wonderfully perverse track. It was appropriately one the most plugged songs on the pirate station Radio London in its final hours on August 14, 1967. "Dandelion" is a charming flower power song and is in tune with the peace-and-love tenor of the era. Brian Jones provides beautiful touches on the saxophone, the mellotron, and one of the many keyboards upon which the track was built. At the end of each of the songs, there is a fading snippet drawn from its companion track. For a rushed production that had been pieced together over sessions in June and July, in between their court and personal battles, it is a memorable record and often overlooked in their canon.

The Rolling Stones were not the first drug bust in 1960s pop music (the Lovin' Spoonful's Zal Yanovsky and the Scottish folk troubadour Donovan were both busted, on separate continents, for possession of pot in May and June 1966, respectively), but the Stones's public profile and notorious reputation made them easy targets for straight society, who wanted to demonstrate the evils of drug use to a youth generation who, by the end of the decade, would be further adrift from straight society than could have been imagined in 1967.

THE ROLLING STONES: *THEIR SATANIC MAJESTIES REQUEST* (DECEMBER 1967)

Andrew Loog Oldham produced all Rolling Stones records from their debut single "Come On" to the mid-1967 psychedelia of "We Love You"/"Dandelion." His production skills were developed by trial and error, and he did not possess the aesthetic instinct or technical mastery of a Phil Spector, George Martin, or Brian Wilson. Still, he provided the band with an unmistakable sound that made them second only to the Beatles in terms of popularity and sales. Upon his departure as manager, Oldham painted the split as amicable, but the Stones were in far worse shape than anyone could have imagined. Allen Klein, whom Oldham had brought on as a business partner in 1965, secured the band's finances in his control, acquired the masters to their entire output recorded for Decca, and ultimately "owned" the band more than the band owned themselves.

While Oldham was not a technical or creative leader, by leaving them to self-produce their next album, it became clear that they needed a guiding hand if they were to survive beyond 1967. *Their Satanic Majesties Request* is perhaps the most self-indulgent Rolling Stones album in their extensive catalog and is one of the most divisive albums among fans. Although it is their most diverse and eclectic record, given the various personal and legal challenges faced by the band, it is no small miracle that they created as many high points as are found on this album.

Released in December 1967 as their sixth U.K. and eighth U.S. album, *Their Satanic Majesties Request* was the Stones' attempt at full-blown psychedelia, from its exotic gatefold cover with a 3-D photograph to the music contained within. The album features psychedelic sunshine pop ("She's a Rainbow") with a string arrangement provided by future Led Zeppelin bassist John Paul Jones; pregoth drones ("In Another Land"); a bona fide psychedelic masterpiece ("2000 Light Years from Home"); roots-flavored songs ("Citadel" and "2000 Man"); pure incoherence in the guise of free improvisation (both versions of "Sing This All Together" and "Gomper"); and a semivaudevillian send-off with "On with the Show."

In Bill Wyman's exhaustive memoir/diary "Rolling with the Stones," he recalls much of the album was recorded with one or more of the group absent from any given session, and he remarks on the various entourages that accompanied the three leaders of the group that served to slow all and any work on the album to a crawl. His only composition to appear on a Rolling Stones album, "In Another Land," was released as a single and prefigures the darkly inventive style of songwriting he would feature on solo albums in the decade to follow.

The highly elaborate cover was photographed and directed by Michael Cooper, the photographer responsible for the *Sgt. Pepper's Lonely Hearts Club Band* album cover, who was a fixture on the London psychedelic scene, having been introduced to the rock elite through art dealer Robert Fraser; like Fraser, he was present at the Redlands bust.

As the Stones entered 1968, they returned to their riff-based roots with their next single, "Jumpin' Jack Flash." It was that single's B side, "Child of the Moon," that would be the band's final foray into psychedelia. The song was begun during sessions for *Their Satanic Majesties Request* but was not included on the album and was saved for the B side of their May 1968 "comeback" single.

SANTANA: *ABRAXAS* (SEPTEMBER 1970)

Santana does not fall squarely into psychedelia, nor does it fall into progressive rock. This late 1960s San Francisco group played a fusion of Latin rock and was the first commercially recognized band of that genre. Following Jefferson Airplane and the Grateful Dead, Santana was, along with Sly and the Family Stone, the next generation of bands to emerge from the city's evolving psychedelic scene. The San Francisco–based band, led by guitarist Carlos Santana, was managed by Bill Graham, and thanks to his persistence, they made their international debut at Woodstock. Carlos Santana has led a version of Santana since 1966 and has worked with more configurations of players than perhaps any other artist of the rock era. The list of musicians who have, at one or other time, played in Santana during the band's half century of existence numbers close to fifty. By 1969, Latin and Afro-Latin rhythms were becoming more prominent in popular music, and Santana was one of the early proponents of the genre.

Carlos Santana was born in the state of Jalisco, Mexico, and lived both there and in the border city of Tijuana through his teen years.

His family moved to San Francisco in the mid-1960s, where Carlos started the Santana Blues Band. This evolved into Santana, and by 1966, the band was playing at the Avalon Ballroom and was soon under Bill Graham's management. Graham's influence helped the band come to the attention of Columbia Records, and in 1969, they released their largely instrumental self-titled debut album. It was their second album (and first post-Woodstock), *Abraxas*, released in 1970 that features some of their most well-known work and a rich variety of musical styles. "Black Magic Woman/Gypsy Queen," composed by Fleetwood Mac's erratically brilliant Peter Green ("Gypsy Queen," combined with "Black Magic Woman" on Santana's album, was composed by Gabor Szabo), was their first top 5 hit. With a lead vocal sung by keyboardist Gregg Rolie, the album reached No. 1 on Billboard's album charts. The album also featured Santana's most frequently recognized song, the Tito Puente composition "Oye Como Va." Their third LP, *Santana III*, was the last album with the original lineup and last under Graham's management. Carlos never limited the band to any one style of music, and he has managed to maintain a loyal following even when their works were not critical favorites.

In the early 2000s, when the record industry began its significant decline with the rise of file-sharing platforms, Santana experienced one of the band's most successful periods with the albums *Supernatural* (1999) and *Shaman* (2002), which featured duets with Rob Thomas and Michelle Branch, respectively. In the past decade, Santana has reunited the Woodstock-era band and released *Santana IV* to mark the continuation of the band that had recorded *Santana III* over forty years earlier. One of the biggest arena bands of the 1970s and 1980s, Journey, was an offshoot of Santana. Keyboardist and vocalist Gregg Rolie and guitarist Neal Schon left Santana following 1972's *Caravanserai* to form Journey, which would later that decade go on to become one of the most successful bands of the era.

SMALL FACES: "ITCHYCOO PARK" (AUGUST 1967)

Along with the Who and the Kinks, Small Faces was one of the mod greats of England's beat music scene, but they were the least resilient group of the three and lasted barely over three years. Small Faces consisted of Steve Marriott (guitar, vocals), Ronnie Lane (bass, vocals), Ian McLagan (keyboards, vocals), and Kenney Jones (drums, vocals). Their name reflected the members' vertically challenged stature, but it in no way described the power and drive of their records. The U.K. and U.S.

releases of their catalog did not align until their final album, one of psychedelia's lauded releases, *Ogdens' Nut Gone Flake* (1968). Their self-titled first album and its singles were released on Decca, where they were managed by one of the field's most infamous agents, Don Arden. After a typically Arden-esque break, the band was signed by Immediate Records, a label set up by the Rolling Stones' manager, Andrew Loog Oldham. Their first album on Immediate was also self-titled, which was cause for just a bit of confusion in cataloging their modest output. Their second U.K. album was released in the United States as *There Are but Four Small Faces* and features an altered track listing from its English counterpart; it includes the hit single "Itchycoo Park"/"I'm Only Dreaming."

"Itchycoo Park" is a classic sunny psychedelic pop single from the late summer of 1967. It was a top 20 single in Britain, the United States, and many European territories and a No. 1 single in Canada. Coauthored by Ronnie Lane and Steve Marriott, the location of said Itchycoo Park has been claimed to be a park near the suburban London home of guitarist Marriott; "Itchycoo" is a reference to the nettles/needles that shed from the trees in the park. McLagan's Hammond organ and Jones's phased drums are a perfect underpinning to the Marriott/Lane guitar/bass interplay. The B side, "I'm Only Dreaming," is a perfect companion song in terms of both style and theme.

The album *Ogdens' Nut Gone Flake*, released in May of the following year, is considered by some as one of psychedelia's classic albums, but it is a more complex and dense record than the perfected sunshine psychedelia of "Itchycoo Park." Side one features six exceptional psychedelic songs, but it is the album's second side where the record loses focus. The two sides feel as if they were created for two entirely different records. Side two is a fairy tale about a boy named "Happiness Stan," and Stanley Unwin reads narrative interludes between the songs. The entire side is not terribly different from Brian Wilson's twelve-minute contribution to the album *Holland* (1973), "Mt. Vernon and Fairway (a Fairy Tale)," a record Wilson claimed was influenced by Randy Newman's seminal work *Sail Away*, but it could have easily been influenced by side two of *Ogdens' Nut Gone Flake* from five years earlier. On *Ogdens' Not Gone Flake*, every track on side one shows how brilliantly this band evolved from a mod fixture to a progressive, psychedelic outfit.

Sadly, this was the last album of original music that Small Faces would release for nearly a decade. Steve Marriott left the group in the middle of a show on New Year's Eve 1968, frustrated at the band's inability to shed their pop image. Upon leaving Small Faces, he joined forces with Peter Frampton to create the 1970s supergroup Humble Pie. Lane, McLagan, and Jones continued with Ronnie Wood (guitar) and Rod Stewart (vocals), both of whom had recently departed from the Jeff Beck Group. The newly configured five-piece band dropped "Small" from its name and became simply Faces. This incarnation of the group had success as a touring fixture in both the United Kingdom and the United States, but Rod Stewart had greater success with his solo albums and ended his run with the band. Ronnie Wood left the group in 1975 to tour with (and ultimately join) the Rolling Stones, where he has remained to the present day.

Small Faces was a noteworthy influence on the Britpop movement in the early 1990s, but the band also influenced the Jam and the Jam's creative front man, Paul Weller, in his 1990s solo work. The Jam recorded a version of "Get Yourself Together," and Weller's mid-1990s solo albums, *Wild Wood*, *Stanley Road*, and *Heavy Soul*, all contain trace influences of Marriott's songwriting and vocal style.

THE SOFT MACHINE: *THE SOFT MACHINE* (DECEMBER 1968)

The Soft Machine is one of the most overlooked and generally forgotten groups of the psychedelic era. They were at the forefront of the English psychedelic scene and played many of the scene's early shows with Pink Floyd both at the Roundhouse and UFO. Although they were at the birth of psychedelia, their sound is often described as progressive rock or jazz fusion. The sheer variety of their music makes it difficult to categorize them in one or other camp, but that is a complete waste of time; in doing so, we lose the amazing music of this unique band.

The band underwent a number of lineup changes from its beginnings to the early 1980s, but the name resurfaced in the 2000s. This entry is focused on the core group who recorded the first studio album: *The Soft Machine* (1968). The lineup for the first album consisted of Kevin Ayers (bass, vocals), Mike Ratledge (keyboards), and Robert Wyatt (drums, vocals). Guitarist Daevid Allen had left the group before they made the first album and was not replaced until mid-1968, when Andy Summers joined the group for a brief period. The membership of the group appeared to be in perpetual change, and this no doubt contributed to the band's lack of commercial success.

The Soft Machine was a Canterbury-based band and should have had a chance at the same exposure and success as Pink Floyd. However, looking at the years 1967–1972, Pink Floyd had successful albums, but they were not a massive act until 1973's *Dark Side of the Moon*. They played all over the globe and sold impressive numbers of records, which were a reflection of their discipline and desire to achieve success. The Soft Machine was dealt a hand with difficult management, and they lacked a consistent recording profile. They released some singles in 1967, the first produced by Chas Chandler, the manager they shared with Jimi Hendrix, and then a follow-up single produced by Kim Fowley. They recorded a number of tracks with Giorgio Gomelsky, whose own legacy was tied into his ownership of the Crawdaddy Club, an early English blues venue, and his management of the Yardbirds (it was Gomelsky who brought the Graham Gouldham–penned "For Your Love" to the band, which prompted the departure of Eric Clapton). Gomelsky founded Marmalade Records, and although he produced a set of demos for Soft Machine, nothing came of them. They remained unreleased for over three years, by which time Robert Wyatt had left the band. By the time their debut LP was released, it was through ABC Probe (in North America) and Barclay (France). Their second album was also released through these less influential labels. They were picked up by Columbia (in the United States) and CBS (in the United Kingdom) for their third through seventh albums, at which time they moved to Harvest Records, the progressive imprint at EMI that should have released their output from the beginning.

If psychedelia had been the passageway that swallowed pop, beat, and rock music and enabled it to exit into hard rock, progressive, glam, and other genres, then Soft Machine was the first group to lead the charge into progressive rock. They married the unyielding intensity of psychedelia to an anarchic mélange of sound and created a sound that would set a model for many genres of groups in the next decade. Before "Jam Band" became an eye-rolling exercise in male-dominated excess, Soft Machine was taking improvisatory excess into wonderfully exciting territory. Unlike Cream, who maintained a blues core in all their work, Soft Machine was never tied to any American genre. They were peers with Pink Floyd, playing many of the same shows, and on friendly terms with the group. Floyd drummer Nick Mason produced solo albums by a few of its members, and some of Soft Machine played on the first Syd Barrett solo album, *The Madcap Laughs*.

Soft Machine, not unlike the virtuoso power trio Cream, consisted of a fragile collection of egos. They toured with Jimi Hendrix through North America for a good portion of 1968 and even recorded their debut album in New York. Back in London, between U.S. tours, they added Andy Summers to the band to replace Daevid Allen. Summers had played with protopsychedelic Zoot Money and with the San Francisco version of Eric Burdon & the Animals on the *Love Is* album. Back in London, Summers joined Soft Machine and was on the band's second U.S. tour with Hendrix, but Kevin Ayers demanded that Summer be removed from the group. Summer was relieved of his duties, and the band reverted to a trio. Despite being sacked from the band, Summer went on to greater success in the late-1970s as the guitarist for the Police. No sooner did this take shape than Kevin Ayers choose to leave the band. At the end of their 1968 tour in the United States, Soft Machine faded out of existence for the remainder of the year. Ratledge and Wyatt reformed the group in 1969, adding Hugh Hopper on bass. From this point forward, Soft Machine would be a constantly shifting configuration of players. Wyatt would leave in 1971 followed by Ratledge in 1975–1976.

By 1971, Robert Wyatt, whose childlike high tenor on lead vocals was a timbral hallmark of the band's sound, had left the group to pursue other projects. In 1973, an inebriated Wyatt fell from a fourth-floor window and was left a paraplegic. His drumming career now finished, he pursued a career as a vocalist and gathered a solid cult following. Pink Floyd hosted a benefit concert for Wyatt in November 1973, and he continued to work with an interesting array of artists. His solo rendition of the Monkees' "I'm a Believer" remains his most popular solo record. Nearly a decade later, producer Clive Langer and Elvis Costello wrote the song "Shipbuilding" for him, which he released as a single in 1982.

Much of the Soft Machine catalog has been made available in the past few decades, and the first three albums are worthy of a deep listening to acquire a full picture of English psychedelia circa 1966–1967. Although Soft Machine arrived on the psychedelic scene with Pink Floyd, they would not achieve the level of success that Waters, Gilmour, Wright, and Mason mastered in the 1970s. They provided an entrée for some of the early progressive rock greats with Yes and King Crimson, but they would again remain more of a cult band than the star acts that Yes and, to a certain extent, King Crimson would become into the early 1970s.

TYRANNOSAURUS REX: *MY PEOPLE WERE FAIR AND HAD SKY IN THEIR HAIR ... BUT NOW THEY'RE CONTENT TO WEAR STARS ON THEIR BROWS* (JULY 1968)

Prior to Marc Bolan becoming a massive star of the teen glam scene from 1970 to 1972 in T. Rex, he fronted the psychedelic/folk duo Tyrannosaurus Rex. They were the most low-fi psychedelic band on the scene thanks to their all-acoustic setup. Bolan played acoustic guitar and sang while

Steve Peregrine Took (born Stephen Ross Porter) accompanied him on bongos and other hand percussion. Prior to Tyrannosaurus Rex, Bolan was the guitarist for the early psychedelic flower power band John's Children. Managed by former Yardbirds manager Simon Napier-Bell, John's Children only managed one album on the U.S. independent label White Whale (that label's biggest act was the Turtles), but that album was performed by session musicians hired by Napier-Bell with only one member of the group on the recordings. Bolan left that aimless and unpromising concern to take up with Stephen Porter, who soon adopted the Tolkien-influenced name of Steve Peregrine Took, and together they created a fresh and original sound that blended folk with psychedelic themes.

Signed to the EMI subsidiary Regal Zonophone, Bolan released three albums under the unwieldy moniker of Tyrannosaurus Rex. Their first single, "Debora" (1968), is perhaps the best song from this configuration of the band. Bolan and Took had a very tight sound for an acoustic duo, which was a reflection of both Bolan's songwriting style that borrowed from early rock and roll tropes and Tony Visconti's production. Their debut album, *My People Were Fair and Had Sky in Their Hair . . . But Now They're Content to Wear Stars on Their Brows*, bears the long-winded, ethereal, sci-fi/fantasy references that helped to make it a hit with the psychedelic crowd. Tony Visconti produced the album (and would produce Bolan's work as T. Rex up to 1974), and his signature clean and bright sound was a perfect fit for Bolan's songs. (Visconti went on to produce David Bowie's *Man of Words/Man of Music*, *The Man Who Sold the World*, and other albums in Bowie's catalog, including his stunning final work, *Blackstar*). The album was a success in the United Kingdom, where it reached the top 20. Later, in October 1968, Bolan released *Prophets, Seers & Sages: The Angels of the Ages*. It did not chart at the time of its release but has been accorded appropriate recognition in recent decades. This was followed with *Unicorn* (May 1969), the last album to feature Took, whom Bolan fired before their fourth and final album as Tyrannosaurus Rex. All three albums carry the air of fantasy literature blended with Bolan's rock and roll rhythm guitar approach. No one in the U.K. psychedelic scene had a sound like this, and while their albums achieved modest success in the United Kingdom, they never found a solid audience in the United States.

The narrative for the band becomes cloudy at this point, and most narratives overlook the significant changes Bolan brought to his career in 1970. Took was fired by Bolan before the 1969 sessions for their fourth album, *A Beard of Stars* (March 1970). He replaced Took with percussionist Mickey Finn while also adding electric guitar, organ, and bass to his arrangements. His sound was moving from that of a cross-legged guitar-playing hippie to one clearly hinting toward rock stardom. Visconti had produced all four albums, and on each successive release, Bolan's sound became more focused as a rock sound rather than the whimsy of folksy psychedelia.

By December 1970, the band's name was abbreviated to T. Rex, and the release of the group's first album under a more easily marketed name signaled the arrival of glam rock's first superstar. Although this was the first rock album for T. Rex, it featured songs that went back to Bolan's time in John's Children. There remains a hint of Tolkien's influence with the opening and closing track of the album, "The Children of Rarn," but "Jewel" and "One Inch Rock" demonstrate where Bolan was headed in this new incarnation. The album features Bolan and Finn in addition to Tony Visconti on bass and piano and Howard Kaylan and Mark Volman, aka "Flo and Eddie," formerly of the Turtles and later of the Mothers of Invention. It was the next album, *Electric Warrior* (September 1971), where Bolan morphed into the teenage market's favorite glam artist. The single "Get It On" launched Bolan's career into overdrive, and it remained there for the next two years. Beginning with 1973's *Tanx*, Bolan starts to incorporate soul and funk elements into his work, and he added female backup singers to the group. He would record one more album with Visconti, *Zinc Alloy and the Hidden Riders of Tomorrow—A Creamed Cage in August* (February 1974).

Declining sales resulted in the band being dropped by Reprise Records in the United States. Neil Bogart released one cobbled together T. Rex album on his new Casablanca label, but after that, Bolan found himself without a label in the United States, where he had begun to both live and work, absorbing more soul influences and marrying them with his interest in science fiction. While living in Los Angeles, Bolan became a tax exile, developed a cocaine problem, put on weight, and by all accounts became a generally unpleasant person. Mickey Finn and most of his band had left him by 1975, and his career faded. Bolan's merger of blue-eyed soul with glam had difficulty finding a place and fitting in with the sounds of the mid-1970s.

Bolan returned to the United Kingdom and was reenergized by the arrival of punk rock. By 1977, he was promoting some of these bands on his limited-run Granada TV show, *Marc*. His final album, *Dandy in the Underworld* (March 1977), was a partial return to T. Rex's winning sound, and the album made the top 30 in the United Kingdom, his first chart showing in over three years. This success was short-lived.

Bolan died in a car crash in September 1977. Marc did not drive, but a Mini driven by his second wife, Gloria Jones, hit a post, followed by a tree, while crossing a bridge in SW London, killing Bolan instantly. His funeral was attended by his longtime friend David Bowie, who had recently appeared on the last episode of *Marc*, where they performed "Heroes."

David Bowie was an artist who changed his persona on every one of his records. Marc Bolan stayed relatively true to his basic rock and roll forms and continued with them until his sound became "in" again, which appeared to be happening with the release of *Dandy in the Underworld*. When it did, the punk and new wave scene was a natural draw for him, and his premature death, barely a decade after he had launched himself as an acoustic psychedelic hippie, robbed the music world of one of psychedelia's more colorful troubadours.

VANILLA FUDGE: *VANILLA FUDGE* (AUGUST 1967)

Vanilla Fudge was a unique contributor in the development of psychedelic rock, and this New York–based band is one of the region's few entries in this volume. While certain qualities in their sound were not dissimilar to those heard in many garage bands, their truly unique sound and cover versions of other artists' hit songs were enormously effective, both commercially and artistically, and have secured the band's legacy. Other artists in this volume performed cover songs, but none made covers the core of their repertory. No other cover band could match Vanilla Fudge's power or originality, and under Shadow Morton's production, their debut album succinctly captures one extraordinary facet of this era. Prior to Vanilla Fudge, Shadow's biggest success was with the Shangri-Las, with whom he produced evocative minidramas, and his ability to create a dramatic canvas of sonic otherworldliness benefited their best work.

The band, originally called the Pigeons (upon the advice of their manager and their label, they changed it to Vanilla Fudge), achieved a certain level of success on the regional circuit through 1965–1966, but with active management (who had long ties to the Lucchese crime family) and the marketing support of Atlantic Records, they were a chart success by late 1967. Their approach to covering the hit songs of other artists was certainly uncommon for the period. More of interpretations than authentic covers, Vanilla Fudge performed songs originally recorded by the Beatles, the Supremes, Curtis Mayfield, and the Zombies at slower tempi with infinitely heavier and tension-filled instrumental arrangements. The original band consisted of Mark Stein (keyboards, lead vocals), Vince Martell (guitar, vocals), Tim Bogert (bass, vocals), and Carmine Appice (drums, vocals). They ended their run in 1970, and each went on to other projects; most notably, Bogert and Appice went to play with Jeff Beck in Beck, Bogert, and Appice. Carmine Appice later became one of the top drummers of the 1970s, playing with Rod Stewart through his most commercially successful period in the late 1970s and early 1980s. The band has reformed in various guises since the 1980s, and the current lineup features three of the four original members, with Tim Bogert now replaced by Pete Bremy.

Their self-titled debut album has remained available in the marketplace, but in the era of remasters and enhanced editing of classic recordings, this album, as of this writing, has not been cleaned from the multigeneration master used in the 1980s-era transfer to compact disc. The Zombies were also a keyboard-fronted group, but Vanilla Fudge's Mark Stein used a Hammond B-3. Although the instrument was favored and used by many musicians, Vanilla Fudge was the first group to place the instrument at the front and center of their sonic wash, which gave the band a sound that approximated the collapse of a black hole. Nothing could escape the sonic fence Bogert and Stein built into every song. Jon Lord of Deep Purple moved from a Vox Continental to the Hammond B-3 in 1966 and has stated that Vanilla Fudge was an influence in shaping the sound of Deep Purple Mk. I.

Vanilla Fudge opens with a fantastic teeth-grinding cover of the Beatles' "Ticket to Ride." The peppy single released by the Beatles just two years earlier is given the full gothic-stoned treatment. This is followed by their moody cover of Curtis Mayfield's "People Get Ready," with a delivery laden with a cathedral-like solemnity. Next is their cover of the Zombies' biggest U.S. hit, "She's Not There," in a reading that dispenses with any shade of optimism that was present in the original. Side one closes with a heavily deconstructed interpretation on Sonny Bono's "Bang Bang." In addition to the band's extraordinarily loud and thick instrumental palette, their vocals are not so much sing-speech as scream-speech, which creates a fantastic counterpoint to their instrumental sound bed. On "Bang Bang" we hear their most complex and diverse vocal stylings.

Side two is an entirely different musical animal. Each of the songs is bridged with brief (less than twenty-five seconds in length) transition pieces titled "Illusions of My Childhood, Pts. 1–3." The first track on side two is a mind-blowing interpretation of the Supremes hit "You Keep Me Hanging On." Vanilla Fudge took the Holland-Dozier-Holland classic and turned it inside out into a seven-and-a-half-minute masterpiece. The throbbing organ and bass lines feel like a tourniquet around your head with no sign of release. This song was selected for the single from the album and was released in a shortened form (edited by Atlantic's master producer Arif Mardin) for AM radio. This is followed by another of their half-minute transition works into the song "Take Me for a Little While" by the little-known New Jersey–based songwriter/producer/arranger Trade Martin; it was originally recorded by Eva Sands. It's an effective song for club dancing, but sandwiched between Holland-Dozier-Holland and the final track, the Lennon/McCartney classic "Eleanor Rigby," it can easily be overlooked. "Eleanor Rigby" is a tour de force track and the longest on the album. The arrangement is so heavily deconstructed that you are never sure where it is headed, thanks in part to its very low-key and sinister arrangement. They close out the song with a quote from the Beatles' "Strawberry Fields Forever." They sing, in a barely present and somewhat de-energized manner, "Nothing is real . . . nothing to get hung about."

On the whole, the album is a wonderful acid-drenched tour through the latest of the American and British songbooks. "You Keep Me Hanging On" has remained on oldies radio programs, and after Hendrix, this song is an easy go-to for any filmmaker who wants to evoke a particular moment in the late 1960s. It was given a second and very effective lease on life when the rerecording of the song was used in the final episode of the television show *The Sopranos* (2007) and again in the first episode of the final season of the excellent period piece television series *Mad Men* (2015).

Sadly, Vanilla Fudge could not sustain the success or focus of their debut album. They followed up with the experimental and pretentious *The Beat Goes On*, which was nothing more than an aimless collage. Frank Zappa created similar work on his 1967 solo LP, *Lumpy Gravy*, and while constructing these collages is tiring and difficult manual labor, the end result seldom matches the intention or effort. The band saw this as a failed experiment and returned to their earlier style for their third album. While closer in spirit to their debut, the weaknesses on *Renaissance* are the result of having so many works composed by the band members with only a few cover tunes to complete the LP. Although Deep Purple may have borrowed certain elements from Vanilla Fudge for their sound circa 1968, the fact that Purple quickly developed into strong and prolific songwriters ensured that their sound would not remain stagnant. With Vanilla Fudge, the well-intentioned albums that followed after their debut simply do not match the quality or energy of that first album. They released excellent cover versions of Donovan's "Season of the Witch" and Dusty Springfield's "The Look of Love" (the latter is the B side to Mark Stein's excellent "Where Is My Mind," released the following year), but could not translate this power to their later work.

THE VELVET UNDERGROUND: *THE VELVET UNDERGROUND & NICO* (MARCH 1967)

The Velvet Underground's legacy has been packaged in the oft-repeated and apocryphal myth (often attributed to Brain Eno) that their debut album, *The Velvet Underground & Nico*, only sold ten thousand copies, but "everyone who bought one of those 10,000 copies started a band." This was the simple (and correct) acknowledgment of the impact this album had upon generations of musicians, from glam to electronica, to punk and beyond. Never mind that, in various sources, the number ten thousand is inflated to twenty-, thirty-, or fifty thousand; the point remains. The Velvet Underground's albums did not sell in great quantities, but their influence transcended the commercial model of "album sales equals success."

The Velvets were the antithesis to any generally accepted definition of *psychedelia*. They were not about peace and love nor was anything present in their music or image that could be described as pretty. They presented a nihilistic underbelly of life in New York City and packaged it in terse, poetic verse accompanied by an assaulting soundtrack of auditory stimuli that could easily have been mistaken as free-form music or endless drones. If the visuals of psychedelia are represented by washes of bold colors, rich fabrics, and vibrant styles, these would never have applied to the Velvet Underground. The band members wore black, and to Middle America, they looked more like delinquent undertakers than pop stars. They emerged from the bohemian and avant-garde scene in New York City and were a microcosm of the same literary and art crowd that traveled to London in 1965 to help ignite Britain's psychedelic movement.

The Velvet Underground consisted of Lou Reed (guitar), John Cale (bass, keyboards, viola), Sterling Morrison (guitar), and Maureen "Mo" Tucker (percussion). Lou Reed would become one of the most prolific and influential songwriters at the end of the last century, but in 1965, he was a poet who, while at Syracuse University, was a devotee of Delmore Schwartz. John Cale was born in Wales but came to the United States on a music scholarship to study at Tanglewood. His musical preferences at university, prior to coming to the Berkshire Music Center, were centered on the avant-garde, and once he arrived in New York City, he collaborated with LaMonte Young, Terry Riley, John Cage, and Tony Conrad. In 1963, he was one of the pianists engaged by Cage to perform Erik Satie's *Vexations*, a work that, according to the composer, is to be played 840 times. The band was completed with Sterling Morrison, an acquaintance of Reed's from Syracuse University, and Maureen "Mo" Tucker on percussion. Tucker was one of the few women playing rock and roll in the 1960s, and her unorthodox playing techniques enabled her to create the seismic heartbeat of the group's sound.

The band's earliest performances involved their playing at film screenings organized by underground filmmaker Piero Heliczer. Music journalist Al Aronowitz, impressed with the band at Heliczer's showings, helped them secure a December 1965 residency at Café Bizzare. This is where Andy Warhol saw them for the first time, and just two days after meeting him, they were fired from that gig. Fortunately, they received an invitation to the Factory, where Warhol decided he should manage them, and he ultimately served as both manager and producer of the group's debut album, *The Velvet Underground & Nico*. This album is basically an edited studio version of their live show, and though Warhol lacked the technical skills needed to produce the album, he had "produced" this group through all their performances in *Andy Warhol's Up-Tight* and the *Exploding Plastic Inevitable*.

Warhol added Christa Päffgen to the band. Known as "Nico," she was an alluring German chanteuse who found herself at Warhol's Factory and was inserted into the Velvets as a member of the band. Her presence on the first album provides a ghostly vocal air, but she was an awkward addition. Her inclusion in the band was a gesture of Warhol-directed flair intended to provide the Velvets with an ever-greater dramatic stage presence via her role as the tragic, Teutonic, post-Dietrich femme fatale. The teenaged Nico had appeared in Fellini's *La Dolce Vita* (1961) as an unintentional extra who ended up with substantial screen time. She made her way to London, where the Rolling Stones' manager, Andrew 'Loog' Oldham, signed her to his label, Immediate Records, and through him she found herself among Warhol and the Factory crew.

The Velvet Underground began in 1965 when Reed, Cale, Morrison, and Angus MacLise created the band on Ludlow Street in New York's Lower East Side. MacLise left the group just prior to their first appearances at Piero Heliczer' film showings and was replaced by Maureen "Mo" Tucker. They became a fixture at Warhol's Factory, and in winter 1966, they began to provide the live musical score for *Andy Warhol, Up-Tight*. By April 1966, the year-and-a-half-long collaboration with

Warhol had evolved from *Andy Warhol, Up-Tight* into the *Exploding Plastic Inevitable* (EPI), a "multimedia event," a "happening," or a "performance" (however you might choose to describe it) that brought a downtown, avant-garde sensibility to the masses. Warhol associate Paul Morrisey claims that Andy brought the Velvets into his productions because they were making no money from his films, and he felt that by adding the Velvets he was making his shows more accessible and attractive for audiences. One goal had been to get a regular club residency for the band so they could make regular money, 25 percent of which was supposed to go to Warhol.

Although the Velvet Underground was not an extension of Warhol's creative progeny, their presentation within Warhol's production gave many the belief that the band was Andy's creation. Warhol's films were projected on the band as they performed a "soundtrack" to the evening's event. Warhol; his lighting designer, Danny Williams; and filmmaker Jonas Mekas contributed to the creation of a new lighting and performance aesthetic through their work with EPI. The Dom, the Gymnasium, and the Cinematheque were the regular locations where the visual components of the EPI were refined. Their techniques were among the first uses of theatrical lighting techniques in popular music, and their practices would become a standard for rock concerts in the late 1960s and are the bedrock for today's current stadium concert extravaganzas.

Andy Warhol's *Exploding Plastic Inevitable* was, at its largest, a twelve-person ensemble that performed across the United States. The core members of this ensemble (the Velvet Underground, Andy, Nico, Gerard Malanga, Ingrid Superstar, Barbara Rubin, Paul Morrissey, and, later, Mary Woronov and Ronnie Cutrone) were largely in place by early 1966. Edie Sedgwick, the star of several Warhol films, left the Factory just as the *Up-Tight* show was about to go on the road. Warhol's name was enough for EPI to be booked at locations from coast-to-coast. One of the lesser-known performances of EPI involved their participation in the "World's First Mod Wedding," a publicity stunt dreamed up by former Motown publicist Al Abrams. This occurred at the Michigan State Fairgrounds on November 20, 1966, and involved Warhol officiating over the wedding of a go-go dancer who wore a painted paper gown he designed and painted.

The band began to record the album at Scepter Studios in New York City and continued recording in May 1966 at T.T. & G. Studios in Los Angeles. They tried to sell the album to Atlantic and Elektra, but when producer Tom Wilson (Bob Dylan, Simon & Garfunkel) moved from Columbia to Verve Records, he was able to sign them to the label. The Velvet

Underground was not Warhol's creation, but he served as their ad hoc manager and producer of their first album, *The Velvet Underground & Nico*, also known as the "banana" album for the Warhol artwork that graces the cover of the album.

Verve Records, at that time a subsidiary of MGM Records, was also the home for Frank Zappa and the Mothers of Invention, who also worked with Tom Wilson. Although Zappa and the Velvets represent the extremes of psychedelia's artistic pendulum, the antipathy between the groups was without equal. In no world could one imagine Lou Reed and Frank Zappa sharing, expressing, or acknowledging the others' extraordinary skills and talents, so their mutual disdain for each other's work remains a part of their respective legacies. *The Velvet Underground & Nico* was completed by summer 1966, but MGM Records, with two of the field's most progressive bands on its label, managed to create more problems than it solved. The album's release was delayed until mid-1967, at which time EPI was winding down, and Warhol was beginning to move on to other projects.

Production delays were caused by the label's managerial incompetence and having no idea how to market a new type of popular music. The production challenges that were a result of assembling Warhol's removable banana peel on the album sleeve also delayed its release. It was immediately pulled upon its release because downtown performance artist Eric Emerson did not give permission for his likeness to be used on the back-album cover. The image was a still from an EPI show, where Emerson's face appeared in Warhol's film. MGM, concerned with legal action (that surely would not have transpired), pulled the album and airbrushed the photo to remove Emerson's image. By the time the album was rereleased, the interest in and momentum of EPI was at its end, and Warhol's interest in the band had begun to change. The subject matter of many of the album's songs ("Heroin," "Waiting for the Man") precluded its inclusion in mainstream media outlets, and other songs ("The Black Angel's Death Song") were too noncommercial and dissonant for radio play. The album was destined for obscurity while the Velvets continued on as a performing band. The album was out of print before the decade was out and would not be widely available until the mid-1980s.

"Sunday Morning" was the last song recorded for the album, but it is the first track on side one. It was the sweetest lullaby they would create until "Pale Blue Eyes" on their self-titled third album. The celesta played by Cale gives little indication of the sonic assault that is about to occur on the remainder of the album. "Waiting for the Man" is an effective yet simple song about scoring heroin in Harlem ("Up to Lexington,

1-2-5 . . . feel sick and dirty, more dead than alive"). "Femme Fatale" was composed for Nico to sing and is followed by the equally quixotic "Venus in Furs." This song, titled after Leopold Sacher-Masoch's novella, is a deliciously bound description of female dominance and sadomasochism.

The dysfunctional dynamic of Nico, Andy, and Lou was a constant in the band's career during this period. Warhol wanted her, as did Nico, to sing nearly every song, but Reed did not want her singing at all. She sings the lead on three of the album's eleven tracks, but her contributions bring a mood and shape to the entire album that transcends many of the iconic albums released in that year. As the group's name was borrowed from a book Tony Conrad brought to the Ludlow Street flat, it made sense that they would create a song that references the most widely known literary work on sexual submission and domination. "Run, Run, Run" is another scoring drugs song, this time in Lower Manhattan. Reed's four characters (Teenage Mary, Marguerita Passion, Seasick Sarah, Beardless Harry) are each suffering a form of withdrawal, and each is trying to decide how or what he or she will do. The first side of the album closes with "All Tomorrow's Parties." This was Warhol's favorite song on the album and was another vehicle for Nico to take the lead vocal. In an edited version, this song served as their first single. The track features Nico's insistent monotone, which helps to balance the mélange of instrumental textures that accompany her.

Side two opens with "Heroin," one of the truest and most romantic songs ever composed about drug use. This was an early composition for Reed and is one of the first he played for Cale soon after their first meeting. Though Reed's songs can be mistaken for autobiographical tales, this was not Reed's glorification of the drug, but it likely inspired countless hopeful rock stars to initiate a heroin habit. "There She Goes Again" opens with a riff that is a direct quote taken from Marvin Gaye's "Hitch Hike," but it has a far simpler arrangement when compared to Gaye's classic. "I'll Be Your Mirror" is a lovely, and self-explanatory song that Lou wrote for Nico. "The Black Angel's Death Song" is one of two cacophony specials on the album, and it is here where Cale's Appalachian viola fiddling with Reed's fingerpicking rhythm behind his singing turn the work into a narcotic-roots composition. "European Son" picks up from "Black Angel's Death Song" with an insistent rhythm that gives way to a barrage of sound effects that Cale created in the studio. It is loud and sounds as if it will fall apart at any moment, but it is a perfect closing track for a most extraordinary album. "European Son" was dedicated to poet Delmore Schwartz, even though he allegedly hated rock and roll. The album opens on side one with the tender lullaby "Sunday

Morning," but it comes to an anarchic conclusion with the final two tracks on side two.

Once released, *The Velvet Underground & Nico* was not marketed or promoted, and sales were all but nonexistent. The *Exploding Plastic Inevitable* ended. Nico returned to Ibiza, and the band began to distance themselves further from Warhol's crowd. Under Steve Sesnick's management, the group began to tour regularly, and 1968 would be a year of sheer energy, during which time a wealth of new songs were recorded by the band. The most significant change of that year was Reed's unilateral firing of John Cale ("Despite all the amputations . . .").

THE VELVET UNDERGROUND: *WHITE LIGHT, WHITE HEAT* (JANUARY 1968)

As thousands of kids flocked west to experience the social changes wrought by the hippies in California, it was reported that New York City had a calm, comfortable, and relaxed tenor during the Summer of Love. Sterling Morrison described the westward exodus as follows:

> In addition to the usual eastward migration of the vapid chic set . . . to the Hamptons, another and even more welcome exodus took place—westward, to San Francisco. Inspired by media hype, and encouraged by shamelessly deceitful songs on the radio (Airplane, Mama's and Papa's [*sic*], Eric Burdon), teenage ninnies flocked from Middle-America out to the coast; hot on their heels came a predatory mob from N.Y.C. Roughly speaking, every creep, every degenerate, every hustler, booster, and rip-off artists, every wasted weirdo packed up his or her clap, crabs, and cons and headed off to the Promised Land. . . . Then descended upon the hapless hippies (and their dupes). . . . In Manhattan, all was suddenly quiet, clean, and beautiful—like the world of Noah after the Flood. (Bockris and Malanga 1983, 86)

Morrison's description also recognizes the geographic shift of the music scene from New York to the West Coast of California. The music that emerged from New York in the late 1960s into the 1970s, while lesser in quantity than what came from Los Angeles, would slowly evolve to create a perfect collection of new, earth-shattering genres. Glam (New York Dolls, Lou Reed), soul and funk (Nile Rogers and Bernard Edwards), punk (the Ramones, Television, CBGB's), and rap all came to the fore in the decade that followed the Summer of Love and this surely was assisted by an exodus that probably was not dissimilar to what Morrison described, leaving a fresh slate for the emergence of new creative genres.

Toward the end of 1967's Summer of Love, the Velvets recorded their sophomore album, *White Light/White Heat (WL/WH)*, at Scepter Studios on Fifty-Fourth Street in Manhattan. In the decades since its release, this album has likely had a greater impact on the field than their debut album. It is loud, unrelenting, and fueled by amphetamine-soaked tales that are woven throughout the record. Nico was gone, so it was the quartet who recorded the album in three days with Tom Wilson at the production desk. The dynamic level is unrelenting, and the distortion present on each song is, despite the engineer's best efforts to remedy it, the most identifiable timbre of the album. Although Nico was no longer a part of the Velvet Underground, she had been signed as a solo artist to Verve Records, where she recorded *Chelsea Girl* (October 1967) with the assistance of Reed, Cale, and Morrison, who provided songs and played or arranged a number of tracks.

It is likely that John Cale met the then emerging designer Betsey Johnson back in 1966, when her designs were the hippest of the hip fashions. She and Cale married in April 1968, and she took charge of outfitting the group in a stylized set of black outfits. Although the band had always worn black, their pedestrian clothing reflected the band's generally impoverished status. With Betsey, each member of the group had a set of clothes that identified him or her as an individual, and in Lou Reed's case, she would influence many of his image choices throughout the 1970s. Betsey admittedly had difficulty connecting with Lou, but she was responsible for giving the band a striking stage look that provided them with a post-EPI image, something they lacked since leaving Warhol's shows. Despite the break from Warhol's management, the band's unique friendship with Andy continued. He contributed the concept and photograph for the cover of *White Light/White Heat* (January 1968) and a photograph of the band taken at the Factory that was used on their self-titled third album in 1969.

They engaged Steve Sesnick as their new manager, which enabled Lou to fire Andy. Reed told Warhol they no longer needed him, and legend has it that Warhol called Lou a "rat," which was apparently the worst insult he could muster. Relations within the band began to disintegrate once Sesnick took over management and resulted in Cale leaving the group in September 1968. The band was in Los Angeles in the early summer months of 1968 when they read about Valerie Solanas's attempted assassination of Andy Warhol. After this, life with Warhol changed, and the fluid open-door policy that Andy had at the Factory, an openness that had enabled the Velvets and others to enter his creative orbit, came to an end.

White Light/White Heat is the final Velvet Underground album to come from the Reed/Cale partnership and their last contribution to the psychedelic canon. Cale was involved in recording sessions in the summer of 1968, five selections of which are available on the *VU* and *Another View* compilation albums from 1985 and 1986, respectively. In those songs, you can hear more humor and lightness in their work, drawing yet another line under their Warhol/psychedelic period. Aside from a few live performances (that included shows where they backed Nico), Lou Reed and John Cale would not make another album together until 1990's stunning *Songs for Drella*, their memorial tribute to Andy Warhol. Their creative partnership was a perfectly combustible combination that created indescribably beautiful art or just as easily fell apart because one or other party could not subject himself to the level of criticism and creative intimacy that is required to create work of the quality the Velvet Underground delivered so capably. Lou Reed insisted on being the alpha within the group, and the delicate creative balance created by the two front men was ruined.

This would not be an isolated incident in response to Sesnick's goading and manipulation of Lou Reed, but would become a lifelong issue for him, as throughout his entire career, he left behind a rich trail of discarded collaborators. The relationship with Cale resulted in music that is as powerful today as it was when it was first created a half century ago. Cale blames Steve Sesnick for having focused the band entirely toward Lou, referring to the group as "Lou's band," which was a catalyst in the breakdown of the Reed/Cale partnership.

White Light/White Heat is the perfect Velvet Underground album because it is a culmination of the ideas they first began to design in their Ludlow Street flat in 1965. The opening title track is a playful look at amphetamine usage with droll call-and-response vocals as Cale's heaviest bass playing drives a stake right through your body. "The Gift" is a wonderful short story about innocent long-distance love that has no idea how, in the real world, it is outranked by lust and passion. The text is spoken, not sung, by Cale in his best BBC Wales compere voice over a gently grooving accompaniment that evolved from the band's improvisational sessions. In the stereo mix, you can pan to either channel to hear just the narration or the music. "Lady Godiva's Operation" is Reed's retelling of the Lady Godiva legend through his most complex and surreal lyrics. The first half of the song is sung by Cale with a straightforward description of Lady Godiva, in a wistful, narrative tone that could have been delivered by Donovan. In the second half, Reed and Cale alternate vocal duties, and the song veers off into a black description of a botched surgery. "Here She Comes Now" is most like "Sunday Morning" from the first album and is the most peaceful song on *WL/WH*. The simple title is loaded with crossed meanings. What is it about? Unrequited attentions? Female orgasm? Does the "she" reference the effects of drugs, as in "the effect" is coming on. This song could easily have fit onto their self-titled third album, but on *WL/WH*, it provides the one respite from the album's otherwise furious assault.

Side two opens with "I Heard Her Call My Name," an emphatic love song from a speed-addled Reed. The traditional song structure features backing vocals that punctuate Reed's story in a style you could find on any number of Motown or girl group records. Lou's guitar playing on this track is closer to Hendrix's incendiary style than anything else he would record, excluding *Metal Machine Music*, either with the Velvets or as a solo artist. The album concludes with their pièce de résistance, the seventeen-minute "Sister Ray." This work was recorded in a single uninterrupted take. With Cale on the organ, no bass was played, though you would never know this because their wall of cacophony is all the listener can manage to hold. Like so much of the album, the entire group is playing at full volume with full force, as if each member is fighting to overcome the others. With "Sister Ray," it must have been clear to the group that no one person could outplay everyone else, so they all play at an equal and unrelenting sonic and rhythmic pace. If other Velvet Underground songs dealt with drugs or sexuality, this song incorporates themes of drug use, violence, homosexuality, and transvestitism. Lou intended the song to represent utter debauchery and decay and succeeded in this quest. The descriptions of the various drag queens, the cooking of heroin and the many failed attempts to mainline the drug, and multiple descriptions of oral sex, anilingus, and bondage are pure prose to the core. For all its dark subject matter, the band sounds like they are having unrestrained fun on this track. Knowing this piece would be completed in one unbroken take, each of them is in sync with the others, and through their well-honed improvisational skills, they create an oppressive yet delicious sense of decay and perversion. This work precedes the arrival of heavy metal and punk and would remain one of Reed's greatest achievements. The song would be covered by numerous other artists and was played in their shows until Reed left the band.

The first half of 1968 was difficult for the band because they remained on the sidelines of obscurity while bands such as the Nazz, the Mothers of Invention, and Buffalo Springfield, who had opened for them a just few years earlier, were now scaling the charts. Few, if any, radio stations would touch records from the Velvet Underground. MGM had no idea how to market the band. Distribution was barely existent, and promotion was virtually absent. People heard of the band from seeing them live or from knowing one of those purported ten thousand who had purchased a Velvet Underground album.

Sesnick continued to alienate Cale from Reed, and as John was living most of his life with Betsey, it was easy for Sesnick to create fictional scenarios to play on Lou's well-developed, heroin-soaked paranoia. Lou gave Sterling Morrison and Maureen Tucker an ultimatum: they could be with John or they could stay with him. Both Morrison and Tucker later regretted how they did not fight back or stand up in John's defense, but Lou made the first move. John played his last shows with the Velvet Underground on September 28, 1968. Whether John Cale quit the band or was fired will never be resolved within the historical narrative of the band.

The post-Cale, post-Warhol, postpsychedelia Velvet Underground hired a young Boston-based bass player, Doug Yule, to play bass and sing. In March 1969, they released their first album without John, the self-titled *The Velvet Underground*. This album bore more of an unplugged folk-rock sound and featured songs on more intimate topics ("Pale Blue Eyes," "Jesus," "I'm Set Free") than anything Reed had composed for their first two albums. They moved from MGM/Verve Records to Atlantic Records, and their final album, *Loaded*, was released on the Cotillion label in November 1970 though Reed had left the band by the time of its release. *Loaded* became the most popular and widely known of their four albums and was the only original Velvets release to remain in print throughout the 1970s and 1980s. Verve Records had pulled their first three albums from the catalog by the early 1970s, so *Loaded* became their studio LP calling card to represent the band until their commercial resurgence in the mid-1980s.

THE WHO: *THE WHO SELL OUT* (DECEMBER 1967)

The Who may be an unexpected inclusion in this volume, but their late 1967 album, *The Who Sell Out*, is a masterpiece that captures a Warholian sense of absurd consumerism amid the freewheeling sounds of London in 1967. It also thumbs it to the conventional marketplace through its thematic reliance on products and advertisements, of which the majority were used without the permission of their respective copyright holders. In short, it is pure punk idealism clothed in the colorful finery of the day. This album goes beyond pop art, mods, psychedelia, or hard rock, as all of it is captured here and is digested in second and third servings. Like their best work from that decade, *The Who Sell Out* is unabashed fun and introduces more than a few themes and tropes that would be developed in greater detail on *Tommy*. Accidental? Inspired? It is a true band album, an ensemble work created by the band's four distinct personalities that Pete Townshend would enshrine in 1973's *Quadrophenia*, except that here each of the four is captured flogging a specific product: Pete with Odorono underarm deodorant; Roger nearly submerged in an enormous tub of Heinz Baked Beans; Keith, the band's youngest member, applying an oversized tube of Medac to treat his enormous pimple; and John swathed in a leopard skin tunic, with a teddy bear in one arm and the other wrapped around a fulsome leopard skin bikini–wearing model, hoping the Charles Atlas method will enable him to become the muscle man whom all the girls will notice.

More than seven months were required to construct this album, and without the option of remaining close to their preferred studios, manager Kit Lambert had the group recording while on tour. Therefore, studios in London (where they used CBS, IBC, De Lane Lea, and Pye Studios), New York City, Nashville, and Los Angeles were used over April–October of that year, and recording documentation is sparse because the band was literally on the go. It is likely that no one in 1967 thought anyone a half century down the line would be listening to or writing about this album. The 1995 reissue provides a fresh stereo mix of the album with ten bonus tracks, and the 2009 deluxe edition features the stereo mix in addition to the long-out-of-print monophonic mix. As was the pattern for rock albums until the late 1960s, the monophonic mix was in many cases a reflection of the band's preferred mix and the one into which they placed their attentions to get the album just right. Stereo mixes seldom had the artists' input, and as a by-product of creating a stereo version of the album, the new mix could, and often did, sound quite different from the intended monophonic mix. On *The Who Sell Out*, there are a number of differences in the monophonic mix, some quite subtle, others less so. Bonus tracks on the mono disc feature more previously unreleased mixes and versions of songs that appeared both on singles and on the album.

The Who arrived on the rock scene one or two years behind the Beatles and the Rolling Stones. Their first single, "Zoot Suit" b/w "I'm the Face," was released in mid-1964 under the name the High Numbers. Adopted by members of Britain's mod subculture, they were at first tagged as a mod band. Like the Beatles, the Rolling Stones, and the Yardbirds, the Who was influenced and inspired by black American music. But unlike their slightly older British compatriots, the Who leaned toward the soul and R & B of the Tamla Motown variety and artists such as James Brown. After changing their name back to the Who and acquiring new managers in Kit Lambert and Chris Stamp, they recorded and released some of the most iconic singles of the era: "I Can't Explain"; "Anyway, Anyhow, Anywhere"; and "My Generation," the last of which remains a timeless rock anthem. They were the first open anarchists in the rock world and often destroyed their equipment at the climax of their shows. More than a novelty theatrical act, the Who possessed an enormous musical sensibility and evolved into one of the most important groups of the rock era.

The album that followed *The Who Sell Out*, the double-album set *Tommy*, would become their calling card and financial savior, but it is a work that eventually took on a life of its own, though it had its origins in *The Who Sell Out*. The two most enduring interpretations of *Tommy*, Ken Russell's 1975 film of the same name and a 1992 musical under the production aegis of Des McAnuff, are removed from the band's original work, but regardless, *Tommy* could not have been created in a vacuum. So what was its author thinking in the months leading to his masterpiece? *The Who Sell Out* is the through-composed step Townshend used en route to *Tommy* (1969), the aborted *Lifehouse* project in 1970–1971, and *Quadrophenia* (1973).

The Who's 1966 album, *A Quick One*, was only their second long player, and for years it was unfairly looked over as an inferior product from the band. While not a masterwork, it contains a few works—"Disguises," "So Sad about Us," and a cover of Holland-Dozier-Holland's "Heat Wave"—that are their farewell to the mod scene that comprised their initial fan base. The album may lack any thematic cohesion and features songs composed by all four members (in response to a publishing deal arranged on their behalf by Chris Stamp), but it is a necessary component in Townshend's creative arc. In an era when British pop albums featured between twelve and fourteen tracks per disc, *A Quick One* carried a paltry ten tracks, the last of which, the nine-minute "A Quick One, While He's Away," was composed to bring the record to a respectable length required for a long-playing album. This work, a rock motet, if you like, is a compressed narrative work spread over six connected movements and concerns a sailor, his unfaithful wife, and an engine driver. Although the studio recording of this song can tire after repeated listening, the various live performances released in the years that followed are fantastic and amazing examples of what can be performed on stage by a single quartet.

In the months prior to the release of *The Who Sell Out*, the band released a couple of singles that, with the exception of the April release "Pictures of Lily," are generally unremarkable and would later surface on compilations and on the deluxe CD edition of *The Who Sell Out*. This album is the first time we see Townshend's lasting genius in full display, as the very structure of the record was unlike anything else ever committed to disc. It is presented as a real-time capture of a pirate radio station, where songs and commercials are interspersed throughout, and the first side in particular conveys an experience that was likely familiar to most British kids, who could only hear rock music, American R & B, ska, and the like on pirate radio.

Pirate radio, a form of illegal and unlicensed radio broadcasting, was the main conduit through which British teens first heard their music in the mid-1960s. Until the BBC was restructured in 1967 with four stations to serve a wider English listenership, pirate radio stations made use of a legal loophole that allowed them to broadcast from international waters using anchored ships or disused sea forts. Radio Caroline and Radio London are the two most widely remembered pirate stations, so the Who spoofed a Radio London broadcast hour and pinched actual radio jingles used on Radio London, interspersing them throughout the album.

The album begins with one of the real Radio London jingles, which they used without credit or permission, and leads into "Armenia City in the Sky," a song composed not by Townshend but by Speedy Keen, who would go on to lead Thunderclap Newman and whose Townshend-produced hit "Something in the Air" would become a classic thanks to its effective use in the soundtrack for *The Magic Christian*. But as the opening track, "Armenia City in the Sky" features a plethora of psychedelic colors with backward guitar washes of echo and other sound effects. This is perhaps the best Pete Townshend song composed by someone other than Townshend.

Another Radio London sound bite is used to link into the first "commercial-in-a-song," John Entwistle's "Heinz Baked Beans." In barely over a minute, John takes us through a family dialogue in which a child, a husband, and a grandfather all ask what they will have for their tea, the answer of course being "Heinz Baked Beans." Entwistle's bass playing and brass fanfares are accompanied with martial drumming, cinema organ, and old-timey banjo strumming. Another pinched Radio London jingle and we are off to one of Townshend's mildly naughty songs, "Mary Anne with the Shaky Hands," a companion song of sorts to their 1966 single "Pictures of Lily." Aside from the topic of our heroine, who gives perfectly wonderful happy endings, it is easy to overlook the actual song, the tight instrumental accompaniment, and the perfect, spot-on vocals. This is followed by Keith extolling the joys of Premiere Drums, his preferred drum maker.

Just a few seconds pass before we have another ripped-off Radio London sound bite. "Odorono" is a witty Townshend tune that extols the virtues of using underarm deodorant, a necessity for the auditioning heroine of the song. No matter how beautifully dressed and prepared she is to deliver a perfect performance, a good dose of pong (body odor) would be enough to scuttle the entire prospect. This is punctuated with another Radio London jingle, and though these jingles were recorded by a company in Texas, the "smooth sailing" of the arrangement could have come from the BBC Light Programme. While all tongue in cheek, "Tattoo" is a mildly humorous tale of two boys who go off "past the barber and gymnasium" to get their first tattoos. In the decades before artistically applied ink became the norm on bodies of both genders, tattoos were strictly masculine affairs with crudely drawn figures on male skin that was far from smooth and likely to wrinkle and stretch, deforming whatever artwork was enshrined on the wearer's arm, chest, back, or whatever body part chosen to subject to the talents of the ink handler.

Despite its minor key construction, "Our Love Was, Is" is Townshend's effort at creating overcast sunshine pop. The lyrics make every attempt to be sincere in their expression of love toward one's intended, but quickly enough, the song is derailed into a noisier and more raucous expression of the "famine . . . frustration" of love. Another pinched jingle is followed by the shortest advertisement, this one for Rotosound Strings, which are necessary to "hold your group together." This is used as a leap-off point for the one classic psychedelic song on *The Who Sell Out*, "I Can See for Miles." The unbridled heaviness of this song has given it longevity beyond that afforded to the album. It is easy to overlook the excellent vocal work of this song, which is all quite high in the vocal register and in tune.

Side two begins with a rough advertisement for the Charles Atlas bodybuilding method. "I Can't See You" is a perfectly agreeable sunshine pop tune from Townshend. The sincere, spot-on delivery of vocals, a clean arrangement, and enough variety of content give this song much more than we might otherwise afford to a love song from the Who. Entwistle's "Medac" is wonderfully off-kilter. The Radio London jingles are now finished, and the commercials-in-a-song are nearly complete. For the last third of the album, the Who takes the listener into darker territory to provide more than a hint about the arrival of *Tommy*. "Relax," with its dominant organ ostinato, becomes a wonderful psychedelic freak-out, a cacophonous mess that resettles back to the first theme of the song and a barely extolled request to "Relax." John Entwistle's excellent "Silas Stingy" follows "Relax," and like his best gothic work, this song is about a sad man whose stingy nature still manages to leave him with absolutely no money. All of John's tropes are here, swirling organ, brass, great vocal harmonies (his vocal colorings cover the range from his guttural baritone to his controlled falsetto), and a complex arrangement that ends on a major chord to conclude the song. "Sunrise" is Townshend's dry run in the lead-up to *Tommy*; his solo album, *Who Came First*; and the incomplete *Lifehouse* album. The delicate guitar plucking with his lead vocal (in place of Daltrey's) makes this an intimate chamber work, a love song that, even for Townshend, is unusually intimate and personal. Lacking any other members of the band, "Sunrise" is an awkward fit amid the Who's psychedelic exercises, but it is a perfect aperitif in advance of our first proper introduction to what will come the following year in *Tommy*.

There are many tracks, most of which were made commercially available on various Who compilation records and re-issues of *The Who Sell Out* beginning in 1990s, that use the name "Rael," including the one originally released in 1967. This version was retitled "Rael 1" for the 1995 reissue. The bonus tracks on that album featured "Rael 2," and on the 2009 edition, there is "Rael Naïve." In combination, there are preliminary mixes and other versions, none of which are surprising because this song would become the Who's bridge en route to the creation of *Tommy*. Other advertisement pieces and Radio London jingles that were left off the original album round out the 2009 double-CD set. When *The Who Sell Out* is looked at as a complete work in its original form, the many fragments and pieces that were left behind in 1967 demonstrate how this album is an important work, not only for the psychedelic canon but in Townshend's creative trajectory. At the end of 1967, rock music was in transition from the freedom that had been infused into popular music to a more serious, and at times darker, genre. *The Who Sell Out* is a final poke in the eye to those who rejected the power of rock and roll in exchange for peace and love.

THE YARDBIRDS: *LITTLE GAMES* (JULY 1967)

The Yardbirds may be an unlikely inclusion in this volume, but their contributions to rhythm and blues, psychedelia, and hard rock, in addition to their role as a launchpad for three of the rock era's greatest guitarists, Eric Clapton, Jeff Beck, and Jimmy Page, places the band as a major contributor to the psychedelic movement. *Little Games*, the final album released during the band's tenure, and only in the United States, is the Yardbirds' most eclectic and progressive record. With Jeff Beck's removal/departure from the band, they were reduced from a quintet to a quartet and settled into their final configuration with Jimmy Page as the band's sole guitarist. Following the release of this album, Page, with manager Peter Grant, reconstructed and renamed the Yardbirds as the New Yardbirds in mid-1968 before settling on the name Led Zeppelin. Keith Relf and Jim McCarty were less interested in the heavier sound driven by Page and left the group by mid-1968. One of Page's songs on *Little Games*, "White Summer," is a precursor to "Black Mountain Side" from Led Zeppelin I, released two years following *Little Games*, and shows the band moving into entirely new territory. The Yardbirds officially ended in July 1968, but the Page-led band performed concerts as the New Yardbirds until October of that year, when Led Zeppelin was born.

The Yardbirds never reached the heights of success achieved by the Rolling Stones, and in the decades following their 1968 demise, they were better known for their trio of groundbreaking guitar virtuosi than for their albums and singles. Unlike the Rolling Stones, who preceded them as the house band at the Crawdaddy Club, the Yardbirds had difficulties in evolving beyond their core R & B roots but also battled with unequal levels of technical proficiency among its members. The Stones were also rhythm and blues purists, but that quintet was more equally balanced in terms of technical proficiency and versatility. Brian Jones's unique talents as a multi-instrumentalist and Mick Jagger's near-perfect emulation of the dialect and phrasing of American blues singers put them in a league quite distinct from the Yardbirds.

While U.S. releases of albums by artists such as the Beatles or the Rolling Stones often appeared in collections that were generally unrelated to their releases in the United Kingdom, the Yardbirds albums released in the United States bore absolutely no resemblance to their English counterparts and were out of print for over twenty years after the band officially ended in mid-1968. In the United States, they were released on Columbia's (CBS) Epic Records imprint, and in the United Kingdom, they were on EMI/Columbia. By the time *Little Games* was released in North America in July 1967, EMI did not bother to release it for the English market, and for many years, it remained unavailable to fans on both sides of the Atlantic.

The band's first hit single, "For Your Love," in the spring of 1965 precipitated Eric Clapton's departure from the band. The Graham Gouldman–penned single is a pure pop classic with an arrangement that features bongos and the harpsichord and is a perfect soundtrack for

Swinging London. With Clapton's departure, Jeff Beck was hired to fill his place in the band, and with him, they produced their self-titled debut studio album (the first album release of the Yardbirds in 1964 was *Five Live Yardbirds*). Released in the United Kingdom simply as *The Yardbirds*, it would become known as *Roger the Engineer*, in reference to the album sleeve artwork that featured Chris Dreja's pencil sketch illustration of recording engineer Roger Cameron. The record was reconfigured for release in the United States as *Over Under Sideways Down*, minus two tracks from the U.K. album. All songs featured on the album were composed by the group's members, but their style was still rooted in their blues origins.

Following the departure of bassist Paul Samwell-Smith, Jimmy Page agreed to cover on bass until guitarist Chris Dreja could master the instrument. Once Dreja took over bass duties, Page moved back to guitar, and the band entered its brief Beck/Page guitar lineup. With both guitarists in gear, the music began to take on a more contemporary, prepsychedelic edge with songs such as "Happening Ten Years Time Ago." In early 1966, prior to Page joining the band, they released one of the first psychedelic singles, "Shapes of Things." Another pop earworm produced by Giorgio Gomelsky, "Shapes of Things" became one of the two Yardbirds songs, along with "For Your Love," to be sustained on FM radio long beyond the band's lifetime. Beck left the group in the last weeks of 1966, which left Page as the sole guitarist, and the now four-piece unit entered its slowly unraveling final phase.

Producer Mickie Most, who in 1967 was producing Donovan's most memorable albums, came to the Yardbirds on a directive from CBS to produce the album. Most's legacy is a point of contention among fans of the various artists he produced, but for this album, his work was not well received and remains a black eye on the band's discography. Both Page and drummer Jim McCarty distanced themselves from the record, and its poor chart performance did nothing to enhance its image among the band's core fan base in the decades that followed. Mickie Most used future Zeppelin bassist John Paul Jones in lieu of Chris Dreja on many of the album's sessions at both Olympic Studios and De Lane Lea Studios.

The album was released in midsummer 1967, following *Sgt. Pepper's Lonely Hearts Club Band*, *The Doors*, *Are You Experienced*, and *Surrealistic Pillow*, and when compared against those albums, *Little Games* has many strong qualities in its favor. Jimmy Page's guitar work is the highlight of the album and provides us with a glimpse of the sounds he would unleash with Led Zeppelin. There are two covers, the album's title track and "No Excess Baggage," but all other original tracks are clearly of the era and would be at home on most any psychedelia-themed playlist. The Yardbirds lead vocalist, the late Keith Relf, never tried to emulate black American singers, as Mick Jagger had so effectively done for the Rolling Stones. His purely English vocal qualities are more convincing, confident, and effective on *Little Games* than they were on the band's prior recordings, perhaps because the songs are so unlike anything the group had recorded to that point. Most makes the best use of double-tracking Relf to provide the songs with timbral variety and depth. This album would not have been delivered in its final form had Jeff Beck remained in the group; his absence provided Jimmy Page with room to provide wonderfully subtle and rich playing that lifts the entire album and is worthy of repeated listening.

The album was released both in mono and stereo and had a short print run. It was out of print before Page launched Led Zeppelin, but as that group achieved their stratospheric levels of fame, *Little Games* became the hard-to-find curio of Page's pre-Zeppelin career and ended up on a variety of bootleg collections. Since the 1990s, the album has been available in both mono and stereo mixes and has received a more generous opinion among fans of both the Yardbirds and Jimmy Page.

THE ZOMBIES: *ODESSEY AND ORACLE* (APRIL 1968)

Odessey and Oracle, like the Kinks' 1968 release, *The Kinks Are the Village Green Preservation Society*, is an autumnal psychedelic masterpiece and one of the most enduring albums of the psychedelic era. Like the Kinks, the Zombies were part of the British Invasion and had a U.S. No. 1 single early in 1965 with "Tell Her No," a song that is as fresh today as it was over a half century ago. Swept into the rush of the British Invasion, they were massively popular in the United States but had less success in their home country, where they released only one album. *Begin Here* was the U.K. album on Decca. In the United States, a reconfigured collection imaginatively titled *The Zombies* was released on the London Record subsidiary, Parrot Records.

The Zombies stood out from their English compatriots with a sound that was unlike any other British Invasion group. Piano and organ were at the forefront of the band's sound, and the harmonies found in Rod Argent's songs were clearly pop but infused with a soul-like moodiness. Like so many blues-based English beat groups in the early 1960s, they played a number of American blues and soul tunes in their shows and on their early singles, but for all their Englishness, they would never sound convincing when singing "Roadrunner," "Summertime," or "You Really

Got a Hold on Me," no matter how earnestly they tried. They did not rely on a shtick (like Freddy and the Dreamers) or a cartoonish front man (Herman's Hermits) but instead were a sharply dressed group who appeared to be enjoying what they did, no matter the coolness they tried to convey to their audiences. Their appearances on *Ready, Steady, Go!*, *Shindig*, and other shows are a prime example of mid-1960s cool.

The Zombies consisted of Rod Argent (keyboards), Paul Atkinson (guitar), Chris White (bass), Hugh Grundy (drums), and Colin Blunstone (vocals) and originally formed while at school in St. Albans, outside London, in 1961. The Beatles' "Love Me, Do," released in the fall of 1962, forever changed the trajectory of pop music, and for the hundreds of kids across England who played in bands, it demonstrated how they could create their own sound and identity. The Zombies took this directive and had one of the first beat groups led by a keyboardist, their primary songwriter Rod Argent. Liverpool's Gerry and the Pacemakers also had a pianist, but Les Maguire did not lead the band with his slick chops. For the Zombies, Argent's moody harmonies provided a core around which the rest of the group's sound fit into place, and Colin Blunstone's plummy and adept vocal stylings conveyed a range of emotions that could reach beyond the themes of teenage romance. Their early appearances show them borrowing the then fashionable high-button jackets and tapered trousers first displayed by the Beatles, but their sound was nothing like the Beatles, the Rolling Stones, or the Kinks.

Rod Argent and bassist Chris White were the primary songwriters for the band, and between 1964 and 1966, they turned out numerous singles. But with each release, they found their popularity waning, especially in their homeland. By 1967, their relationship with Decca had ended, and so they signed with the then relatively new CBS UK label. They secured the right to produce themselves and went into Abbey Road in the summer of 1967, soon after the Beatles had finished recording *Sgt. Pepper's Lonely Hearts Club Band*. The band's spirits were not at their peak during the recording of *Odessey and Oracle*, a result of their new label providing a miserly budget to make the record, fewer bookings for live appearances, and the commercial decline of the previous year where their singles were unable to attract fans. Although the album was recorded by a band at a crossroads, they had ultimately decided to disband by the time the album was released in the United Kingdom in spring 1968. There is a wonderful BBC studio track of the Zombies recorded by Kenny Everett (who called *Odessey* "the album of the century") for the closing segment of his show in which they nonchalantly mention they have broken up. Colin Blunstone is very matter-of-fact while talking about the failure of the album (*Odessey and Oracle*) in the charts.

The album was released in the United States in June of that year, with no success, but someone at Columbia decided to release "Time of the Season," the album's final track, as a single. By winter 1969, "Time of the Season" had made the No. 1 spot in the United States. The album was rereleased in response to the success of "Time of the Season," and the now disbanded Zombies had the biggest success of their career. CBS tried to convince them to regroup, but they wisely decided to reject that opportunity. CBS released a few additional songs under the Zombies name, but those faded into obscurity (without a live band to promote them) along with *Odessey and Oracle*.

The album retained a diehard fan base in both the United Kingdom and United States, for whom the album was an overlooked masterpiece. During the 1970s and into the 1980s, finding Zombies records in the shops required persistence and hunting skills. Decca/London released *The Zombies—The Best of . . .* for the Canadian market in 1982, in a dreadful stereo mix (all their singles were recorded in mono), and for many years, this was the only available long player from the Zombies. (In 2002, the Big Beat label released *The Zombies—The Decca Stereo Anthology*, which contained all their Decca sides in a tastefully mastered stereo mix. The album righted the sonic wrongs of the 1982 release and gave those songs their long-overdue presentation.) Rod Argent had, post-Zombies, gone on to modest success with his hard rock band, Argent, but the Zombies existed more in memory than reality unless you were one of the lucky few to have acquired a used copy of *Odessey and Oracle*.

Although CBS signed the band and gave them the freedom to self-produce, they provided a miserly recording budget of £1,000 (£18,000 or $22,000 in 2019), so the always disciplined and prepared group put their skills to the test, as there would be no room for error or multiple retakes. Abbey Road was still working on four-track machines, and not being the Beatles, who were given virtually unlimited studio access, the Zombies were booked into the studio for three-hour increments; so their well-rehearsed songs were recorded in workmanlike fashion. One advantage to their work at Abbey Road was the access they had to instruments they did not themselves possess. For example, the mellotron used by the Beatles was still in the studio and was used to great effect on this album.

The album opens with "Care of Cell 44" (originally titled "Prison Song" and then "Care of Cell 69," but the title was changed by their publisher), a seemingly dark song about a man coming home from prison to see his love. It was released as a single and vanished without a trace. The line "Watching the laughter play around your eyes" in a song about being released from prison and into freedom is pure magic. The harpsichord, mellotron, and Beach Boys–like backing vocals lift this song into glorious perfection.

The sublime love song "A Rose for Emily" is a borrowed title from a William Faulkner short story, though the song has no connection to Faulkner's story. The arrangement is unusually simple, with block chords on the piano with backing vocals. "There's loving everywhere, but none for you . . ."—Rod Argent is seldom given credit for his lyrics, but on this album, he was at his best. Chris White's "Maybe after He's Gone" has a beautiful arrangement, and Colin's vocals have an angelic air in the final round. White also composed "Beechwood Park," which carries an air of autumnal psychedelia and is not dissimilar to the evocative writing Ray Davies was developing at this time that would be borne out on *The Kinks Are the Village Green Preservation Society*, *Arthur (or the Decline & Fall of the British Empire)*, and *Muswell Hillbillies*. White's bass playing on the album is extraordinary, but it is only in this, the fourth song on the album, that we hear Paul Atkinson's guitar work. His understated playing had always been the timbral foil to Argent's keyboards on so many of their early hits, and on *Odessey and Oracle*, his playing was initially not as prominent. But on this song, his unique sound shines through. For a song with a distinctly English sense of place, White claims to have written it while on tour in the Philippines; so being halfway across the globe in a steamy tropical land somehow enabled him to evoke such clear memories of an England that even then was disappearing.

"Brief Candles" is another of Chris White's evocative songs of place. Like "A Rose for Emily," "Brief Candles" is a title borrowed from literature, but in this case, Aldous Huxley. Rod, Chris, and Colin share lead vocal duties and give the song a baroque-like air. Argent's "Hung Up on a Dream" closes side one of the album. The interplay of piano, mellotron, and guitar is simply fantastic, and Colin's vocal is absolutely perfect on this track. It is the first time on the album where the Zombies deliver a song that sounds psychedelic, ironically, on an album that captures psychedelia in its most delicious perfection. When listening to *Odessey and Oracle* on vinyl, this song gives side one a sense that a chapter has ended, and when you turn the record over, a new experience awaits you.

Side two opens with "Changes," a track that wears its *Pet Sounds* influence in full color. The entire band sings backing harmonies, the only time all five are featured in this configuration on a Zombies song. Blunstone recalls recording the vocals in Studio 3 at Abbey Road, which was kept on a strict schedule. He shares that once the clock hit the allotted end time, studio techs would enter the studio and set up for the next session, even if a take was in progress. He recalls that during one vocal take when they were all around the microphone, the studio technicians came in and began to move the piano located right next to them. White confirms what many listeners have observed on this song, namely, that they were out of time, and on the stereo mix, this error is clearly apparent. Rod Argent's "I Want Her, She Wants Me" was originally recorded by the Mindbenders, another British Invasion group, but the composer did not care for the changes they made to the song; so the Zombies recorded it for this album. Rod sings the lead vocal with Colin joining him on the chorus.

The next song, "This Will Be Our Year," is another upbeat, romantic song, this time from Chris White. Colin Blunstone describes the song's "enduring beauty and optimism," qualities that are not that often heard in psychedelia. The subject in psychedelia is often very internal and personal. Unless one was going to prattle on about the Be-In or a mass group event, songs that play upon the optimism possible in everyday life are few in the canon, save for "This Will Be Our Year" and a handful of other miniature gems. There are two distinct versions of this song on its various releases, one with a brass arrangement by their old producer at Decca, Ken Jones, which was the only outside force marshaled for the album. The brass parts are on both the thirtieth and fortieth anniversary mono mixes, but they are missing on the stereo mix for each edition.

With "Butcher's Tale," we enter the final turn to the end of the album. "Butcher's Tale" is the dark horse song on the album, and though overlooked at the time of its release, the song was very prescient for the time. When CBS released the album in the United States, this was the first single released, but it made no impact on the U.S. charts. Chris White, inspired by the stories of the Battle of the Somme in the Great War, composed this very personal anti-war song. He had lost his uncle in that battle, and his commentary on the futility of war was in line with the feelings of many in the anti-war movement; however, few would have connected the experiences of World War I and the Vietnam War. Colin did not want to sing this and felt his voice did not fit the song, so White sang it to Argent's harmonium accompaniment. The subtitle of the song "(Western Front 1916)" was changed by the record company to "(Butchers Tale 1914)," a change that automatically wiped out its connection to the Battle of the Somme.

Although Rod Argent wrote a majority of the band's songs, Chris White had the ability to cover a range of emotions quite differently from Argent's more subtle undertones. White could take us from the pastoral "Beechwood Park" to "Butcher's Tale" and then to "Friends of Mine," one of the most upbeat songs on the album. He wrote this about selected friends who were in the first flush of love, and the names of these people were recited in the backing vocal. It is a perfect balance to "I Want Her, She Wants Me," with its optimistic view of romance and love. Of the eight couples mentioned in the song, the second, "Paul and Molly," is likely about guitarist Paul Atkinson, who was married about this time.

"Time of the Season" is the song that sustained the decades-long legacy of *Odessey and Oracle*, and thanks to CBS, who seldom could get it right with artists who were not a priority, the single was released and became the band's posthumous hit single. The Zombies recorded this album in Studio 3 at Abbey Road with Geoff Emerick, the Beatles' primary engineer, at the boards for the album. "Time of the Season" was the last song composed for the album, an emergency tune needed to complete an otherwise finished album. Rod Argent went back to his flat and composed this tune, and because the band did not have time to rehearse the song in advance, getting it down in the studio became a pressure with time and money running out. Colin and Rod had their set-to because Colin was not immediately getting the song and had difficulty finding the song's not-so-simple phrasing. However, it was completed to the satisfaction of everyone, and with this, the Zombies closed out their recording career for the decade.

Drummer Hugh Grundy recalls that the song began to get airplay in Boise, Idaho, six months after the album was released in the United States. From there, the song rippled across the country, and before long, the single had worked its way to the top of the charts. The success of the song led CBS to ask the Zombies to reform and continue, but they had all gone on to new careers and projects; thankfully, they declined the offer.

The original cover released in the United Kingdom was a colorful painting by their friend Terry Quirk. It was done quickly, and he misspelled "Odyssey" as "Odessey." By the time the mistake was caught, the covers were already in preparation, and there was no time to make a change. The band kept up a pretense that it was an intentional take on "Ode," and, if anything, young fans probably had difficulty in learning how to correctly spell "Odyssey." When initially released in the United States, the cover used the colorful graphics found on the U.K. edition, but with the band name and title spelled out on the top of the sleeve.

When they rereleased the album the following year (its initial sales were so poor that it was pulled from circulation following its initial pressing), after the success of "Time of the Season," they used a ghastly design that pulled one image from Quirk's cover and enhanced it to fill the whole sleeve, adding a border around the figure. It was an absolute disaster of a design choice.

Rod Argent confirmed that Al Kooper returned to the United States from a scouting trip in the United Kingdom and had in tow over two hundred albums. He pulled this one, handed it to Clive Davis at Columbia/CBS, and described it as "a rose among thorns." Davis admitted to having passed on it when originally released, and to Davis's credit, it eventually was released. It was not released on the Columbia or Epic labels, the prime marquees at CBS, but on the lesser-known subsidiary, Date Records. After the initial flush of success for "Time of the Season," the album was once again removed from print and remained so until various (and sometimes sonically inferior) editions began to show up on compact disc. Reissues on the Ace or Big Beat labels have restored the album to its original glory and its rightful place among other masterpieces of the period.

CHAPTER 3

Impact on Popular Culture

The impact of psychedelia would reach beyond the usual topics of music, fashion, media, and youth culture. The sheer numbers of baby boomers who came of age in the 1960s would drive the ongoing impact of rock music in its various forms, which included, among others, the psychedelic movement. Universities and colleges were filled to near capacity with young students, while the United States maintained a standing army that continued to swell as greater numbers of young men were sent to Vietnam and all corners of the globe to support America's role in the Cold War. The changes in fashion that accompany any freshly minted cultural movement were pushed to new boundaries when bold and bright colors were integrated into the fashions for both men and woman, and the media was ready to feast on the opportunities set into motion as a result of psychedelia.

The emergence of FM radio as a medium on which to broadcast rock music in stereo began to gain momentum in the late 1960s and reshaped the FM band as a model for music, talk, educational, and commercial broadcasting. The term *album-oriented rock* (AOR) was created precisely because FM stations did not limit their playlists to songs under three minutes, and before the end of the 1970s, FM radio listenership had outpaced AM radio. Many music stations on the AM band moved to the sonically superior FM band in the 1980s, leaving AM for minority-language and music, sports, news, and political broadcasting. American kids first experienced the Beatles and the Rolling Stones on AM radio while less than a decade later they would experience the music of Santana or Pink Floyd in stereo on numerous FM stations.

Commerce also changed, both in England and the United States, in response to the shifting economies that were fed by the psychedelic movement. The record industry changed its business model when it was apparent that millions of dollars from the sales of rock music were being regularly deposited into their coffers, so major labels in the United States had to adapt to a new commercial model; they borrowed sales and marketing methods from the pages of the burgeoning independent record companies. In 1967, record sales totaled more than $1 billion of product, double the amount shifted just a decade earlier, and LP sales outstripped the sales of the ever hearty and seemingly indestructible singles market. The Beatles' extraordinary and unrelenting success required that record labels look at how they ran their businesses. Rock and roll was no longer an American genre centered around Elvis Presley, Chuck Berry, and a handful of artists; it was now an English practice that was enormously popular among teenagers and young adults of the baby boom generation, and it would move millions of dollars' worth of records.

The Beach Boys, followed by the Beatles, changed the model of pop artist (the Beach Boys and the Four Seasons were among the few American groups who survived and flourished during the British Invasion). It was no longer mandatory that the songwriter be distinct from the recording artist. Performers who could generate their own material became the rule more than the exception, and when the majors latched on to popular music (Elvis Presley at RCA, the Beatles and the Beach Boys at EMI, the Rolling Stones at Decca/London, and the Kinks at Pye/Reprise), the record companies became enormously wealthy on the sales of rock and roll; yet, they were blind to the almost instantaneous changes that began to occur in popular music.

One factor responsible for the popularity of psychedelic music can be directly traced to numerous independent record labels that arose in the 1960s. In the United States, independent labels released the prepsychedelic garage rock of the Seeds (GNP), the Turtles (White Whale), and the 13th Floor Elevators (International Artists), while medium-sized companies such as Liberty, Cameo-Parkway, Phillips, and Dot also released a number of new and exciting artists from this period.

The major record labels in the pre–rock and roll world of the United States in the 1960s included Columbia (CBS), RCA, Capitol, and, to a lesser extent, Liberty, Dot, Mercury, Atlantic, and Warner Bros. Each company already had their niche in the marketplace. CBS made a fortune on Broadway cast albums and middle-of-the-road (MOR) artists. Jazz was king at Atlantic and Mercury. Capitol was a jazz and light music label that also scored well in country music. Although these genres sold reasonably well over the course of the 1950s and early 1960s, with rock and roll, these companies would reap riches of the sort never seen in their line of business. Classical music was subsidized by mainstream sales at all the labels, but these sales began to decline both in the number of releases and in total sales. By the 1970s, American labels had all but given up on classical music and relinquished the genre to English, Dutch, and German companies, who led the field not only in commercial recordings but also with technological developments in both recording and playback hardware.

Despite the transnational realignment of the music business, it would be the mid-1960s before the major labels put much effort into understanding rock music. Even then, it was only when they noticed their sales had begun to dry up in their otherwise dependable specialty areas that they realized the market for records had shifted from older and more affluent customers to the exploding teenage market. RCA had Elvis Presley, and Capitol had the Beatles and the Beach Boys; however, it would be a few years before they realized these acts were not an anomaly but were the future. Capitol Records did try to make a dent (with limited success) with garage rock and psychedelic groups such as Quicksilver Messenger Service, the Chocolate Watchband, Music Machine, and Pink Floyd, but most labels were simply out to make a quick sale to the teen market before the "fad" wore out.

It was not until 1965 (a decade after they bought Elvis Presley's contract from Sun Records) that RCA took a chance on the San Francisco folk-rock group Jefferson Airplane, and Columbia made a serious effort to promote popular music when it signed the Byrds and Donovan. Aside from a few signings at the majors, it was the independent and niche labels who took a chance on the newest psychedelic bands. Medium-sized labels such as Elektra, Atlantic, and MGM enabled psychedelic music to break-out as both a financial and cultural force in the United States. It was quite different in the United Kingdom, where EMI, Decca, and Pye were more daring in their releases of beat and garage rock in the years leading up to 1966.

The substantial difference in business practices between England and the United States was down to one simple medium—radio. In the United States, radio was a multilevel commercial resource for all ages. Urban centers had multiple stations that broadcast a combination of music, sports, and news as part of a larger commercial service. In England, the monopoly designed by the BBC set limited hours per day for playing records because their arrangement with the Musicians Union required that a majority of the music that they broadcast be performed in studios managed by the BBC. It was the pirate radio business model that emerged in the early 1960s where British teens were introduced to the idea that radio existed to play their music. Beginning with Radio Luxembourg in the mid-1950s (the station had been in operation since the 1930s, but beginning in the 1950s, they broadcast American rock and roll) and from 1964 to 1967 with Radio Caroline and Radio London, pirate radio was the sole resource available to English teens to hear the best popular music. The Marine Broadcasting Offences Act of 1967 put an end to pirate stations while also loosening the restrictions on the BBC's policy for programming popular music. These stations were at the peak of their popularity just as psychedelic music was at its peak both in terms of popularity and cultural influence.

In 1965, Clive Davis was the administrative vice president of CBS Records and one of the first executives at the majors to realize artists like Donovan and Janis Joplin were the future of the music business; he was determined that Columbia would embrace new artists and promote a current voice in music. He was instrumental in redirecting Columbia Records away from the influence of rock and roll–hating Artists & Repertoire (A&R) director Mitch Miller, who left the label in 1965 in part because he did not want to handle rock music and saw his own once sizable sales numbers shrinking with each passing month. Davis had proved his mettle to the company in 1963, when he was given the task of reining in Bob Dylan, who had threatened to leave Columbia Records in response to the poor sales of his debut record. His skills of negotiation led to other sucesses and resulted in his becoming the administrative vice president for Columbia Records.

Columbia signed the Byrds in 1965, and in 1966, Davis personally made his first rock signing to the label with Donovan, who would release a string of successful albums on Epic/CBS. He invested in a number of smaller and less successful groups (Moby Grape, the Peanut Butter Conspiracy, and Pacific Gas and Electric), but his belief in the artistry and power of Janis Joplin led him to put her recordings on the front line of promotion and marketing at Columbia. He went on to sign Santana and Sly and the Family Stone, two groups less frequently considered contributors to psychedelia. Before he was fired from CBS in 1973, he also managed to acquire Pink Floyd for their North American releases. The risks taken by Warner Bros., Elektra, and Atlantic ensured these labels would grow from being modestly sized niche labels into major players in rock music and would by the 1970s, coalesce into a marketing, sales, and distribution powerhouse as WEA (now known as Warner Music Group),

The business of buying and selling records also changed. To accommodate the massive number of records demanded by the youth market, savvy entrepreneurs opened shops that were solely dedicated to sales of records. The flood of new recording artists coming to market required record retailers to adjust how they did business. In the United States, independent record retailers may have thrived in their limited markets, but until the mid-1960s, it was typical for most Americans to buy records through appliance stores, drugstores (Woolworth's), department stores (Sears), and musical instrument stores (Wallach's Music City). Beginning in the 1950s with the wealth of jazz recordings available in the newly introduced long-playing (LP) format, and followed in the 1960s with the massive sales of pop music and rock and roll on both 45 rpm singles and long-playing albums, the world of retail record sales had evolved to a point where music fans could visit shops that only carried music and allowed their customers to listen to and compare products. In the 1950s, the Commodore music shop was already in its second decade and was the source for the best records in Midtown Manhattan. Sam Goody would become one of the early chain record stores in the Eastern United States. In Los Angeles, Wallach's Music City was a nirvana for music fans. At Wallach's, you could buy instruments, sheet music, records, and music playback equipment. The opening of Tower Records in the 1960s brought to consumers the world of large-scale, discounted records in virtually all genres of music. It was a perfect commercial storm to complement the explosion of popular music in the 1960s.

In England, where retail record sales had been a thriving business from the very start of the era of commercial recordings, two World Wars and a battered economy changed how music was consumed. Aside from the now deceased His Master's Voice (HMV) record store on Oxford Street, buying records outside of London meant you bought records through drug stores, furniture stores, or by mail order, like American music fans. The popularity of jazz and rock and roll enabled a new kind of retailer to emerge in the United Kingdom. Brian Epstein's NEMS music stores helped to shape a new model for the record retail business by providing a store that carried any record you may want. His success at selling music in Liverpool was known to the label bosses in London, who noted that Mr. Epstein's shop could move any and all product. New retailers emerged to serve a new youth culture, such as Musicland Records, one of the first English record shops to expand their R & B store to include psychedelic music. One Stop Records and Town Records were started by young entrepreneurs who cashed in on the demand for this music, but perhaps the most influential shop was on the King's Road. The Chelsea Drugstore was located down the road from hip clothier Granny Takes a Trip, and it ignored the conventional rules of urban commerce. It was open sixteen hours a day, seven days a week, and had three floors of various goods and services and included a record shop. The store was immortalized in the Rolling Stones' 1969 classic "You Can't Always Get What You Want" and served as inspiration for Stanley Kubrick when he required a record store from the future in *A Clockwork Orange*. While independent record shops could hold a few customers, the Chelsea Drugstore's large footprint could accommodate a critical mass of the psychedelic generation, but it too would fade away and close in 1971.

One of the more unusual marketing success stories concerns the Moody Blues. Although the Moody Blues were often derided by critics and fans of "real" psychedelic music, their digestible proto-baroque-psychedelia-en-route-to-progressive rock was enormously successful. Decca granted the band their own vanity label, Threshold, through which they would make their mark both as a lifestyle brand and as a record label. They opened a series of suburban record shops under the Threshold name that were focused on the label's releases (primarily the Moodies) but also carried a wealth of psychedelic records. They opened shops in Chichester, Birmingham, Surrey, and Swindon, making it far easier for kids in the provinces to get the latest discs without having to rely on the limited access of nonspecialty shops or having to travel into London. Threshold, like the Beatles' Apple Records and the Beach Boys' stillborn Brother Records, was supposed to serve as a platform for new artists, but it ultimately served as the label on which the Moodies released their own records, starting with *To Our Children's Children's Children* in November 1969. The stores proved themselves to be a successful retail shop that provided the latest music for fans who otherwise might not have easy access to these records. The spirit of the independent retailer was most fully realized with Sir Richard Branson who launched his Virgin brand with the Virgin Records shop in 1971 that, before the end of the decade, would evolve into the Virgin Megastore. The Virgin brand would be affixed to multiple goods and services and enabled Branson to succeed in the commercial marketplace long after his competitors had closed shop.

Since Al Jolson appeared in *The Jazz Singer*, music and movies have been well-suited companions. Rock and roll artists as early as Elvis Presley found film to be a complementary medium for their work. The Frankie and Annette movies from American International Pictures were a perfect blend of lightweight comedy with hit songs of the day. The Beatles' *A Hard Day's Night* (1964) demonstrated how music could be captured as a visual language, and Richard Lester, the film's director, pioneered many techniques that would be used over a decade later in music videos.

Psychedelic music was an ideal match for both the small and large screens. The adoption of color television in the United States during the mid-1960s also lent itself to a medium where the visuals were awash in color. The Monkees were a manufactured fictional group modeled on the Beatles circa *A Hard Day's Night* and had a half-hour show on the NBC television network from 1966 to 1968. The visuals for their show were bold and colorful, and while their music was decidedly unpsychedelic, television was their medium, not music. When the television show ended in 1968, they had four No. 1 charting albums, and, in the process, this fictional band became a real band who broke away from their fictional small-screen counterparts to perform live in concert. By 1967, their television show had become more surreal as viewer ratings declined. After the show finished its run in early 1968, they set to making a feature-length film, *Head*. The accompanying soundtrack had psychedelia-infused works and is one of their most innovative albums.

Psychedelic themes and imagery were central in a number of films from the late 1960s: *Easy Rider* (Dennis Hopper, 1969); *Zabriskie Point* (Michelangelo Antonioni, 1970); *2001: A Space Odyssey* (Stanley Kubrick, 1968); *The Trip* (Roger Corman, 1967); *Magical Mystery Tour* (the Beatles, 1967); *Head* (Bob Rafelson, 1968); and *Psych-Out* (Richard Rush, 1968). Antonioni's *Blow-Up* (1966) captured a slice of the scene in Swinging London, while Peter Whitehead's *Tonite Let's All Make Love in London* (1967/1968) was a semidocumentary film that attempted to offer a more realistic view of London's new scene. *Yellow Submarine* (George Dunning, 1968) was a spectacularly disembodied experience in which the animated Beatles traveled on a journey through Pepperland. The animation techniques used in this movie were of the highest quality and captured the intensely beautiful colors that paralleled a psychedelic experience.

There are plenty of B and C movies that run the gamut from exploitation films to self-indulgent exercises and attempt to capture the heightened sights and sounds of a hallucinatory experience, but do not warrant discussion or inclusion in this volume. The film *Monterey Pop* perhaps is the best concert movie to feature many of the period's leading musical artists, and the film *Woodstock* shows the end of the 1960s in its marvelous and muddy glory. The dark underbelly of the psychedelic era was captured in Albert and David Maysles film, *Gimme Shelter,* which documented the final weeks of the Rolling Stones' 1969 US tour. The film climaxes with the Rolling Stones' free concert at Altamont Speedway where a fan, Meredith Hunter, was killed by the Hells Angels who had been secured by the Stones to handle security. Psychedelia was composed of, and informed by, so many literary, musical, social, and media elements that its influence would never disappear but instead imbed itself through various pathways into mainstream music, film, art, and fashion before it experienced a renaissance in the aftermath of the punk and new wave movements of the late 1970s.

CHAPTER 4

Legacy

The psychedelic music of the 1960s never really ended; over the next two decades, it was transformed and absorbed into other genres and styles of music. While the genre was in its later stages with Hendrix and Joplin, it began to evolve in new directions before the decade was out. The English band Yes successfully bridged psychedelia into progressive rock. The group was the successor to one of England's late-period psychedelic groups, Mabel Greer's Toyshop, who never released any records during their brief existence; however, appearances on John Peel's influential BBC radio programs exposed their sound to a larger audience. When Chris Squire and Peter Banks joined from another psychedelic outfit, the Syn, the core group of what would soon become Yes was in place. With the addition of Jon Anderson on vocals, they quickly moved into the first iteration of Yes with the additions of Tony Kaye and Bill Bruford on keyboards and drums, respectively. Their first three albums presented a band that was clearly a descendant of the rapidly fading (save for Pink Floyd and Soft Machine) psychedelic scene, but they also managed to breathe new life into a sound that would become the core of progressive rock.

This period in the band's evolution is brilliantly captured on the album *Something's Coming: The BBC Recordings 1969–1970*. These recordings contain songs from their first two studio albums, *Yes* and *Time and a Word*, and featured the original lineup of Jon Anderson (vocals), Peter Banks (guitar, vocals), Chris Squire (bass, vocals), Tony Kaye (organ, piano), and Bill Bruford (drums). Although Banks appeared on their sophomore long player, he was fired before its release and was replaced by Steve Howe, formerly of the freakbeat/psychedelic band Tomorrow. The third album, and first with Howe, *The Yes Album* (1971), showed the band moving away from the elegant, private school anarchy of their first two albums toward a more virtuosic progressive rock sound. While this album was a departure from its predecessor, Tony Kaye's Hammond organ remained a central timbre in the band's sound, and the song structures were not dissimilar to songs on their first two albums. Howe's expansive virtuosity gave the group a broader palate of sound, and the album featured their first major hit, "I've Seen All Good People." Following Kaye's departure, the band's overall sound dramatically changed with the addition of Rick Wakeman, and the first album with the Howe/Wakeman lineup, *Fragile*, became (and remains) a central work in progressive rock.

One of Yes' contemporaries on the London scene was the Robert Fripp–led band King Crimson. Formed in 1968 from the almost successful postpsychedelic outfit Giles, Giles and Fripp, King Crimson would feature a perpetually evolving membership, with Fripp as the band's one constant. Notable musicians who appeared with King Crimson throughout the 1970s to1990s included Bill Bruford, Adrian Belew, John Wetton, Boz Burrell, Greg Lake, Peter Sinfield (early Roxy Music collaborator), Mel Collins, and Tony Levin. The group made its live debut as one of the six opening acts for the Rolling Stones' legendary Hyde Park concert in 1969 (this was the Stones' first live performance since 1967, the first with new guitarist, Mick Taylor, and occurred two days following the death of the Stones' original guitarist, Brian Jones).

King Crimson has an unusually fragmented history, with different iterations of the band in each decade of the 1970s, 1980s, 1990s, and 2000s. In their first decade, they were an influence on the first generations of Yes and Genesis. While King Crimson has been accorded the respect and acknowledgment of peers and fans, they never achieved the same level of commercial success or recognition equal to those two groups. Robert Fripp, the central member for any version of King Crimson, would become more widely known for his unique sound (Frippertronics) and for the breadth of his collaborations. Fripp was one of the most influential musicians of the last half of the twentieth century and would become one of the architects of ambient music. He recorded a pair of seminal albums with Brian Eno, *No Pussyfooting* (1973) and *Evening Star* (1975), in addition to providing irreplaceable contributions to other Eno albums, including *Here Come the Warm Jets* (1973), *Another Green World* (1975), and *Before and After Science* (1977). His work with Eno led to collaborations with David Bowie and Talking Heads. He also appeared on Peter Gabriel's second and third solo albums, was a guest on Blondie's *Parallel Lines*, and produced albums by the vocal trio the Roches.

Another offspring of psychedelia came through the former West Germany. Groups emerged from West Germany who adopted elements of the progressive psychedelic scene, jazz, and experimental music and transformed it into the early forms of techno or, as Julian Cope described it in his book on the subject, "krautrock." Bands from Dusseldorf (Kraftwerk, Neu!), Cologne (Can), and Berlin (Cluster, Tangerine Dream) were among the prolific pioneers of early techno. Producer Conny Plank and a recording studio (Hansa Tonstudio) informally known as "Hansa by (at) the Wall" also are central to the development of the genre.

Can was the Germanic extension of a sound not dissimilar to that created by Soft Machine, and Cluster was a pioneer of early ambient music. In the 1980s, Can bassist Holger Czukay collaborated with Jah Wobble, David Sylvain, and the Eurythmics. Brian Eno collaborated with Cluster's two founders, Hans-Joachim Roedelius and Dieter Moebius, on two of his early ambient projects, *Cluster & Eno* (1977) and *After the Heat* (1978). Kraftwerk is the most widely known and commercially successful band of the genre, and they pioneered a robotic techno sound. The symbiosis that existed between the work coming from Dusseldorf and the emerging electronica being generated in Detroit by the Belleville Three helped to create the modern forms of techno that are known around the world. Neu! began as an offshoot of the early Kraftwerk (the English group Ultravox borrowed the graphic impact of Neu! on their first two albums as Ultravox! and worked with Neu! and Kraftwerk producer Conny Plank on their third, fourth, and fifth albums).

Kraftwerk achieved a level of international success that no other German group would match. Their first two albums were experimental rock albums and did not feature the electronic sound for which they would become known. Their fourth album, *Autobahn* (1974), was their first international hit record, and their sixth album, 1977's *Trans-Europe Express*, solidified the Kraftwerk sound. They were an influence on artists from David Bowie and Iggy Pop to the postpunk act Joy Division/New Order and inspired the development of the new romantic sound with bands such as Ultravox, the Human League, Japan, and others. Other hit albums, *The Man Machine* (1978) and *Computer World* (1981), followed, but after *Electric Café* (1986), the band released no new music until *Tour de France Soundtracks* (2003). Cofounder Florian Schneider left the group in 2008, leaving Ralf Hütter to work with an entirely new band that has continued to tour as of 2019.

Berlin replaced London and San Francisco as a city where "new" music was being reshaped and redefined, and musicians flocked to Berlin to best capture the sonic space of the city, similar to how bands flocked to San Francisco and London in the previous decade. *Low* (1977), *Heroes* (1978), and *Lodger* (1979) are David Bowie's "Berlin" Trilogy, even though *Heroes* was the only album recorded in its entirety in Berlin. Parts of *Low* were recorded in Berlin, and *Lodger* was recorded in Switzerland and New York. But they are a triptych that sprang from a single creative vein in Bowie's catalog. The work with Eno (on all three) and Fripp (on *Heroes*) is among Bowie's greatest, and along with his 1980 album *Scary Monsters (and Super Creeps)*, which also features Fripp, these records marked the end of Bowie's classic period.

Ultravox collaborated with Conny Plank on *Systems of Romance* (1978), *Vienna* (1980), and *Rage in Eden* (1981), bringing full circle the German successor to late psychedelia into the postpunk new wave movement of the late 1970s. In 1976, the full-scale arrival of punk rock in the United States, with the Ramones, Patti Smith, Television, and other groups from the CBGB's scene, and in England, with the Sex Pistols, Buzzcocks, the Clash, and countless other bands, set the stage for a revival of psychedelia. Punk helped to save rock music from the hopelessly overblown and disconnected forms of rock music that had become the norm in the 1970s. In the way psychedelia in England was developed on substantially different aesthetic and creative lines than its North American iteration in the 1960s, London- or U.K.-based punk had a radically different agenda and set of goals than its American counterpart. In the way 1960s psychedelia was borne from the electric and energetic forms of popular or beat music, psychedelia in the late 1970s was borne from the immediacy that punk rock brought to the mannered and bloated rock scene of the mid-1970s. Although there would be American new wave–based psychedelic bands, they did not achieve the same popularity or success as their U.K. peers, and they came onto the scene as the U.K.-based psychedelia was transforming itself into something new. As a result, there was little shared common ground across the continents between neo-psychedelic bands.

In the United States, the West Coast was home to a movement that was coined the Paisley Underground. This consisted of bands who drew inspiration from classic groups such as the Doors, Love, or the Byrds. The neo-psychedelic groups the Dream Syndicate, Green on Red, the Rain Parade, the Three O'Clock, and the Bangles all achieved a level of regional success, though the Bangles achieved mainstream popularity after Minneapolis-based Prince took them under his mentorship and authored their first Billboard hit, "Manic Monday." The Cramps were an unusual and fantastic hybrid of rockabilly and psychedelia. A majority of the late 1970s to early 1980s neo-psychedelic groups are largely forgotten, and while Prince's work was closer in spirit to the space funk of Parliament-Funkadelic than it was to the neo-psychedelic scene, his enormously successful recording career; his vanity label, Paisley Park; and his work that followed the film and accompanying soundtrack to *Purple Rain* demonstrated that he was a creative and spiritual heir to Jimi Hendrix. He was an otherworldly talent with a universal sexual appeal who could play Hendrix-styled psychedelia, funk, soul, rock, blues, or any form of music he chose to adopt, playing nearly every instrument on his albums. He also promoted other artists, such as Morris Day, the Time, Vanity, and the Bangles. And from Cleveland there was Pere Ubu, who blended a psychedelic/performance art aesthetic with a panoply of other influences.

In the late 1970s, a new breed of English psychedelic bands emerged from the punk and new wave scene. Early punk pioneers the Stranglers displayed a Doors-like sound with an emphasis on the organ in the center of their sonic fingerprint. There were also unremarkable bands such as Mood Six, but from Liverpool, Echo & the Bunnymen and the Teardrop Explodes were born from the remnants of an earlier, unrealized band, the Crucial Three. Its successor, A Shallow Madness, featured Ian McCulloch and Julian Cope, the two leading figures of Liverpool's neo-psychedelic scene.

The Teardrop Explodes had a fluid makeup with Cope, Gary Dwyer (drums), and David Balfe (keyboards) as the constant members across the majority of their records. They released three singles in 1979–1980 on the Zoo Records label (a Liverpool-based label founded by David Balfe and Bill Drummond) before they signed to Mercury Records in 1980. These singles had limited distribution but later were available on an unsanctioned compilation *Piano* (drawn mostly from vinyl transfers) but were given a cleaner release on the 2010 reissue of their 1980 debut album, *Kilimanjaro*. This album was produced by Balfe and Drummond under their creative moniker, the Chameleons. The soon-to-be hit producers Clive Langer and Alan Winstanley produced additional tracks on the album.

While the songs on *Kilimanjaro* are strong, the different production values between the Chameleons with Langer and Winstanley were noticeable. As a result, the album has a slightly schizophrenic feel, and the stripped-down psychedelia of their early singles was replaced by a more pop-friendly sound on *Kilimanjaro*. All the singles released from the album were strong tracks, with "Reward" reaching No. 8 on the U.K. singles chart. The album also featured "Books," a song composed by Cope with former bandmate Ian McCulloch, which was featured in a darker, moodier version on Echo & the Bunnymen's debut album, *Crocodiles* (1981), titled as "Read It in Books." Clive Langer produced the band's sophomore release, *Wilder* (1981), which featured a cleaner and more direct sonic fingerprint than their debut album. If their album sound leaned toward a more pop psychedelic feel, their singles demonstrated that Cope and company did not lose their experimental side. Single sides from 1981 to 1983, such as "Christ vs. Warhol," "Window Shopping for a New Crown of Thorns," "Ouch Monkeys," and others, were more rewarding songs for many fans.

Julian Cope and Ian McCulloch reportedly quit working with each other because of ego clashes, and in the case of the Teardrop Explodes, Cope's ego could not resist his sacking members of his band on a regular basis. Despite the disruptions to band personnel, the band recorded a wealth of new tracks that received a release on U.K.-only EPs, and an aborted third album, released posthumously in 1990 as *Everybody Wants to Shag . . . The Teardrop Explodes*, showed that the band was still expanding their sonic imprint. Although they were one of the most volatile bands of the neo-psychedelic scene, their reputation has far outlasted their brief existence, and their rare and hard-to-find tracks have appeared on various CD reissues.

Julian Cope pursued a very prolific career as a musician, author, and critic. His first two solo albums on Mercury were, despite their miniscule sales and gutted critical reviews, minor masterpieces. His next phase had him signed to Island Records, where they tried to make him a mainstream eighties pop star and were somewhat successful with "World Shut Your Mouth" (1985). To the irritation of Island, he released two brilliant lo-fi bootleg albums, *Skellington* (1989) and *Droolian* (1990), the latter as a fundraiser for 13th Floor Elevators front man Roky Erickson, who was rotting in the Texas penal system on a trumped-up charge of mail fraud. Cope's magnum opus, *Peggy Suicide* (1991), set the course for the remainder of his career.

Recorded against the backdrop of the infamous poll tax riots of 1990, *Peggy Suicide* represents a rebirth in Cope's canon. He perfected a neo-neo-psychedelic sound on *Peggy Suicide* and throughout the 1990s with *Jehovahkill* (1992) and *Autogeddon* (1994). A wealth of BBC Radio sessions that have been collected on various compilation albums show that Cope continued to be a groundbreaking artist. Beginning with *Peggy Suicide*, Cope adopted a harder sound reminiscent of Detroit bands MC5 and the Stooges. Garage rock bands such as the Seeds and sonic assault specialists Blue Cheer informed his work going into the new millennium. His refusal to tour the United States has made him a minor cult figure in North America, though he occasionally appears in concert in the United Kingdom and has resisted efforts to reunite the Teardrop Explodes for the oldies/nostalgia circuit.

Cope authored two volumes of memoirs, *Head-On* and *Repossessed*, and three volumes on music: *Krautrocksampler*, *Japrocksampler*, and *Copendium*. The first two volumes were among the earliest English-language publications on German and Japanese rock music. The self-identified arch-druid also authored *The Modern Antiquarian*, about stone circles and monuments of prehistoric Britain, and *The Megalithic European* covers the same topic on prehistoric sites on the continent. He continues to release new music on his Head Heritage label but has not had a U.K. charting album since 1996.

In the early 1980s, it might have appeared that Ian McCulloch was the more bankable and consistent artist when compared to his mercurial former bandmate Julian Cope. After being sacked by Cope from A Shallow Madness, McCulloch joined forces with Will Sergeant and Les Pattinson to form Echo & the Bunnymen, who played their first gig at the legendary Liverpool club Eric's, where they opened for the Teardrop Explodes. Their first single, "The Pictures on My Wall"/"Read it in Books" (1979) was released on the Zoo Records label and was produced by the Chameleons, aka Bill Drummond and David Balfe (the latter from the Teardrop Explodes and former bandmate in A Shallow Madness). Their debut album, *Crocodiles* (1980), is a brilliant album and is remarkable for its aesthetic and sonic cohesion. Echo & the Bunnymen was a stable band in that the four original members remained with the group until 1988, so albums over their first eight years followed a creative arc that concluded in 1988 with their most popular, self-titled album.

Echo & the Bunnymen had an image, with a well-coiffed lead singer and guitarist, Ian McCulloch; a guitarist with fantastic sonic abilities in Will Sergeant; and an understated but rhythmically obsessed bassist in Les Pattinson. With drummer Pete de Freitas, their albums conveyed an aural consistency one might expect on a concept album, but without the narrative themes. The follow-up to *Crocodiles*, the atmospheric and spacious *Heaven Up Here*, is in many ways a superior album, but it did not generate any hit singles, though the Hugh Jones–produced album was a New Musical Express Best Album awardee in 1981. Will Sergeant's guitar work is sonically diverse and is the central timbre across the band's reverb-heavy sound. The album is darker than its predecessor, but one of the standout tracks from this period is the B-side to "A Promise," the psychedelic minimalist drone "Broke My Neck," which was released in its original length on the 7" single. The 12" single "Broke My Neck (Long Version)" is a psychedelic masterpiece and a tour de force for Sergeant.

It would be nearly two years before Echo & the Bunnymen released *Porcupine*, a slow and bleak album that continued with themes they introduced on *Heaven Up Here*. The striking cover artwork featured photographs of the band captured on frozen waterfalls in Iceland. "The Back of Love" b/w "Fuel" and "The Subject" was released almost a year prior to the album and pointed toward a more aggressive and manic sound for the band, but when *Porcupine* was released the following year, "The Back of Love" was the fastest song on the album. Ian Broudie's production values captured a broad, spacious, and ghostly sound. Warner Bros. rejected the first version of the album, so they added layers of strings provided by L. Shankar, which gave the album a decidedly South Asian color. At the start of 1984, they released what may be their most enduring single, "The Killing Moon." The original version was a perfectly wonderful song, but the nine-minute 12" "All Night Version" is of the mood and ambience of "Broke My Neck (Long Version)" from 1981. The more consciously produced sound from David Lord resulted in a sonic masterpiece that presaged the sound of bands such as the Smiths.

Released in spring of 1984, *Ocean Rain* was a further departure for the band. The dark moodiness of their first three albums was replaced with a more traditional sheen thanks to the addition of a string accompaniments recorded in Paris. Not unlike the Doors' *The Soft Parade*, the dramatic change in instrumental arrangements makes this album somewhat perplexing for many fans. Keeping with tradition, the album scored Top 10 in England and barely made the Top 200 in the United States. The band had begun to come apart in the wake of this album, and in the three years that separated *Ocean Rain* and its follow-up, *Echo & the Bunnymen*, the band succumbed to various personal challenges. McCulloch's drinking began to derail his once carefully cultivated image, and his singing became ragged. Drummer Pete De Freitas descended further into drug dependency and had left the band at one point before asking to return. In a state of "barely there," they released what would be their most successful album and biggest single, "Lips Like Sugar." McCulloch left the group the next year, and Pete De Freitas was killed in a motorcycle accident. Sergeant and Pattison carried on with the name and new members and recorded what may have been their most psychedelic sounding album, *Reverberation*. The original trio reunited in the mid-1990s and released *Evergreen*. Pattinson left the group the following year while Sergeant and McCulloch continued to record into the new millennium.

The Psychedelic Furs were the most commercially successful group from the English neo-psychedelic scene. The London-based band sounded closer in spirit to early Roxy Music than to any 1960s psychedelic outfit, but they had a sound like no other band at the time. With CBS Records in their corner, they were destined to either become megastars or hollow caricatures of themselves. While en route to the former, their legacy sadly followed the latter. Their first two Steve Lillywhite–produced albums are excellent examples of the genre. They were noisy and dense but loaded with pop hooks and lead singer Richard Butler's raspy voice. The first eponymous album from 1980 had experimental techno-influenced songs ("India"), clever lyrical commentary ("Soap Commercial," "Imitation of Christ") and driving glam hard rock (the brilliant "Blacks/Radio"). The six-piece band made a lot of noise, and with Lillywhite's trademark gated drums (a texture he designed in collaboration with Hugh Padgham), the album had an enormous and intoxicating sound. The following year delivered *Talk, Talk, Talk*, a more restrained album with more pop hooks than its predecessor. The U.S. version of the album opened with a song that would, six years later, provide a lasting payday for the band, "Pretty in Pink." More desperate romanticism arrived in the moody verses of "No Tears," "Dumb Waiters," "She Is Mine," and "All of This and Nothing."

CBS/Columbia worked the band endlessly across North America in the hope of finally breaking into the lucrative new wave market, which to the majors was more a demographic than a musical movement. They had modest success with Elvis Costello and were embarking on greater successes with the Clash, but they fell flat with the Boomtown Rats and the Fabulous Poodles. Bands such as Journey, REO Speedwagon, Kansas, and Blue Oyster Cult were their top-dollar bands, so they surely deluded themselves into believing the Psychedelic Furs would be a success in a genre for which they had no understanding. CBS' international arms in England, Australia, and elsewhere proved to be more dependable resources until they began to mint millions of dollars with Michael Jackson's *Thriller*. CBS had pinched some of Motown's biggest stars, the Jacksons (including Michael as a solo artist), Diana Ross, and Marvin Gaye, and in the 1980s, they became one of the most successful labels in black music, a genre they also knew nothing about just a decade earlier.

In 1982, The Psychedelic Furs welcomed the release of their third album, the Todd Rundgren–produced *Forever Now*. The band was slimmed to a quartet and delivered an album with a more studio-driven sound; and while the singles "Love My Way" and "Goodbye" had dependable hooks, the album was not as strong a record when compared to their first two collections. In addition, CBS quit marketing them to the college-aged/art music crowd and turned its attention to a younger demographic, which ultimately had more financial success for the label. *Mirror Moves* followed nearly two years after *Forever Now*, with a band now slimmed to a trio by the departure of drummer Vince Ely. By this time, any psychedelic pretense of the band was a distant memory, and they were packaged as "neo-goth-art-lite-synth" band. The album was produced by Giorgio Moroder protégé Keith Forsey, who had achieved a great deal of success throughout his career in disco and with new wave artists such as Billy Idol. The Furs rerecorded their 1981 single "Pretty in Pink" for the 1986 John Hughes film of the same name, and in the process, they solidified their sound as a bland and utterly forgettable new wave band. Although this record made them a good bit of money, it killed the raucous early Roxy Music-influenced sound they had perfected on their first two albums.

The Soft Boys were a Cambridge-based band fronted by Robyn Hitchcock. They released two studio albums in their brief tenure, *A Can of Bees* (1979) and *Underwater Moonlight* (1980). After the breakup of the band in 1980, guitarist Kimberley Rew went on to international pop success with Katrina and the Waves, and Robyn Hitchcock created one of the most comprehensive catalogs of any postpunk/new wave artist. Both as a solo artist (1981–present) and in fronting Robyn Hitchcock and the Egyptians (1984–1993) (solo works and group albums overlapped each other), he created an extraordinary range of music that was anchored in a surreal and classic psychedelic sound. Cambridge native and Pink Floyd founder Syd Barrett was an influence on his work (the Soft Boys recorded Barrett's "Vegetable Man," one of Barrett's "lost" tracks with Pink Floyd that was, until 2015, available only on bootleg collections).

Unlike Echo & the Bunnymen (Warner Bros.) and the Psychedelic Furs (CBS), the Soft Boys never had the backing of a major label, and their records became cult classics. Both Warner Bros. and A&M Records gave Hitchcock's solo and Egyptians' catalogs some support in the 1980s and early 1990s, but his music never broke into the mainstream. A&M released an Egyptians compilation in 1996, and the following year, Rhino Records released a compilation of songs from his non-A&M catalog. Hitchcock continues to release new recordings on Yep Roc. Despite the lack of commercial success and releases on a variety of independent labels and major labels, he remains a consistent draw on the club circuit in the United States, England, Europe, and Australia. His work encompasses influences from Bob Dylan, Bryan Ferry, John Lennon, and others. He has released nearly two dozen studio recordings (in addition to more than a dozen live and compilation albums) and remains one of the most iconoclastic and fiercely independent artists. Perhaps more than any of his peer neo-psychedelic artists (excluding Julian Cope), he has encompassed the surreal and altered reality of early psychedelia in a body of music that is wholly contemporary.

The least well-known, though maddingly prolific, Anglo-Dutch band the Legendary Pink Dots (LPD) is a true psychedelic band that has lasted for nearly forty years with over fifty studio albums and more than forty compilation collections in their discography. None of their significant output has been released on a major label, but not unlike Robyn Hitchcock, LPD have an extensive and very dedicated following. Their sound borrows from early psychedelic pioneers Pink Floyd and Soft Machine but also bears the influences of ambient, industrial, progressive jazz, freeform, noise rock, and other forms. Their longevity has therefore been an influence on many artists in those genres. With a small core of regular long-term band members, they rotate through numerous guest musicians who enable them to create whatever hybridized style they decide to follow at a given time.

Psychedelic music lives on in the work of artists who followed the neo-psychedelic scene with psychedelic funk and hip-hop, trance, trip-hop, shoegazing, drone, acid trance, rave, and an endless variety of musical forms that has dominated popular music since the 1990s. Along with rhythm and blues and hip-hop, psychedelia has been the most influential form of popular music over the past seven decades.

Bibliography

Blake, Mark. *Pink Floyd—Pigs Might Fly: The Inside story of Pink Floyd.* London: Aurum Press, 2013. Kindle edition.
Bockris, Victor, and Gerard Malanga. *Up-Tight: The Velvet Underground Story.* New York: Quill, 1983.
Cale, John, and Victor Bockris. *What's Welsh for Zen: The Autobiography of John Cale.* London: Bloomsbury, 1999.
Carlin, Richard. *Godfather of the Music Business: Morris Levy.* Jackson: University Press of Mississippi, 2016. Kindle edition.
Cartwright, Garth. *Going for a Song: A Chronicle of the UK Record Shop.* London: Flood Gallery Publishing, 2018.
Cavanagh, John. *The Piper at the Gates of Dawn.* New York: Continuum International, 2003.
Clapton, Eric, with Christopher Simon Sykes. *Eric Clapton: The Autobiography.* London: Century, 2007.
Coleman, Ray. *Brian Epstein: The Man Who Made the Beatles.* London: Viking, 1989.
Cope, Julian. *Copendium: An Expedition into the Rock 'n' Roll Underworld,* London: Faber and Faber, 2013.
Cope, Julian. *Head-On: Memories of the Liverpool Punk-scene and the story of The Teardrop Explodes (1976–82)/Repossessed: Shamanic depressions in Tamworth & London (1983–89).* London: Thorsons, 1999.
Cross, Charles R. *Room Full of Mirrors: A Biography of Jimi Hendrix.* New York: Hyperion, 2005. Kindle edition.
Davis, Clive, with James Willwerth. *Clive: Inside the Record Business.* New York: Ballantine Books, 1974.
Doors, The, with Ben-Fong Torres. *The Doors.* New York: Hyperion, 2006.
Drummond, Paul. *Eye Mind: The Saga of Roky Erickson and the 13th Floor Elevators, the Pioneers of Psychedelic Sound.* Los Angeles: Process Media, 2007. Kindle edition.

Echard, William. *Psychedelic Popular Music: A History through Musical Topic Theory*. Bloomington: Indiana University Press, 2017. Kindle edition.
Einarson, John. *Forever Changes: Arthur Lee and the Book of Love*. London: Jawbone Press, 2010. Kindle edition.
Everett, Walter, ed. *Expression in Pop-Rock Music: Critical and Analytical Essays*. New York: Routledge, 2008.
Forde, Eamonn. *The Final Days of EMI: Selling the Pig*. London: Omnibus, 2019. Kindle edition.
Gelder, Ken, and Sarah Thornton, eds. *The Subcultures Reader*. London: Routledge, 1997.
Gray, Michael. *Mother!:The Frank Zappa Story*. London: Plexus Publishing, 1994.
Greenfield, Robert. *A Day in the Life: One Family, the Beautiful People, and the End of the Sixties*. Philadelphia: Da Capo Press, 2009.
Greenfield, Robert. *Timothy Leary: A Biography*. Orlando, FL: Harcourt, 2006.
Gulla, Bob. *Icons of R & B and Soul: An Encyclopedia of the Artists Who Revolutionized Rhythm*. 2 Vols. Westport, CT: Greenwood Press, 2008.
Harris, John. *The Dark Side of the Moon: The Making of the Pink Floyd Masterpiece*. Cambridge, MA: Da Capo Press. 2005.
Houghton, Mick. *Becoming Elektra: The True Story of Jac Holzman's Visionary Record Label*. London: Jawbone Press, 2016. Kindle edition.
Jack, Richard Morton. *Psychedelia: 101 Iconic Underground Rock Albums 1966–1970*. New York: Sterling Publishing, 2017.
Joynson, Vernon. *The Acid Trip: A Complete Guide to Psychedelic Music*. Lancaster, England: Babylon Books, 1984.
Kesey, Ken. *One Flew Over the Cuckoo's Nest*. New York: Viking Press, 1973.
Kopp, Bill. *Reinventing Pink Floyd: From Syd Barrett to the Dark Side of the Moon*. Lanham, MD: Rowman & Littlefield, 2018.
Kostelanetz, Richard, ed., with John Rocco, asst. ed. *The Frank Zappa Companion: Four Decades of Commentary*. New York: Schirmer Books, 1997.
Kubernik, Harvey. *1967: A Complete Rock Music History of the Summer of Love*. New York: Sterling Publishing, 2017.
Leary, Timothy, Ralph Metzner, and Gunther M. Weil, eds. *The Psychedelic Reader*. New York: Citadel Press Books, 2007.
Lewis, Miles Marshall. *33 1/3: There's a Riot Going On*. New York: Continuum International Publishing, 2006.
Lewisohn, Mark. *The Beatles Day by Day: A Chronology 1962–1989*. New York: Harmony Books, 1990.
Lewisohn, Mark. *The Complete Beatles Chronicle*. London: Hamlyn, 2003.
Lowe, Kelly Fisher. *The Words and Music of Frank Zappa*. Westport, CT: Praeger Publishers, 2006.
Marten, Neville, and Jeff Hudson. *The Kinks: A Very English Band*. London: Bobcat Books, 2007.

Mason, Nick. *Inside Out: A Personal History of Pink Floyd*. San Francisco: Chronicle Books, 2017.

Morgan, Robin, and Ariel Leve. *1963: The Year of the Revolution: How Youth Changed the World with Music, Art, and Fashion*. New York: HarperCollins, 2013.

Neill, Andy, and Matt Kent. *Anyway, Anyhow, Anywhere: the complete chronicle of THE WHO 1958–1978*. New York: Sterling Publishing Company, Inc, 2002.

Perry, Charles, Barry Miles, and Jon Savage. James Henke and Parke Puterbaugh, eds. *I Want to Take You Higher: The Psychedelic Era*. San Francisco: Chronicle Books, 1997.

Povey, Glenn. *The Complete Pink Floyd: The Ultimate Reference*. New York: Sterling Publishing, 2017.

Richards, Keith. *Life*. New York: Little, Brown, & Company, 2010.

Sanders, Daryl. *That Thin, Wild Mercury Sound: Dylan, Nashville, and the Making of* Blonde on Blonde. Chicago: Chicago Review Press, 2019. Kindle edition.

Savage, Jon. *1966: The Year the Decade Exploded*. London: Faber & Faber, 2015.

Scott, Paul. *Motherless Child: The Definitive Biography of Eric Clapton*. London: Headline Publishing Group, 2015.

Southall, Brian. *Jimi Hendrix: Made in England*. Ovolo Books, 2012. Kindle edition.

Stein, Mark, with Larry Schweikart. *You Keep Me Hangin' On: The Raging Story of Rock Music's Golden Age*. La Vergne, TN: Lightening Source, 2012.

Tamarkin, Jeff. *Got a Revolution!: The Turbulent Flight of Jefferson Airplane*. New York: Atria Books, 2003.

Thompson, Dave. *Cream: The World's First Supergroup*. London: Virgin Books, 2005.

Thompson, Dave. *Smoke on the Water: The Deep Purple Story*. Toronto, ON: ECW Press, 2004.

Walley, David. *No Commercial Potential: The Saga of Frank Zappa*. New York: Da Capo Press, 1996.

Wolfe, Tom. *The Electric Kool-Aid Acid Test*. New York: Picador, 1968. Kindle edition.

Wyman, Bill. *Rolling with the Stones*. New York: DK Publishing, 2002.

Zanes, Warren. *Revolutions in Sound: Warner Bros. Records, The First Fifty Years*. San Francisco, CA: Chronicle Books, 2008.

Zappa, Frank, with Peter Occhiogrosso. *The Real Frank Zappa Book*. New York: Poseidon Press, 1989.

Index

Abbey Road (EMI Studios), 41, 178–179, 181–182
ABKCO, 145
Acid Rock, xii, 14, 21, 24, 91
Adler, Lou, 112
Alice in Wonderland, 88
All-Night Rave, 7
Allen, Daevid, 152–153
Alpert, Richard (Baba Ram Das), 1
Altamont Free Concert, 9, 192
Ambient, xii, 125, 194–195, 203
Amboy Dukes, The
 "Baby Please Don't Go," 127
Anderson, Signe Toly, 85–86
Animals, The, 21, 44, 96–97, 115, 134, 154
 Love Is, 80–81
Antonioni, Michelangelo, 142, 191
 Blow-Up, 134
 Zabriskie Point, 134
Argent, Rod, 129, 177–183
Arthur Brown Set, The, 16, 52
Artwoods, The, 54, 62
Asher, Jane, 18, 38
Asher, Peter, 18
Atco Records, 84, 125
Atkinson, Paul, 178, 180, 182

Atlanta International Pop Festival, The, 8
Atlantic Records, 53, 55–56, 84, 125, 157, 159, 162, 169, 185–188
Avalon Ballroom, 7, 82, 127, 150
Avory, Mick, 101
Ayers, Kevin, 152, 154

Bach, Johann Sebastian, 84, 144
Back from the Grave, 124
Baez, Joan, 25, 45–46, 67
Bailey, David, 17
Baker, Ginger, 54–56, 59–60
Balin, Marty, 7, 9, 85–86, 89, 93
Bangles, The, 196–197
Barbarians, The, 126
Barrett, Syd, 13, 42, 46, 59, 70, 107, 132–142, 151–153, 202
 Barrett, 136
 The Madcap Laughs, 135–136, 153
 Opel, 136
BBC, 57, 65, 71, 104, 117, 123, 132, 134, 140, 142, 167, 172–173, 178, 187–188, 193, 198
Be-In (Human Be-In), xi, 9, 51, 92, 181

Beach Boys, The
  Anderle, David, 29
  Asher, Tony, 28, 30
  Brother Records, 29, 33, 190
  Dumb Angel, 28–30
  "Good Vibrations," 27–30
  Pet Sounds, 14, 27–30, 32, 38–39, 43, 160
  SMiLE, 28–35, 39
  Smiley Smile, 30–34
  The SMiLE Sessions, 31, 35
Beatles, The
  Beatlemania, 21, 35–36
  Epstein, Brian, 36, 38, 40, 115, 189
  Help, 38–39, 47, 62, 65
  "Hey Jude," 71
  Let It Be, 42
  Magical Mystery Tour, 40, 42, 191
  Revolver, 14, 28, 35, 37–39, 41, 43, 48–49
  Rubber Soul, 14, 38–39, 47
  Sgt. Pepper's Lonely Hearts Club Band, xi, 13, 27, 33, 39–42, 69, 102, 121, 137, 149, 176, 178
  The Beatles (The White Album), 34, 39, 58, 105
  Yesterday and Today, 39
  "You Know My Name (Look Up the Number)," 42
Beau Brummels, 21, 24, 128
Beck, Jeff, 63–64, 70, 97–98, 152, 158, 174, 176–177
Bee Gees, The, 81
Belleville Three, The, 195
Belli, Melvin, 113–114
Berkeley, 23, 121
Berry, Chuck, 19, 101, 186
Bhagwat, Anil, 37
Big Brother and the Holding Company, 21, 24, 82, 86, 98
Big Three, The, 54
Bito Lido's, 23
Black Panthers, The, 4, 9

Black Sabbath, 60
Blackmore, Ritchie, 61–64, 66
  Ritchie Blackmore Orchestra, 63
Blake, Peter, 41
Blind Faith, 60
Blondie, 194
Blood, Sweat & Tears, 126
Blue Cheer, 198
  Vincebus Eruptum, 42–43
Blues Incorporated, 54
Blues Magoos, The, 128
Blues Project, The, 125–126
Blunstone, Colin, 129, 178, 181
Boetcher, Curt, 128
Bogart, Neil, 145
Bogert, Tim, 158
Bolan, Marc, 16, 154–157
  John's Children, 16
  Marc (television show), 156–157
  T. Rex, 156–157
  Tyrannosaurus Rex, 154, 155
Boone, Steve, 112
Botnick, Bruce, 111
Bowie, David, 7, 52–53, 97, 155, 157, 194–196
Boyd, Alan, 31
Boyd, Joe, 8, 19, 131
Brave New World, 23
Brecht, Berthold, 76
Bremy, Pete, 158
Brill Building, 12, 24, 25
British Invasion, The, 15, 18, 22
Britpop, xiii, 152
Broadway, 14, 24, 70, 186
Brooker, Gary, 132, 143–144
Brooks, Rosa Lee, 96, 109
Brown, Arthur, 52–53
Brown, Pete, 55
Bruce, Jack, 54–57, 59–60, 90
Brumbeat, 20, 114
Brunswick Records, 97
Buddha Records, 145
Buffalo Springfield, 23, 56, 60, 72, 108, 169

Burdon, Eric, 21
  Black Man's Burdon, 81
  Eric Burdon Declares WAR, 81
  "Spill The Wine," 81
Burundi National Orchestra, 53
Bushy, Ron, 84
Buzzcocks, 196
Byrds, The, xii, 15, 23–24, 38, 48–52, 56, 60, 64–65, 67, 92, 94, 186
  The Notorious Byrd Brothers, 50–52, 92, 94
  Younger Than Yesterday, 48–50

Café Bizzare, 161
Café Wha? (Greenwich Village), 96
Cage, John, 139, 161
Cale, John, 77, 160–161, 163–167
  At Berkshire Music Center (Tanglewood), 160
Cambodia, 5, 10
Cameo Parkway Records, 145, 186
Campbell, Glen, 96
Can, 195
Capitol Records, 28, 31–32, 39, 53, 101, 109, 125, 128, 142, 186–187
Captain Beefheart, 17
Carnaby Street, 17, 38, 102, 146
Casablanca Records, 145, 156
Casady, Jack, 58, 85–89, 92, 94, 100
Cash, Johnny, 12, 44
Castaways, The, 126
Cavern Club, The, 35
Chandler, Chas, 96, 99–100, 153
Chicago Eight (Chicago Seven), 3–4
Chitlin' Circuit, The, 96
Chocolate Watchband, The, 21, 128, 187
CIA, 5
Cinematheque, 162
Civil Rights Act, The, 5
Clapton, Eric, 17, 28, 54, 56, 90, 113, 153, 174–175
Clark, Gene, 48, 50

Clark, Ossie, 17
Clarke, Arthur C., 51
Clarke, Michael, 50–51
Clarke, Tony, 116, 119–120
Clash, The, 7, 12, 196, 201
Clinton, George, xii, 129–131
Cluster, 195
CND (Campaign for Nuclear Disarmament), 18
Cochran, Eddie, 43
Cocker, Joe, 64
Cold War, The, 5, 137, 185
Collins, Gail, 56–57
Columbia Records (CBS), 13, 43–45, 75, 80, 99, 113, 128, 150, 153, 162, 175, 179, 183, 187–188, 201
Columbia Records (EMI), 16, 131–132, 153, 175
Commodore Music Shop, 189
Conrad, Tony, 161, 164
Conscription (The Draft), 17, 19, 20, 32, 85, 111
Constanten, Tom, 82
Cooper, Alice, 52–53
Cooper, Michael, 41, 149
Cope, Julian, 123, 127, 139, 195, 197–199, 203
Coppola, Francis Ford, 77
Cordell, Denny, 144
Cosby, Bill, 63
Costello, Elvis, 154, 201
Cramps, The, 196
Crawdaddy Club, 153, 175
Crazy World of Arthur Brown, The, 16, 19, 52–53, 64
Cream, xii, 19, 65, 90, 95, 98, 105, 109–110, 153
  Disraeli Gears, 54, 56, 57–58, 102
  Wheels of Fire, 56–58, 105
Crosby, David, 9, 48–51, 60, 94
  Crosby, Stills & Nash, 50, 60
  Crosby, Stills, Nash & Young, 9
Cryan' Shames, The, 127
Curtis, Chris, 61–62, 65

Davies, Dave, 17, 101–102
Davies, Ray, 17, 100–102, 104–108, 140, 180
Davis, Clive, 68–70, 99, 126, 183, 188
De Lane Lea Studios, 170, 176
Decca Records, 16, 62, 97, 101, 115–117, 148, 151, 177–179, 181, 186, 190
Deep Purple, xiii, 16, 45, 52–54, 59–66, 158–159
  Shades of Deep Purple, 60–66
Densmore, John, 72–73, 75–76, 79
Deram Records, 116, 143, 144
Derek and the Dominos, 60
Deviants, The, 64
Disc and Echo, 31
Dixon, Willie, 77
Doherty, Denny, 112
Dom, The, 162
Donovan (Leitch), 17, 66–71, 138, 148, 160, 168, 176, 187–188
  Barbajgal, 67, 70–71
  Cameron, John (Donovan's arranger), 68
  A Gift from a Flower to a Garden, 69–70
  Sunshine Superman, 66–69
Doors, The, xii, 7, 15, 23, 50, 53, 71–80, 108, 111, 121, 176, 196, 200
  Doors, The, 71–77
  Strange Days, 77–80
Dowd, Tom, 56
Dream Syndicate, The, 196
Dreja, Chris, 176
Drifters, The, 25
Dryden, Spencer, 86–88, 90–92, 94–95
Dunbar, Aynsley, 97
Dunbar, John, 18
Dunwich Records, 126
Dylan, Bob, xii, 11–13, 25, 28, 34, 43–49
  Blonde on Blonde, 14, 28, 43, 45–46, 48

Easy Rider, 125, 191
Echo and the Bunnymen, 197–200, 202
Echols, Johnny, 109, 111
Edge, Graeme, 114, 118–119
Edwards, Tony, 62
Electric Kool-Aid Acid Test, The, 2
Electric Prunes, The, 21, 125
Elektra Records, 19, 72, 74–76, 78, 111, 124, 131, 162, 187–188
Elliot, Cass, 69, 112
Emerick, Geoff, 37, 41, 182
Emerson, Lake & Palmer, 60
Epic Records, 68–69, 70–71, 175, 183, 188
Episode Six, 16
Eric Burdon & The Animals, 21, 80–81, 97, 154
Ertegun, Ahmet, 56
Eurythmics, 195
Evans, Rod, 61, 63, 65
Everett, Kenny, 178

Faithful, Marianne, 18
Family Dog Productions, 7
Farfisa Organ, 82, 137
FBI, 4
Feldman, Robert, 125
Fellini, Federico, 161
Fender Rhodes Keyboard, 73, 76, 79
Ferlinghetti, Lawrence, 18
Fillmore, The (West), 7, 9, 58, 76, 82
Finn, Mickey, 156
Fleetwood, Mick, 54
Fleetwood Mac, 54, 150
Flo and Eddie (Howard Kaylan and Mark Volman), 156
Flowerpot Men, The, 62
Flying Burrito Brothers, The, 9, 49, 51
Fonda, Peter, 38
Foundations, The, 52
Four Seasons, The, 25, 128, 186
Four Tops, The, 38, 120

Fowley, Kim, 153
Frampton, Peter, 152
Freakbeat, xii, 16, 53, 124, 193
Fred C. Dobbs, 23
Freddy and the Dreamers, 178
Friedan, Betty, 5
Fripp, Robert, 54, 194, 196
Fulwood, Tiki, 131
Funk, xii, 10, 24, 81, 129, 130, 131, 156, 165, 197, 203
Funkadelic, xii, 80, 110, 129–131, 197

Gabriel, Peter, 52–53
Garage Rock, xi–xii, 16, 21, 25, 42, 82, 84, 108, 126–127, 129, 186–188
Garcia, Jerry, 73, 82, 87–88
Garfunkel, Art, 13, 44, 80, 162
Geffen, David, 114
Germs, The, 42
Gerry and the Pacemakers, 178
Gillian, Ian, 16, 53
Gilmour, David, 134, 136, 140–143, 154
Ginsberg, Allen, 18
Glover, Roger, 16
Goffin, Gerry, 51
Golden Gate Park, xi, 9, 21, 51, 92
Gomelsky, Giorgio, 153, 176
Gottehrer, Richard, 125
Gouldman, Graham, 175
Graham, Bill, 7, 58–59, 76, 89, 127, 149–150
Graham Bond Organization, 54–55
Grahame, Kenneth, 156
Grateful Dead, The, 2, 9, 17, 21, 23–24, 67, 73, 79, 81, 83, 149
Great Society, The, 86–88
Green, Peter, 54, 150
Green on Red, 196
Greenwich Village, xii, 11, 15, 21, 25, 96, 112

Gregg, Bobby, 45
Grossman, Albert, 45
Grundy, Hugh, 178, 182
Grunt Records, 85
Guildhall School of Music, 144
Guthrie, Arlo, 25
Guthrie, Woody, 12
Guy, Buddy, 55
Gymnasium, The, 162

Haight Ashbury, 14, 17, 21, 23, 90
Halladay, Johnny, 67
Hammond Organ (Hammond B3), 46, 63, 65, 82, 113, 141, 144, 151, 158, 194
Harlem Culture Festival, 9
Harrison, George, 37–38, 60
Hart, Mickey, 82
Harvest Records, 131, 133, 136, 153
Hassinger, Dave, 125
Havens, Richie, 96
Hawkins, Edwin, 9
Hawkwind, 53
Haworth, Jann, 41
Hayward, Justin, 115, 117–120
Healy, Dan, 83
HEC Enterprises, 62–64
Helicer, Piero, 161
Hells Angels, 9, 192
Helms, Chet, 9
Hendrix, Jimi, xi–xii, 7, 19, 24, 42, 52–53, 61, 65, 78, 95, 97–100, 105, 109–112, 131, 133, 140, 153–154, 159, 168, 193, 197
 with Arthur Lee, 96
 Band of Gypsies, 52
 with Joey Dee and the Starlighters, 96
 with Little Richard, 96
 with Richie Havens, 86
Hermans Hermits, 178
Highwaymen, The, 60
Hillman, Chris, 48–51
Hillman/McGuinn, 49

Hipgnosis
  Aubrey Powell, 141
  Strom Thorgerson, 17, 141
His Master's Voice (HMV), 189
Hitchcock, Robyn, 202–203
Hoffman, Abbie, 3–4
Hoffman, Albert, 4, 88
Hohner Piannet, 113
Holland-Dozier-Holland, 130, 158–159, 171
Hollies, The, 60
Holly, Buddy, 7
Hollywood, 15, 22–23, 75, 121, 130
Holzman, Jac, 75–76, 78, 111, 124
Hopkins, John "Hoppy," 8, 18
Hopkins, Nicky, 103, 106–107, 147
Hopper, Hugh, 154
Hot Tuna, 85, 88–90
Hot Wax Records, 130
How I Won the War, 40
Human League, 195
Humble Pie, 55, 152

I-Ching, 139
Ike and Tina Turner, 96
Immediate Records, 151, 161
Impalas, The, 25
In-Crowd, The, 16
Incredible String Band, The, 7
India, 73, 86, 201
  George Harrison, 40
  Richard Alpert (Baba Ram Das), 1
Indica Bookshop, 18
Ingle, Doug, 84
International Poetry Festival, The, 18
International Times, The, 8, 19
Iron Butterfly, 84–85

Jagger, Mick, 27, 175, 177
Jam, The, 38, 103, 152
James, Skip, 55, 85
Jansch, Bert, 68
Jarrard, Rick, 87–88
Jeff Beck Group, 70, 97, 152

Jefferson Airplane, xii, 2–3, 7, 9, 17, 21, 23–24, 49, 58, 67, 69, 78–79, 82, 84
  After Bathing at Baxters, 89–93
  Bless Its Pointed Little Head, 69
  Crown of Creation, 51, 93–95
  Surrealistic Pillow, 49, 86–89
  Takes Off, 86, 88–91
  Volunteers, 88
Jimi Hendrix Experience, 52, 78, 95–99, 110, 131
  Are You Experienced, 98–99, 102
  Axis: Bold as Love, 99
  Band of Gypsies, 52
  Electric Ladyland, 95–100
John Mayall and the Bluesbreakers, 54–55
Johnson, Betsey, 166
Johnson, Bruce, 128
Johnson, Robert, 46–47
Johnston, Bob, 14, 44, 48
Jones, Brian, 67, 99, 146–147, 175, 194
Jones, John Paul, 148, 176
Jones, Kenney, 150
Jones, Malcolm, 136
Joplin, Janis, 24, 98, 131, 188

Kama Sutra Records, 113
Kantner, Paul, 49, 85–88, 90–95
Katz, Steve, 126
Kaukonen, Jorma, 58, 85–91, 94, 128
Kaye, Lenny, 124, 129
Keith, Linda, 96
Kent State Massacre, 10
Kesey, Ken, 2, 3, 9, 21, 40
King, Andrew, 18
King, B. B., 9
King, Carole, 51
King Crimson, 154, 194
Kingdom Come, 53
Kinks, The, 63, 150, 177–178, 180, 186

Something Else by the Kinks, 100, 104
The Kinks Are the Village Green Preservation Society, 105–108
Klien, Allen, 64, 248
Knickerbockers, The, 125
Knight, Gladys, and the Pips, 9
Knight, Peter (London Festival Orchestra), 116–118
Kooper, Al, 44–46, 125–126, 183
Koppleman, Charles, 113–114
Korner, Alexis, 54
Kraftwerk, 195
Kreutzman, Bill, 82
Krieger, Robby, 72–73, 75–77, 79
Kubrick, Stanley, 51, 190–191

LaBianca, Leno, 10
Laine, Denny, 114, 116
Lambert, Kit, 52, 97, 101, 170–171
Lane, Ronnie, 150–152
Last Poets, The, 9
Latvala, Dave, 83
Laurel Canyon, 11, 15, 60
Laurie Records, 128
Lawrence, Derek, 63
Lawrence, Linda, 67–68, 71
Leary, Timothy, 1–4, 90, 119
Leaves, The, 127
Led Zeppelin, 7, 60, 148, 175–177
Lee, Arthur, 112
Legendary Pink Dots, 203
Lennon, John, 38, 40–41, 52
  influences, 47
  Lennon & McCartney, 17, 27, 65, 67, 147, 159
  political activism, 4
Lenya, Lotte, 76
Lesh, Phil, 82
Lester, Richard, 40, 190
Levon and the Hawks (The Band), 43, 45
Lightnin' Hopkins, 47
Lingsman, The, 127

Little Anthony and the Imperials, 25
Lodge, John, 115, 117–119
London Fog, 23, 74–75, 79
London Free School, 8, 18
London Records, 102, 177
Lord, Jon, 53–54, 61–66, 158
Love (Arthur Lee), xi, 15, 23, 72, 75, 96, 106, 121, 196
  Forever Changes, 108–111
Love, Mike, 28–31, 69
Lovin' Spoonful, 57, 59, 113–114, 148
  "Summer in the City," 112
Lownds, Sara, 45, 48
LSD, 1, 2, 4–6, 14, 21, 28, 30, 38, 41–43, 68, 73, 83, 86, 88, 107
Lubahn, Douglas, 78

Mabew, Ardian, 143
Maclean, Bryan, 111
Magic Mushrooms, The, 129
Magicians, The, 128
Maharishi Mahesh Yogi, 69, 73
Malanga, Gerald, 162, 165
Malcolm X, 6
Mamas and the Papas, xii, 15, 21, 23, 71, 88, 112
Manfred Mann, 54–55
Manson Family, The, 10
Manzarek, Ray, 72–77, 79
Marcos, Imelda, 36
Marcus Garvey Park, 9
Mardin, Arif, 159
Mark Four, 16
Marmalade Records, 153
Marquee, 55
Marriott, Steve, 150–152
Martell, Vince, 158
Martin, George, 40–41, 148
Masekela, Hugh, 24, 48
Mason, Dave, 100
Mason, Nick, 19, 141, 153–154
Matrix, The, 7, 9
Mayfield, Curtis, 109, 157–158

216   Index

MC5, xiii, 4, 198
McCartney, Michael, 71
McCartney, Paul, 18, 38, 47, 67, 98
   Lennon & McCartney, 17, 27, 65, 67, 147, 159
McCarty, Jim, 175–176
McCoy, Charlie, 45
McCulloch, Ian, 197–200
McGowan, Cathy, 67
McGuinn, Roger (Jim), 49, 51
   McGuinn/Hillman, 49, 50
McKenzie, Scott, 123
McKernan, Ron "Pigpen," 82
McLagan, Ian, 150–152
McVie, John, 54
Meek, Joe, 63
Melcher, Terry, 128
Mellotron, 107–108, 114–120, 141, 146–147, 179–180
Mendl, Hugh, 116–117
Mercury, Records, 128, 168, 197–198
Merry Pranksters, 2, 40
Merseybeat, 15, 20
Metzner, Ralph, 1, 2
MGM Records, 80–81, 121, 124, 163, 169, 187
Michael and the Messengers, 127
Miles, Barry, 18
Miles, Buddy, 100
Mitchell, John, 4
Mitchell, Mitch, 97
Mod, 16, 67, 100, 150–151, 170–171
Moebius, Dieter, 195
Mogull, Arte, 62
Mojo Men (Sly and the Mojo Men), 128
Monkees, The, 50, 154, 191
Monterey Pop Festival, 21, 24, 32, 42, 50, 81, 89, 98–99, 101
Moody Blues, 1, 62, 144, 190
   Days of Future Passed, 114–118
   In Search of the Lost Chord, 118–120

Moog Synthesizer, 29, 50–51, 78, 114
Moon, Keith, 28
Morrison, Jim, 72–77, 79–80, 112
Morrison, Sterling, 160–161, 165–166, 169
Morrissey, Paul, 162
Morton, Shadow, 157
Moss, Wayne, 46
Most, Mickie, 68–71, 80, 176–177
Motown, xii, 9, 38, 77, 130, 162, 168, 171, 201
Mott the Hoople, 62
Mouse (Ronny Weiss), 125
Move, The, 8
Muddy Waters, 55
Mugwumps, The, 112
Music Machine, The, 21, 197
Mydland, Brent, 82

Napier-Bell, Simon, 155
Nash, Graham, 9, 50, 60, 71
Nazz, The, 128–129, 168
NEMS, 115
Neu!, 195
Neuwirth, Bob, 45
New Musical Express, 32, 199
New Order (Joy Division), 195
New York Dolls, 165
Newman, Randy, 151
Newport Folk Festival, 11, 13, 67
Nice, The, 62–64
Nico (Christa Päffgen), 77, 160–167
Nugent, Ted, 127
Nuggets, xii, 52, 124, 129

Oingo Boingo, 100
Oldham, Andrew Loog, 28, 96, 146–148, 151, 161
Olympic Studios, 99–100, 178
Ondine, 76
Ono, Yoko, 4, 52
Oswald, Lee Harvey, 6, 114
Our World, 40

Pa-Go-Go Records, 145
Page, Jimmy, 17, 63, 68, 98, 174–177
Paice, Ian, 61, 63, 65
Paisley Underground, The, 196
Pandora's Box, 23
Pappalardi, Felix, 56–57, 59
Parks, Van Dyke, 28–29, 31, 128
Parliament, xiii, 129–131
   Parliament-Funkadelic (P-Funk), xii, 80, 110, 197
Parlophone, 16, 39, 62–64
Parsons, Gram, 51
Patti Smith Group, 124
Pebbles, 124
Peel, John, 123, 193
Penniman, Richard "Little Richard," 12, 44, 96, 101
Peoples Temple of the Disciples of Christ, 2
Peter and Gordon, 18
Peterson, Dickie, 42
Phillips, John, 21, 112
PiL (Public Image Limited), xiii
Pinder, Mike, 114, 116–117, 119–120
Pink Floyd, xi, xii, 7–8, 13, 17–19, 21, 46, 48, 70, 78, 98, 125, 152–155, 187–188, 193, 202–203, 205–207
   The Early Singles, 131–134
   "Echoes," 142–143
   The Piper at the Gates of Dawn, 136–139
   A Saucerful of Secrets, 139–142
   "Scream Thy Last Stream," 134–136
   "Vegetable Man," 134–136
Pirate Radio
   Marine Broadcasting Offences Act of 1967, 188
   Radio Caroline, 132, 172, 188
   Radio London, 132, 147, 172–174, 188
   Radio Luxembourg, 188

Plank, Conny, 195–196
Polanski, Roman, 10
Polydor Records, 98, 131
Pop, Iggy, 195
Premiers, The, 129
Presley, Elvis, 11–12, 85, 186–187, 190
Prince, 196
Procol Harum, 84, 132
   "A Whiter Shade of Pale," 143–144
Psychedelic Furs, The, 201–202
Psychedelic Review, The, 2
Pye Records, 16, 67, 70, 101–102, 165, 186–187
Pye Studios, 64, 170

Quaife, Pete, 101, 106
Quant, Mary, 17
Question Mark (?) and the Mysterians (Rudy Martinez), 42, 129
   "96 Tears," 144–146
Quicksilver Messenger Service, 21, 24, 82, 187

Rain Parade, The, 198
Ramones, The, 7, 12, 145, 165, 196
Ratledge, Mike, 152, 154
Rawls, Lou, 24
RCA Records, 85, 89–90, 92–93, 125, 186–187
Reaction Records, 55, 98
Reading Jazz Festival, 64
Ready, Steady, Go!, 67, 178
Red Kross, 42
Redding, Noel, 97, 99
Redding, Otis, 24, 125
Reed, Lou, 77, 160–161, 163–169
Regal Zonophone, 144, 155
Regent Street Polytechnic, 98
Reid, Keith, 144
Relf, Keith, 175–177
Remains, The, 126

Reprise Records, 98–99, 101, 105, 107, 125, 156, 186
Revilot Records, 130
Revis Records, 109
Richardson, J. P. "The Big Bopper," 7
Riley, Terry, 161
Riot on Sunset Strip, 128
Ripp, Artie, 113
Roach, Max, 9
Robertson, Robbie, 45
Roedelius, Joachim, 195
Rolling Stones, The, 7, 9, 16, 48, 54, 67–68, 73–74, 96, 98–99, 101, 119, 151–152, 161, 170, 175, 177–178, 185–186, 190, 192, 194
  "Dandelion," 146–148
  Their Satanic Majesties Request, 148–149
  "We Love You," 146–148
Ross, Diana, and the Supremes, 50, 201
Rothchild, Paul, 75, 78
Roundhouse, The, 7–8, 64, 142, 152
Roxy Music, 194, 201–202
Rubin, Barbara, 18, 162
Rubin, Jerry, 4
Rundgren, Todd, 128, 201

Sagittarius, 128
Salvation Army
  Brass Band, 46, 141
  Punk Band, 42
Samwell-Smith, Paul, 176
Santana, Carlos, 9, 185, 188
  Abraxas, 149–150
Satie, Erik, 161
Schmidt, Al, 90
Schroeder, Barbet, 142–143
Scotch of St. James, 98
Screaming Lord Sutch, 63
Searchers, The, 81, 127
Sebastian, John, 112–113
Sedgwick, Edie, 45, 47, 162

Seeds, The, 21, 42, 126, 145, 186, 198
Selective Service Act, 20
Sesnick, Steve, 165–167, 169
Sex Pistols, 12
Shadows of Knight, 126
Shankar, Ravi, 24
Sharp, Martin, 55–59
Shaw, Sandie, 16
Shindig, 126, 178
Shrimpton, Jean, 17
Simon & Garfunkel, 13, 44, 80, 162
Simper, Nick, 61–62
Sinclair, John, 3–4
Slick, Grace, 49, 51, 86–89, 92, 94–95
Sly and the Family Stone, xii, 3, 9, 24, 110, 129, 149, 188
Small Faces, The, 16, 100
  "Itchycoo Park," 150–152
Smashing Pumpkins, 126
Smith, Norman "Hurricane," 138–139
Soft Boys, The, 202
Soft Machine, The, 7, 19, 51
  The Soft Machine, 152–154
Solanas, Valerie, 166
Soma Records, 126
Sopwith Camel, 21, 24
Souter, Joe (Joe South), 45, 65
Spades, The, 127
Spence, Skip, 86–88, 91
Spencer Davis Group, The, 16
Squire, Chris, 16, 193
Stamp, Chris, 97, 101, 171
Standells, The, 125
Stanley, Owsley Bear, 83
Staple Singers, The, 44
Starr, Ringo, 38, 40
Stein, Mark, 158, 160
Stein, Seymour, 96
Stevens, Leigh, 42
Stewart, Abigail, 6

Stewart, Rod, 63, 152, 158
Stigwood, Robert, 55, 58, 98
Stone, Sly (Sylvester Stewart), xi, 24, 128
Stooges, The, xiii, 198
Strangeloves, The, 125
Stranglers, The, 8, 197
Strawberry Alarm Clock, 77
Streetly Electronics, 115
Summer of Love, 2, 13, 32, 78, 165–166
Summers, Andy, 81, 95, 97, 152–153
Summer, Donna, 145
"Swinging London," 18, 39, 102, 104, 107, 126, 146, 176, 191
Syn, The, 16, 193
Syndicats, The, 16

Talking Heads, 194
Talmy, Shel, 101–102
T.A.M.I. Show, 126
Tangerine Dream, 195
Tate, Sharon, 10
Taylor, Derek, 31
Taylor, Mike, 59
Teardrop Explodes, The, 139, 197–199
Television, 165
Temptations, The, xii, 129
Tetragrammaton Records, 53, 63–64, 66
Texas International Pop Festival, 9
Theremin, 29
The Third Rail, 128
Thirteenth-Floor Elevators, 21
Thomas, Dylan, 106
Thomas, Ray, 1, 114, 118–119
Thompson, Bill, 91, 93
Thunderclap Newman, 172
Tin Pan Alley, 24, 67
Tokens, The, 25
Tomorrow, 193
Took, Steve Peregrine, 155
Top of the Pops, 132

Tower Records, 125, 189
Townshend, Pete, 3, 19, 28, 52, 98, 100, 102, 170, 172
Track Records, 52–53, 98
Transcendental Meditations, 40
Traveling Wilburys, The, 60
The Trip (film), 191
Trips Festival, The, 2, 9, 21, 24
Trower, Robin, 143–144
Tucker, Maureen (Mo), 160–161, 169
Turtles, The, 72, 129, 155–156, 186
Twiggy, 17

UFO Club, 8
Ultravox, 8, 195–196
Usher, Gary, 48–49, 50, 128

Vagrants, The, 21, 125
Valens, Ritchie, 7, 129
Van Halen, 100
Vanilla Fudge, xii, 25, 61, 64–65, 81, 85
Vanilla Fudge, 157, 160
Varnals, Derek, 116–117
Velvet Underground, The, 13, 25, 44, 71, 78, 145
The Velvet Underground and Nico, 160–165
White Light, White Heat, 43, 165–169
Vera, Billy, 126
Verve Records, 120, 124, 126, 162–163, 166, 169
Vibrators, The, 42
Village Oldies Record Store, 124
Visconti, Tony, 155–156
Vox (Vox Continental), 72, 76, 82, 84, 113, 126, 158

War, 81
Warhol, Andy, 18, 45, 161–164, 166–167, 169, 198
Warner Bros., 66, 101, 120, 128–129, 186, 188, 200, 202

Warwick, Clint, 114–115
Watergate, 7
Waters, Roger, 48, 98, 133–134, 136–138, 143
Wax, Martha, 91
Weill, Kurt, 75–76
Weir, Bob, 73, 82
Weller, Paul, 38, 152
Welnick, Vince, 82
Westbound Records, 130–131
Whalley, Paul, 42
Whisky a Go Go, 23, 74–77
White, Chris, 178, 180–182
White, Clarence, 49, 51
White Panther Party, 4
White Stripes, The, 126
White Whale Records, 155, 186
Whitehead, Peter, 18, 191
Whitfield, Norman, 129
Whittaker, Robert, 39, 57
Who, The, xii, 3, 8, 16, 24, 52, 74, 97–98, 100–102, 109
  High Numbers, 170
  The Who Sell Out, 169–174
Williams, Hank, 12, 44
Williamson, Sonny Boy, 47
Wilson, Brian, xiii, 27, 35, 39–40, 67, 71, 104, 128, 135, 139, 148, 151
Wilson, Carl, 32
Wilson, Tom, xi, 13, 43–44, 80, 162–163, 166

Winterland Auditorium, 59
Wolfe, Tom, 2
Wonder, Stevie, 9
Wood, Art, 62
Wood, Ron, 62, 152
Woodstock, xi, 3, 9, 84, 95, 100, 149–150, 191
Woronov, Mary, 162
Worrell, Bernie, 131
Wrecking Crew, The, 27, 96, 111
Wright, Richard, 133–134, 136–137
Wyatt, Robert, 96, 152–153
Wyman, Bill, 146, 149

Yanovsky, Zal, 57, 112–113, 148
Yardbirds, xii, 7, 54, 153, 155, 175–177
  Little Games, 174
Yarrow, Peter, 25
Yes, 16, 154, 193–194
Young, LaMonte, 161
Young Rascals, The, 25

Zappa, Frank, 70, 120–124, 129, 159
  The Mothers of Invention, 15, 25, 43–44, 52–53, 69, 91, 163
Zombies, The, 24, 106, 113, 126, 129, 157–158
  Odessey and Oracle, 177–182

About the Author

CHRISTIAN MATIJAS-MECCA is a professor of dance and music at the University of Michigan and chair of the Department of Dance, where he teaches courses on accompanying movement, research methodologies, the integration of music and movement, and the history of music in dance. He is a leading practitioner in dance and music studies and has collaborated with artists from many of the world's leading dance companies. Christian has been an invited speaker at conferences in North America, Europe, and Asia, and under the name Christian Matijas, he has produced albums of original compositions (*Standing Alone*, *Suites for Dance*, and *Na Razie, bez Ciebie*) and music for dance technique classes (*Etoile Solo Ballet Variations* and *Music for Modern Dance*). He is the author of *The Words and Music of Brian Wilson* (Praeger) and a native of Los Angeles, where he earned degrees in harpsichord and early music from the University of Southern California.

www.ingramcontent.com/pod-product-compliance
Lightning Source LLC
Chambersburg PA
CBHW070250230426
43664CB00014B/2474